What is design?
What is creativity?

Whether you design a building
or a watch or a chair, it is an
act of creativity. A fashion
designer can create a building ...
People have the potential to
do anything, if they are creative ...
Design can change a city or
move a culture ... and Australian
design is world class.

Marc Newson

The launch of *Freestyle: new Australian design for living* marks a significant moment for Australian design and for our two organisations. It is the first time such a comprehensive survey of Australian design has been presented both within Australia and internationally. These designers illustrate the creativity and vibrancy that define our design culture and tell us much about what makes Australian design distinctive. Another significant achievement of *Freestyle* is the genesis and development of the project itself. A collaboration between Object: Australian Centre for Craft and Design and Museum Victoria, *Freestyle* is the result of our two complementary organisations combining ideas, inspiration, resources and skills, while pursuing our shared vision. ■ That vision is the *Freestyle* project – an exhibition of 40 of Australia's most interesting designers, this major publication, educational resources and activities, and a range of audience development initiatives aimed at raising the awareness and appreciation of our design culture. Together we have achieved something of a scale, scope and ambition that working alone would not have been possible. ■ For Museum Victoria the project is part of a proud history of showcasing outstanding design through *Designed to Inspire*, Melbourne Museum's program that gives recognition and exposure to emerging and practising Australian designers. The Victorian Government's *State of Design* funding also enables Melbourne Museum to create and deliver a series of design events for the general public and design community, both in Melbourne and regional Victoria. ■ For Object, *Freestyle* represents the culmination of many years of presenting exceptional designers to diverse and growing audiences. The project reflects our philosophy of supporting and showcasing the best of Australian design in its broadest sense – from furniture to fashion, textiles to glass, from the newly discovered to the most established designers. Object is committed to creating outstanding exhibitions that are enjoyed by audiences across Australia and internationally.

We therefore both hope that wherever *Freestyle* travels, the celebration continues – a celebration of our culture, our lifestyle and geography and our creative passion and skill. ■ We would both like to extend our congratulations and thanks to all of the *Freestyle* designers who have been committed collaborators and passionate advocates for the project. Of course they are the raison d'etre for *Freestyle* and it is their talent and creativity that continues to inspire us. ■ Congratulations and thanks should also go to *Freestyle* curator and Object's Associate Director, Brian Parkes, who has spent years researching and undertaking studio visits across the country to learn about the work of hundreds of Australian designers. Brett Dunlop, Manager Melbourne Museum, and Juliet Wilson, Coordinator Exhibitions – Design, both from Museum Victoria, and Annabel Moir, Assistant Curator at Object, have also been key collaborators, integral to the realisation of the project. We would also like to thank all our staff at both Museum Victoria and Object for their dedication and passion for *Freestyle*. ■ The publication of this book is a result of the efforts of its many contributors. We are fortunate to be able to draw on their substantial knowledge and experience of Australian design. We anticipate that this *Freestyle* publication will become an indispensable resource for anyone interested in contemporary Australian design. ■ We have also been fortunate to work with a dedicated team of partners, sponsors and funding bodies to realise this ambitious project. ■ Bombay Sapphire, our *Freestyle* Principal Sponsor, is already well known for its work with the Australian design community through the *Bombay Sapphire Design Discovery Award*, which includes over $30,000 cash prizes and a winner's trip to Milan. Object's relationship with Bombay Sapphire began through the *Design Discovery* project, culminating in the agreement to present the *Bombay Sapphire Design Discovery Award Exhibition* at Object Gallery each year from 2006 to 2008. This exhibition of the work of the 10 finalists, curated by Object Gallery, will also tour to Melbourne Museum as another important component of the Museum's design program. As the *Freestyle* Principal Sponsor, we thank Bombay Sapphire for its generous support and committed involvement with the project. ■ Also passionately committed to design in Australia and integral to the success of *Freestyle* are our *Freestyle* Principal Supporters, the Victorian State Government and Visions of Australia; and our *Freestyle* sponsors, Frost Design, *Vogue Living,* ADS, Image Box, Photo Technica, Kodak, Cafe Sydney and *POL Oxygen*. We have been joined for the first time by Video Education Australasia through the *Freestyle* educational DVD, which will be used in schools and universities across the country. Our Organisational Supporters are also central to this project – the Australia Council for the Arts, Arts NSW, and the Visual Arts and Craft Strategy. Without the support of all these partners and sponsors, *Freestyle* would still be a dream. ■ We believe that *Freestyle* marks the beginning of a new era in the development and appreciation of our design culture, and creates a strong positioning for Australia as a centre of innovation and design excellence. ■ We look forward to seeing how our designers continue to create 'new Australian design for living' and how, together, we can help shape the future of Australian design.

Steven Pozel
Director
Object: Australian Centre for Craft and Design

Patrick Greene
Chief Executive Officer
Museum Victoria

Essays

Australia has always excelled at freestyle – the swimming stroke that is – and we've no shortage of world records and gold medals to prove it. Perhaps this is not surprising given our predominantly coastal lifestyle and the fact that a British-born Australian more or less invented the stroke in the early 1900s.[1] Despite its current refinement as a lycra bodysuit-enhanced, precision movement – as demonstrated by the likes of Ian Thorpe – its origins could be described as a splashy but effective way of moving through water quickly in the absence of restrictive rules.

BRIAN PARKES

Freestyle: new Australian design for living

Contemporary design in Australia is a field not encumbered by the weight of a long history and the resulting restrictive rules that such a history can imply. In Australia, traditional career paths in design are far less trodden than in more established design centres such as Italy, Scandinavia or the United Kingdom, where practitioners can conform or react to but never escape from the history. Here, most successful designers are creating their own particular way of doing things, embracing a freer style or approach to their practice. Indeed, *Freestyle* presents almost as many different ways of developing and sustaining a design practice as the actual number of designers it features. ■ The lateral thinking, entrepreneurial, 'can-do' attitude of many Australian designers has its genesis in those aspects of Australian culture that are the source of significant national pride. From the earliest Indigenous inhabitants to the most recent migrants from troubled parts of the world, Australians have shown a certain capacity to make do with what is available at hand – often turning isolation to advantage and regularly innovating to adapt to the environment or circumstances of the day. Today Australian designers are showing their resourcefulness in the various and often intriguing ways they deal with the design process, manufacturing, choosing and obtaining materials, sales, distribution, marketing, business structure, and the often diverse streams of income that many generate to sustain their livelihoods. ■ We are currently witnessing a 'coming of age' for Australian design. Emerging now – from a nation that values its quality of life – is a locally strong and globally confident new design industry. The last ten to 15 years have seen significant improvements in design education and industry infrastructure. The local domestic market,

traditionally dominated by imported goods, has begun to embrace Australian design, and the quality of Australian design product has been recognised around the world. ░ *Freestyle: new Australian design for living* focuses on objects created for the home and the body. It includes furniture, lighting, textiles, homewares, fashion, jewellery and personal accessories. The 40 designers and design collectives in *Freestyle* provide a representative sample of the character, vibrancy and increasing maturity of contemporary design in Australia. Handmade, one-off and limited edition design objects are featured along with industrially manufactured items and prototypes – reflecting the breadth and nature of design excellence in Australia. These designers have been selected on the basis of both their quality of innovation and the distinctive nature of their work in local and international contexts. The work reflects the tenacity, inventiveness and dedication to quality that are emerging as hallmarks of the most outstanding Australian design.

░ These characteristics are found in the best of Australian architecture and environmental design, graphic and communication design, costume and set design, as well as industrial design for the scientific, medical, automotive and appliance industries. These are all areas in which Australian designers have been recognised and applauded internationally, through prestigious awards, commissions, contracts and publications. While *Freestyle* does not deal specifically with these areas, they each contribute significantly to the growing sense of a broad, mature and supportive design community in Australia, and to the increased awareness of the value of design in the broader public domain. ░ *Freestyle's* particular emphasis on 'design for living' is concerned with objects that are designed and made for use in our everyday domestic life – things that we might *choose* to clothe or adorn ourselves with or to decorate or use within our homes. Most of these items elicit an emotional connection with the user (or potential user) through their tactility, materiality, functionality, craftsmanship or artistic intent. Generally more speculative and personally driven than the work arising from the client/brief-dominated disciplines mentioned above, these varied products 'for living', when seen together en masse, prompt us to consider how they emanate from and contribute to a sense of Australian identity. What *does* our material culture say about us now?

░ There are several key factors that have helped to shape the context in which these Australian designers are working: (1) Australia's extraordinary cultural diversity ensures a rich melting pot of influences, traditions and sensibilities. This is clearly evident in the way modern Australian cuisine, for example, combines elements of Mediterranean, Asian and other styles with local ingredients to create fresh, new and diverse hybrids. Australian designers regularly draw upon their own varied backgrounds or are inspired by the vibrant mix around them. (2) The geographic diversity of the Australian continent – tropical climates in the north, cool temperate zones in the south, vast dry deserts, rolling hills, lush rainforests and sandy beaches – has seen the development of regionally different lifestyles and attitudes. Designers are conscious of these and are equally influenced by the wonderful natural environments that inform them. (3) Australia's relatively small population translates to a limited local market. Australian designers either look to overseas markets as exporters or consciously develop products that are viable in small quantities often aimed at identifiable

niche segments within the market. (4) Australia's physical location in the Asia-Pacific region plays a key role in the nation's trade and cultural exchange. Export and/or manufacturing opportunities for Australian designers are growing rapidly in countries such as Japan, China, India and South Korea. (5) Australia has a limited and diminishing manufacturing base, with some industries, such as commercial production of glassware, no longer operating at all. Australian manufacturers have also been traditionally reluctant to invest in design. Some designers have worked hard to develop productive relationships with them, while many others have developed their own methods of manufacturing. ▪ Despite the high level of independence and individuality represented by the 40 designers in *Freestyle*, a number of consistent characteristics emerge, and it is possible to consider them in five, loosely defined categories. Many of the designers could sit comfortably within more than one category and several of them have shifted from one to another through the evolution of their practice. These categories represent the most persistent approaches, aspirations and concerns of Australian designers today.

SKILLED CRAFTSPEOPLE
Ari Athans, Susan Cohn, Janet DeBoos, Edols Elliott, Gray Street Workshop, Sheridan Kennedy, Maningrida Arts & Culture, Jennifer Robertson, Oliver Smith, Prue Venables ▪ One of the noticeable features of Australian design is the proportionally high percentage of designers who have emerged from, or maintain, a material-specific crafts practice. Working in fields as diverse as ceramics, jewellery, metalwork, furniture, textiles and glass, many of them hover confidently between the realms of art and design. Whether producing unique one-off pieces or products for mass manufacture, these designers are as concerned with expressive content or meaning in the work as they are with its ultimate use. ▪ These skilled craftspeople possess an intimate knowledge of their chosen materials, and a high level of technical proficiency in working with them. This experience-acquired knowledge of the characteristics of a material allows them to create exquisite one-off pieces, but can also enable them to design for limited, or even mass production with a thorough understanding of the tolerances and potential of the particular material. This is true of ceramicists Prue Venables and Janet DeBoos, both accomplished artists with decades of experience in studio pottery, who have also both recently designed tableware for industrial manufacturers – Venables in Japan and DeBoos in Italy and China. ▪ These artist-designers sell much of their work through commercial galleries in Australia and overseas. Their one-off pieces are often quite highly priced and are regularly sought by collectors. This is certainly true of the exquisite work of Sydney-based glass artists Benjamin Edols and Kathy Elliott. Edols is regarded as one of the finest glass-blowers in the world and the duo specialise in producing unique blown and cold-worked pieces, more than half of which are sold through galleries overseas. Like Edols and Elliott, the three jewellers, Julie Blyfield, Leslie Matthews and Catherine Truman (of Adelaide's Gray Street Workshop) maintain a regular exhibiting presence internationally. However, for more than 20 years, the Gray Street partners have continually produced both exhibition and

1 Julie Blyfield, *Pressed desert plant brooch series*, 2005
Oxidised sterling silver, enamel paint, wax.
65 x 60 x 20mm
Photograph Grant Hancock
2 Mabel Mayangal, *Dilly bag*, 2006
Dyed pandanus.
450 x 250 x 250mm
Photograph Benjamin Healley
3 Robert Foster, *F!NK Explosive Vase*, 1999
Explosively formed anodised aluminium.
240 x 120 x 80mm
Manufactured by F!NK & Co., Australia.
Photograph Damien McDonald
4 cloth, *Wattle (sunny) and Copper (abstract) lampshades, Backdrop Wattle (sunny)*, 2003
Screen-print on linen, wire, wood.
Tallest: 650mm

limited-run production work to sustain viable incomes from their practice. This is also the case for Brisbane-based jeweller Ari Athans who, like a growing number of more mercantile artisans, has opened her own studio gallery, giving her greater dialogue with her clients and a higher margin on retail sales.  Many of the designers in this category are likely to have ranges of production work available through specialist retailers and most of them regularly undertake private commissions. Among this group, jewellers Susan Cohn and Sheridan Kennedy, textile artist Jennifer Robertson and silversmith Oliver Smith all share a specific interest in sustainable, production-based practices; each of them is involved in skilfully handmaking both one-off and production items; and each has also successfully designed products for manufacture by other companies either here or abroad. Unique in this group, and geographically far removed, is Maningrida Arts & Culture. Maningrida Arts & Culture represents around 700 Aboriginal artists from north central Arnhem Land. It is one of 50 or so Aboriginal-owned arts centres in remote and regional Australia that affirm and promote the value of local culture and aim to maximise financial returns to artists. Various styles of natural-fibre baskets, bags, mats and jewellery made by the local artists are sold and distributed worldwide through Maningrida Arts & Culture. Utilising laborious craft skills and traditional knowledge of local natural materials, these items are made specifically for a consumer market, but still offer the owner a powerful connection to the land and the culture of the artists who made them.

SELF MANUFACTURERS
Nicola Cerini, cloth, F!NK & Co., korban/flaubert, Stefan Lie, Marc Pascal, Preston Zly, Tiwi Design, Vixen Given Australia's limited manufacturing base it is perhaps not surprising that the model of the designer-maker has become the dominant genre within Australian design. It is within this genre that we see the most diverse and entrepreneurial approaches to design practice. The designer-makers and designer-manufacturers are generally concerned with sustainable in-house production rather than the creation of unique objects. One of the keys to this sustainability is the capacity to design products that can be produced in limited volume as required, with only minimal tooling or set up, thereby maintaining a level of production that can be adjusted to suit the market demand. To a large extent this group represents the backbone of Australian design. Among these are designers and companies such as korban/flaubert, Marc Pascal, cloth, Vixen, F!NK & Co., Nicola Cerini, Preston Zly and Tiwi Design. While many of them outsource the manufacture of some products, or component parts of some products, all of them share an approach to design that is informed by hands-on making processes. With the exception of Tiwi Design, which has been creating contemporary screen-printed textiles based on traditional designs since the early 1970s, these companies have each been around for ten to 15 years, and the adaptability of the designer-maker model has allowed each of them to grow steadily without over-capitalising. Each of them now employs staff to assist with production and/or marketing, sales and distribution. Interestingly, textile designer Georgia Chapman of Vixen actually employs a full-time fashion designer, with whom she collaborates to design all of

the Vixen label garments. ▪ Another advantage of in-house batch manufacturing is the capacity for customising products for commissions or special orders. Lighting and product designer Marc Pascal has consciously worked this possibility into several of his hand-assembled lights, enabling him to produce exclusive pieces for individual clients through variations of colour or material using the same basic components. ▪ The scale of in-house production for some of these companies encourages us to consider them as designer-manufacturers. Most of these have developed their own highly innovative manufacturing processes, and none more so than F!NK & Co.'s Robert Foster. Foster has used high-pressure water forming, controlled explosive forming and a customised 600-tonne press, amongst other methods and tooling, to create multiple products or component parts in aluminium and other metals in his semi-industrial factory/workshop. A similar factory-like atmosphere exists in the workshop of shoe designers Johanna Preston and Petr Zly of Preston Zly, who have been able to cheaply purchase and modify decommissioned factory machinery from the steadily shrinking Australian footwear manufacturing industry. ▪ Not all Australian designer-makers *choose* self-manufacture as their mode of production. For many it is simply a necessity. It provides a means of getting work out into the marketplace for both commercial return and public exposure. The stellar international career of Marc Newson has its origins in the designer-maker tradition, and it remains an important model for emerging designers today.[2] Having graduated in 1998, Stefan Lie is still producing his own furniture and jewellery but has recently fulfilled his objective to begin designing products for other companies. Lie is proving to be a consistent and talented designer.

PROJECT MANAGERS

Jonathan Baskett, bernabeifreeman, Caroline Casey, Jon Goulder, Lorinda Grant, Khai Liew, S!X, Schamburg + Alvisse, Brian Steendyk
▪ This entrepreneurial group of designers market their products under their own brand, but outsource all or most of their manufacturing. Some come from making backgrounds (often designing through making prototypes) and others through more traditional fashion or industrial design education. They tend to seek the highest standards of finish for their work, and invest time and money in developing strong relationships with specialised manufacturers. These designers often seek out highly skilled tradespeople within industry – pattern-makers, sewers, upholsterers, cabinet makers etc. – and form long-term partnerships to produce their designs. Khai Liew's wooden furniture is made by skilled artisans in Adelaide who specialise in antique restoration. Rina Bernabei and Kelly Freeman spend time on the factory floor with sheet-metal workers to encourage them to push the boundaries of what they thought was possible. Brian Steendyk, an architect and product designer, works with experts in a range of fields – from fibreglass and concrete casting to rotationally moulded plastics – to refine his designs prior to committing to production. ▪ With a steadily diminishing manufacturing sector in Australia, it is increasingly difficult for designers to find local manufacturers who have the versatility to work on challenging projects and produce the quality demanded by the higher end of the market – where most of these designers have to compete. Some of them,

1 bernabeifreeman, *Leaf Pendant*, 2002
Punched and rolled aluminium with powder-coated finish, stainless steel.
500 x 150 x 150mm
Photograph bernabeifreeman
2 Schamburg + Alvisse,
Miss Molly lounge sled, 2004
European beech plywood shell, stainless steel, polyethylene, upholstery.
665 x 575 x 745mm
Photograph Schamburg + Alvisse
3 zuii, *Trace - table light,* 2004
Blown glass (clear or tinted), aluminium, low-watt flourescent lamp.
340 x Ø.200mm
Photograph zuii
4 Charles Wilson, *Julep Chair,* 2002
Aluminium, fiberglass, upholstery.
660 x 750 x 780mm
Photograph Marcus Fillinger

such as furniture designers Schamburg + Alvisse and fashion label S!X, are dedicated to working with Australian manufacturers, while others have sought specialist skills elsewhere. For example, most of Jonathan Baskett's glassware is made in a glass-blowing factory in Mexico. Caroline Casey engages skilled local artisans to produce her furniture for the Australian market, and others in Germany for the European market, as a lateral solution to the cost of export shipping. █ The products are mostly made in limited batches – sometimes to order in the case of rugs or some furniture, or for a complete seasonal collection in the case of fashion. An interesting exception to this is the range of plywood furniture that Jon Goulder has been producing in larger volume in China through a factory with which he has spent two years nurturing a relationship. He has helped train the factory's staff and personally invested in improving its equipment. █ Utilising alternative and non-industrial methods of manufacturing is a common feature for many of these designers. An excellent example of this is in the work of clothing and accessories designer Lorinda Grant. Grant's machine-knits are produced through a standard industrial process, but her distinctive hand-knits are actually made by around 100 women in the Bendigo region whom she has taught to 'knit badly' to her specifications.

GLOBAL ROAMERS
Lucas Chirnside and Bianca Looney, Adam Goodrum, Simone LeAmon, Alexander Lotersztain, Nick Rennie, Charles Wilson, zuii
█ Designing exclusively for other companies, with little or no interest in either self-manufacture or investing in having goods produced under their own name, these designers are part of a growing number, here in Australia and elsewhere, whose client base might be anywhere in the world. They are involved in selling their design skills and ideas to various manufacturers in a global market, deriving income through negotiated royalty payments. █ These designers need to be creative with both the design ideas they develop and the ways in which they attract the attention of potential manufacturers. Many of them go to significant expense to enter important competitions or to participate in major design fairs such as the Milan International Furniture Fair or Tokyo Designers Block. They often invest in producing prototypes of speculative, eye-catching products to show at these fairs or to gain useful editorial coverage in the ever-increasing number of design magazines. Nick Rennie, Simone LeAmon, Lucas Chirnside, Bianca Looney and Adam Goodrum are just some of the Australians who have exhibited at the Milan Fair. Each has subsequently achieved significant attention in the design media, and all have entered into or are currently finalising agreements with international manufacturers. In order to be successful, these global roamers have to establish some degree of profile and back it up with a portfolio of great ideas. Each successful project helps significantly to procure the next. █ Designers within this category are in constant negotiation with one or more manufacturers regarding the commissioning or production of a particular design. It can take from several months to several years to move from initial discussions to the commercial release of a finished product. Alana Di Giacomo and Marcel Sigel of zuii have been working with Royal Selangor in Malaysia to develop a new range of pewter wares, which will be on sale

from the end of 2006 (just over a year from when they were first approached). Utilising new communication technologies, computer-aided design software and intermittent overseas trips for meetings, these designers develop and expand their international networks while enjoying a quality of life only possible through remaining in Australia. With a laptop, mobile phone and genuinely global outlook, Alexander Lotersztain is comfortable designing from Brisbane, Byron Bay or Barcelona. His clients include Australian, Japanese and Italian companies, as well as villagers in Africa with whom he is designing exportable lifestyle products to be made by local artisans using traditional techniques and materials, through an exciting United Nations-supported economic development project. Slowly but surely more of these designers are beginning to work with Australian manufacturers – particularly those manufacturers who have begun to recognise the value and advantages of working with Australian designers. Charles Wilson – who, like other designers noted, is negotiating with European manufacturers for several of his smaller products – has been designing furniture for the Sydney-based company Woodmark International for more than ten years. To Woodmark's credit, it has since taken on half a dozen more young Australian designers.

BRANDED HOUSES

Crumpler, Dinosaur Designs, Easton Pearson, Akira Isogawa, Zimmermann These highly influential companies are certainly among the best known names in Australian design, but actually represent something of a minority amongst Australian designers. In refreshingly different ways, each of them is cutting a path for others to follow, providing valuable models that others might adapt to their own needs and strengths. Indeed, more and more designers are joining their ranks each year through the increased confidence in Australian design. For more than 20 years Liane Rossler, Louise Olsen and Stephen Ormandy, the design partners of Dinosaur Designs, have steadily grown their company through constant reinvestment from a regular weekend market stall to an internationally recognised brand name with their own stores in Sydney, Melbourne and New York. With the exception of their modest ranges of glass and textiles, they still manufacture all of their products in-house in their busy Sydney studio. The Melbourne-based bag and accessories company, Crumpler, has achieved a similar pattern of growth without loans or venture capital at an even faster rate, through their decision to manufacture their products offshore. In ten years the company has grown from Stuart Crumpler handmaking batches of 20 courier bags, to having 12 stores around Australia, two in the United States, a satellite office in New York and wholesale clients around the world. These larger-scale businesses are in control of the design, production, marketing and distribution of their products, all have multiple retail outlets and all are active exporters. It would be fair to say that this arena is dominated by fashion design, but this is not to suggest that our fashion designers are any better than their counterparts in furniture, product or any other type of design. Talented and internationally successful though many of them are, it is simply the case that the fashion industry is ideally structured to support a vibrant local contribution: the technology required for production is widely accessible;

1 Akira Isogawa, *Akira Silk Organza Ruffle Dress*, 2006
Spring Summer Resort Collection (shown in Sydney, May 2005)
Photograph Stephen Ward
2 Dinosaur Designs, *Assorted Resin Bangles and Ring*, 1990-2000
Photograph Tim Richardson
3 Easton Pearson, Mercedes Australian Fashion Week Parade, 2002
Photograph Alex Zotos

levels of production are controllable relative to demand; the margin between unit cost and acceptable market price is generally higher than other products produced in limited volume; and garments can be packed and transported more cheaply and with less risk of damage. These characteristics, it should be said, make fashion a genre in which design innovation is not a necessary requirement for commercial success. ■ Several prominent Australian fashion designers have proven to be consistent innovators however, and this has in no way detracted from their success. Pamela Easton and Lydia Pearson, of Easton Pearson, have designed with passion and intuition – rather than following fashionable styles – since they started their label, with $8,000 each, in Brisbane in 1989. They now employ 40 full-time and additional part-time staff, and sell to more than 100 stores worldwide. Similarly, Nicole Zimmermann was at the forefront of reinventing swimwear in Australia in the early 1990s, and continues to innovate with cuts and styles that reflect the sassy verve of Australia's beach culture.

■ Arguably the most outstanding designer working in Australia today is the Japanese born, Sydney-based Akira Isogawa. His work and career can be seen as broadly representative of Australian design today: he is hard working, with equal measures of confidence and humility; his design is informed by a multicultural background and a respectful interaction with other cultures; he seeks the approval of Europe, but is conscious of nurturing the local market; he remains obsessed with the quality of craftsmanship and materials used in his work; he is not constrained by the limits of his field (designing rugs, homewares, costumes for dance etc.), and is a committed collaborator; and he has embraced iconic elements of Australian identity within his work (working with 'Aussie' clothing brand, Bonds). After establishing his label in 1993, Isogawa struggled for many years, despite widespread acclaim, to strike a balance between creative integrity and commercial viability. In recent years he has begun to achieve this balance, and – as with Australian design more broadly – he is now well-placed to take full advantage of the wealth of inspiration, ideas and opportunities that exist. ■ Many of the designers featured in *Freestyle* are truly leaders in their field. The works and compelling stories of these 40 designers have been brought together not because they are the best or the most popular, but because they collectively reflect the diversity, resourcefulness and particular strengths of Australian design now. By providing this snapshot of the industry today, *Freestyle* demonstrates not only the confidence and innovation of Australian designers, but also the increasing cultural and commercial significance of Australian design both here, in Australia, and around the world.

1. In fact, freestyle is not technically a stroke at all, rather a category for competitive swimming in which almost anything goes – the stroke we know as freestyle is actually called 'front crawl' and was referred to as 'Australian crawl' until the 1950s.
2. Marc Newson studied jewellery and object design at Sydney College of the Arts in the early 1980s. The course had a strong emphasis on making and materials, and many of Newson's early furniture pieces – including the first *Lockheed Lounge* (1986) – were handmade by the designer himself.

We are reminded every day that we live in an era of globalisation. In fact, 'globalisation' is simply a new name for a very old phenomenon – international trade and commerce. What is different today is the vastly increased speed and reliability of transport, together with the unprecedented rate of transfer of information due to telecommunications technology.

PAUL MCGILLICK

A Diverse Practice: Contemporary furniture, lighting and product design in Australia

Design, like anything else, exists within a global context, and always has done. But the 'new globalisation' has broken down geographical and cultural isolation to an unprecedented extent, with the result that specific design cultures have come under threat. Their distinctiveness – drawn from the use of indigenous materials, response to local needs, and regional traditions of artisanship – can no longer be quarantined from a burgeoning global culture, where everything is effectively mass-manufactured, instantly available and invariably cheaper. ■ Even Scandinavian furniture design, with its deeply rooted tradition of using local timber within a unique aesthetic, has not been inured from the vagaries of global markets. It has survived so far only through the constant reinvention of itself, coupled with astute marketing, the highly sophisticated application of the latest technology (in an industry that was, until fairly recently, heavily artisan-based) and the preservation of a design ethic in the face of seemingly impossible odds. ■ I refer to the Scandinavian tradition very deliberately because it has been an important influence in Australia, where both designers and consumers have long sensed certain affinities between Australia and Scandinavia: a close connection to the landscape and its light, the use of indigenous materials, a sense of isolation from the mainstream, a small population and a handmaking tradition. But that influence has waxed and waned according to the global profile of Scandinavian design, as well as to political and economic conditions – for example, World War II, import restrictions and tariffs in Australia, and shifts in fashion related to the postwar growth of mass communications. ■ And now there are apparently hotter, sexier and more fashionable design models competing for young

1 *Jon Goulder and Gow*
(Chinese factory worker)
2 Jon Goulder, *Leda seat,* 2003
Plywood and aluminium.
740 x 1760 x 940mm
Photograph Blue Murder Studios
3 *Khai Liew working in workshop*
Photograph Aldo Zotti
4 *Interior of korban/flaubert studio*
Photograph Stefanie Flaubert

designers' attention – models instantly available through telecommunications, promoted by an undiscriminating design press and charged with the promise of wealth and celebrity. Suddenly, the Scandinavian tradition looks a little staid, its rigour too demanding in an era tuned to instant gratification, and its palette too reserved in a world that seems to respond only to the loudest and most lurid. ■ Still, in Australia there is considerable optimism about the future of our emerging design culture, which many feel evinces a freshness and imagination not seen in the metropolitan design centres of the world. If this is the case, then one obvious explanation would be that Australia's isolation and relatively recent emergence as a nation state (colonised in 1788 and federated into a single nation in 1901) means that we simply have to work harder to create points of difference, but also that we work with a certain sense of freedom, without the weight of history and distanced from the hothouse homogeneity and competitiveness of metropolitan design centres elsewhere. ■ Of course, some would argue that Australian design emerged a long time ago. There has been, for example, a strong industrial design sector in Australia at least since the 1950s, which has made, and continues to make, an impact well beyond the shores of Australia. In fact, as a local practice, industrial design goes right back – and not so surprisingly, if you think about it – to the colonial period, when Australia's isolation and dependence on irregular and unreliable imports (for example, of iron, which Australia did not produce for itself until the latter part of the nineteenth century) led to the design and manufacture of products, especially in the agriculture sector, to meet local and immediate demand. ■ Then there is the often overlooked tradition of colonial furniture in Australia. When I look over the list of designers represented in this exhibition, with the exception of the Indigenous designers, I can only see two who are responding to an existing design tradition in Australia. One is Jon Goulder, whose practice has been – at least until recently – artisan-based, and who has inherited a four-generation upholstery tradition, seen in his beautifully crafted wooden *Fruitbowl* (2002) and *Leda seat* (2003) of moulded ply and aluminium.[1] ■ The other is the Adelaide-based Khai Liew, whose practice extends beyond domestic furniture to street furniture and interior design. Khai Liew is worth singling out for several reasons. Like a number of other designers in this exhibition, he comes from somewhere else – Julie Paterson, Michael Alvisse, Alexander Lotersztain and Akira Isogawa being some others. But Khai Liew was effectively forced into exile (from Malaysia, after the race riots of 1969), bringing with him a highly developed sense of tradition. His Chinese Malaysian origins are detectable in his work. But more intriguing was the way in which he looked to another tradition – that of colonial Australian furniture (which, incidentally, includes a sub-tradition of Chinese furniture-makers who came to Australia during the Gold Rushes of the mid-ninteenth century) – as if to fill a vacuum. Khai Liew financed an economics degree by dealing in antique furniture, eventually working both as a dealer and as a conservator, valuer and consultant to private and institutional buyers. He has commented, 'Years of taking furniture apart in the restoration process has enabled me to examine and study the techniques of furniture construction from various countries and cultures, from different artistic movements and centuries. This has been the principal factor in the formation and development of my

design vocabulary.' ■ So, Jon Goulder and Khai Liew are two Australian designers not only responding to tradition, but designing from the inside out – in other words, from an insider's knowledge of how things are put together. But, then, this could also be said of Robert Foster and korban/flaubert, whose products emerge from an empirical examination of materials and technology, with the result that their form and function both become an expression of technological and material potential. ■ Here, then, we are talking about the sources of contemporary Australian design: Where does it emerge from? How does it come to be out there? And are there any characteristics that distinguish it from mainstream international design? ■ Essentially, Australian design gets 'out there' in the same ways as design anywhere else reaches a market. The main difference is the lack of manufacturing support for Australian designers, which, in turn, reflects what has been a lack of market support. Australians are still more inclined to buy an imported product before they will accept a locally-designed and manufactured product – not that this is unique to Australia. It is a species of provincialism found all over the world, and assumes that something from somewhere else and promoted in the world media must self-evidently be superior to the home-grown product. Ironically, with a host of industrial design products – probably because of their anonymity – the Australian consumer is quite undiscriminating and blissfully unaware that numerous everyday products and devices have a local origin. Just try crossing the street: the pedestrian crossing button, now seen all over the world, was designed by Nielsen and Associates. Or – and this could be a glowing endorsement of Bruno Munari's homage to the 'Great Unknown Designer' – the elegant bench-top instant boiling-water and filtered cold-water single tap (which eliminates the need for jugs and kettles and is now a worldwide phenomenon) was developed by Sydney-based Zip Industries, and designed by Sydney-based Bluesky Creative. ■ These are just two examples, chosen at random, which illustrate the strength of Australian industrial design; but what of other design categories, such as furniture and lighting? There can be no doubt that, until recently, manufacturing support has been erratic and generally weak. In fact, one view is that Australian manufacturers actually lag behind the market, which is today much more ready to invest in Australian product. Charles Wilson's first range of furniture for Woodmark in 2002 sold well, he says, 'because of its originality, not in spite of it'. And there are strong signs that specifiers are showing greater interest in Australian design, because they are looking for originality and need alternatives to iconic international brands. Whatever the case, over the last ten years there has been a growth in manufacturer support for Australian design. ■ Hence, one way Australian designers are reaching a market is with the assistance of the slowly growing number of manufacturers who support them through the design, development and prototyping process, and then arrange for the end product to be sold under licence. A prominent example is Woodmark, a company that began manufacturing Danish furniture under licence in Australia, but which is now increasingly looking to Australian designers. It supports important young furniture designers, including Charles Wilson, Matthew Sheargold, Gary Galego and, more recently, Jon Goulder. Charles Wilson's connection with Woodmark began with the *Swivel* chair (1995), which Woodmark

1 *Charles Wilson working in his studio*
Photograph Kell Christiansen
2 *Brian Steendyk with Cero chairs*
Photograph Erik Williamson
3 Charles Wilson, *Boulder* sofa and ottoman, 2004
Cold-moulded foam over plywood, upholstery.
Manufactured by Woodmark International, Australia
600 x 2450 x 900mm
Photograph Anson Smart

manufactured for the showroom, Norman + Quaine, in 1994. Since then, Wilson has designed a series of sofas, chairs and tables notable for their bold scale, fluent and extended line, and focus on functional flexibility. His *Boulder* lounge and ottoman (2006) continues these themes, but with a more organic inspiration originating, he says, in the shape of the grinding stone used for pounding grain – an image Wilson has carried with him since growing up on a farm. This is realised through the scalloped arms and stretched form, using moulded foam on the lounge and echoed in the ottoman. Should we regard this 'vernacular' inspiration as a marker of a distinctly regional – that is, Australian – product? I don't think so, because it is a personal trope and not an element in a common language.

    Nonetheless, this referentialism gives the lounge and ottoman a metaphorical dimension. They go beyond function and aesthetics to set up a dialogue with the user about the way they might be used, but also about wider, implied issues to do with everyday experience and its significance. This is an 'artistic' dimension, and it links Wilson to some other Australian designers, notably korban/flaubert, Robert Foster, Khai Liew, Alexander Lotersztain and Brian Steendyk, who are all primarily functionally driven creative designers rather than 'artist-designers', but whose work engages with the strategies of artworks to hint at an artistic function that enhances the utilitarian and purely aesthetic functions. They initiate a dialogue with the user about form and function, or even (as with korban/flaubert's ruminations on order and complexity) about issues apparently completely extrinsic to the object.   Another way through to the market is in partnership with showrooms that organise the manufacture of the products and then retail them. This is a Scandinavian model – Offecct in Sweden is a good example – which creates a close bond between showroom and designer, making the showroom the focus of a design culture. In Australia, the Sydney showroom, Norman + Quaine, is a notable example. Another is Corporate Culture, which now has showrooms in Sydney, Melbourne, Brisbane and New Zealand. Apart from bringing design, manufacture and marketing together as an integrated process, this model also protects the showrooms from the vagaries of a licensing system that can see them lose a licence despite having invested heavily in a particular designer. Among the Corporate Culture designers are Melbourne furniture designer Ross Didier, Sydney furniture designer Paul Morris, and the Sydney-based furniture design partnership ArnoldLane.

    Anibou, like Corporate Culture, is a showroom specialising in high-end imported design products. But Anibou has also developed a stable of designers with whom it has a variety of relationships. Gary Galego's *Leve* chair (2002) and *Speed* stool (2002) are manufactured by Woodmark, for example, but are retailed through Anibou. Jon Goulder and furniture designer, Leslie John Wright, source their own manufacturers for some products, while lighting designer, Frank Bauer and furniture designer, Johan Larsson, are designer-makers. Caroline Casey was the first local designer that Anibou took on, and she now has a substantial and varied portfolio including sofas, beds, screens, an umbrella stand, lighting, rugs, storage units and a clever adaptation of the ladder in the *Frank O'Neill* bookcase (1994) and *Wishbone* clothes ladder (1995). Casey emerged very quickly and was prolific early in her career, with her work showing

a precocious elegance, innovative strength and high quality finish. She, too, sources her own manufacturers and supervises the production process.

Schamburg + Alvisse, Khai Liew, Koskela in Sydney and Map in Melbourne all represent a third mode in Australian design, combining designer, producer and showroom – in other words, controlling the entire process. For Schamburg + Alvisse, this is especially important because the company is committed to designing sustainable furniture with the highest degree of durability, finish and detailing. Although closely attuned to both the residential and commercial markets, the company is also highly innovative and even experimental, a good example of this being the modular and multi-functional *Stop Playing With Yourself* (2005), which is as much a plaything as it is modular seating. And this mix of creative design and market-led design is true for all these 'designer-showrooms'.

Apart from partnerships, there are some cooperatives or collectives that collaborate to design, produce and market their work. The Brisbane-based Street and Garden Furniture Company, founded by designer and design educator, David Shaw, is one example. Notwithstanding the name, this collective ranges widely and includes personal accessories and homeware products as well as indoor and outdoor furniture. Probably the best known, however, is the Melbourne Movement. Founded in 1999 by RMIT University design lecturer, Kjell Grant, the Melbourne Movement is a collective committed to encouraging and promoting work by emerging designers through exhibitions and forums, and by initiating partnerships with manufacturers and retailers. It also acts as a producer. In this exhibition, Nick Rennie, Lucas Chirnside and Bianca Looney have been assisted through the Melbourne Movement. But the majority of Australian designers still belong to one of two other categories: designer-makers and designer-manufacturers. The most notable designer-manufacturers are korban/flaubert and Robert Foster. korban/flaubert design, develop and manufacture nearly all of their own products (some have been licensed out, but korban/flaubert do all their own tooling), and generally distribute directly. Robert Foster operates in two guises. He is a designer-maker with his more personal objects (such as his ongoing teapot series), but works predominantly through his production company, F!NK & Co., which designs, develops and manufactures mainly tableware and homeware, distributing through retailers. Foster has been fascinated with exploring technological possibilities, exemplified by his use of anodised aluminium in his water jugs, vases, bowls, beakers and serving dishes, in which he not only developed the manufacturing process, but also designed the machine to press the aluminium. The result of his experiments with anodised aluminium has been a series of beautifully refined and brilliantly coloured objects for the home, including table lamps. But F!NK & Co. also produces furniture (aluminium and glass tables, for example) and personal accessories such as the *Buckle Hip Pod* (2001), a cross between purse, wallet and jewellery, made from stainless steel, and the *Blue Ether Handbag* (2001), a cross between a handbag and a briefcase, using anodised aluminium, plastic and rubber. korban/flaubert's furniture and lighting are highly sophisticated, driven by an exploration of the potential of new technology and materials. The products are invariably functional, but always have an idea behind them, making them more than simply utilitarian objects.

1 Street and Garden Furniture Company, *Wave bench* located on waterfront, Burleigh Heads
Photograph Surya Graf
2 *Alexander Lotersztain visiting wood worker in Africa*
3 korban/flaubert, *spiral light*, 2006
Stainless steel
460 x Ø.450 mm
Photograph Sharrin Rees

This 'artistic' or intellectual agenda is most pronounced in a number of korban/flaubert's installations for public spaces in Australia – although these pieces still have a function, usually as seating, sometimes as a screen to delineate different spaces. ▪ The *swaylamp* (2002), described by the designers as 'an animated form, a person filled with light', exemplifies the korban/flaubert agenda. Made from roto-moulded polyethelene with a ballasted metal base, 'it seeks to reduce the "ingredients" for a lamp', setting up an intriguing dialogue between the linear and the curvilinear, a highly formal object that becomes almost anthropomorphic as it sways to the touch. On the other hand, their recent *spiral lights* (2006) and the screens, *array* (2005) and *cellscreen* (2003), are complex structures that seem to penetrate through to the molecular basis of all life. They are an expression of korban/flaubert's fascination with mathematics and geometry, and the fundamental forms of nature. There is always in their work a highly generative ambiguity, a rich tension between the functionality of the object and a powerful urge to throw off functionality and become an object of pure contemplation. *array* is a filigreed stainless steel screen of multiple loops, inspired by the Islamic *mashrabya* screen and South-East Asian textile traditions. Is it a screen or a wall sculpture? Similarly, the *cellscreen* – a cellular, honeycomb structure using anodised aluminium – is inspired partly by the Islamic decorative tradition, but also by complex mathematical sequences, and structures found in nature. The result is a functional screen or room divider, but also a highly decorative object that offers a range of different visual experiences. ▪ The tradition of the design-maker, however, remains strong, and if there is a distinctive Australian design ethos, this is it – or, at least, this is the source of a certain left-of-field, even idiosyncratic, design sensibility. If we take the Sydney-based practice, bernabeifreeman (Rina Bernabei and Kelly Freeman) as an example, it is possible to see connections with the current international mood for a decorative, 'feminine' aesthetic. But bernabeifreeman's perforated, anodised aluminium lights, chandeliers and screens also have a highly defined individuality. This comes partly from their interest in exploring contemporary materials and manufacturing technologies, and partly from a beautifully judged reinterpretation of the patterning of traditional textiles. ▪ This is part of a sensual strand in Australian design, which manifests itself in the organic screens and seating of Stefan Lie, the provocative furniture, lighting and homeware of zuii, and in the tactile lights and vases of Marc Pascal. It is also a feature of the work of Brisbane-based Brian Steendyk, an architect and interior designer who has become very active as a product designer. Steendyk is a highly pragmatic designer whose work – such as the quirky, playful and hugely versatile *Cero* (2001) – is very much about problem-solving for the real world. Nick Rennie and Adam Goodrum, on the other hand, are more focused on anticipating needs or uncovering unrecognised needs, and represent, therefore, the classic creative designer-maker. ▪ Out on his own somewhat is the cosmopolitan Alexander Lotersztain. Born of Polish parents, he grew up in Brazil. Now an Australian citizen, he spends large amounts of time elsewhere – in Africa, where he is working with other designers to help the Khaya people in South Africa to develop marketable products, and in Japan where he has been working with the Idée group.

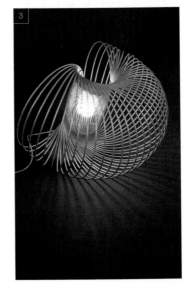

Lotersztain represents a highly ethical strand in Australian design, which is committed to producing sustainable and durable products: for example, his *Crusoe Sofa* (2004) uses recycled Danish boat fenders; the wicker *Soft Sofa* (2002), produced by Idée, also embodies Lotersztain's concern with adapting traditional craft practices to contemporary manufacturing processes; and the custom-made *Coral Light* (2004), which takes an ordinary industrial material, in the form of polyethylene, to create an object that is part art and part light, and capable of being constructed at any scale. In the range of his activities, Lotersztain is unusual in the Australian context, and probably represents where Australian design needs to go – towards a clarity of purpose within an equally clear understanding of its social responsibility, sourced to a vision of design as a mental process, rather than simply a generator of products.　While it is true to say of the overall design scene in Australia that it tends to walk to the beat of international design fashion, it is also true that the best of Australia's new generation of designers have a breezy individuality about them. What they often lack in finish and detail, they just as often make up for with a disarming inventiveness. And if, so far, they lack the confidence to simply play with design and crack the odd joke, they can be disarmingly charming. As to whether there is anything distinctively Australian about this new generation – and whether it really matters, anyway – that will, as always, be decided by others.

1. The designer, Charles Wilson has commented, however, that Goulder, while not trained as an industrial designer, has an industrial designer's sensibility, and points to the *Leda seat* and the way Goulder has cut the timber with an eye to reproduction. Goulder today sources his own manufacturers, and supervises the entire production process.

1 Alexander Lotersztain, *Soft Sofa*, 2002
Wicker/rattan on cane frame.
700 x 2250 x 1140mm

What is the potency of the 'independent' designer? Does this expression imply a major cultural shift in the perception of Australian fashion? The adjective 'independent' proposes autonomy, the ability to stand on one's own. It suggests an approach that recognises local fashion beyond the major arenas of commercial mass production and 'mainstream' culture, offering instead a medium that is perhaps experimental, and potentially unpredictable.

ROBYN HEALY

Making Noise:
Contemporary Australian fashion design

The classification 'independent' is synonymous with the alternate British music industry of the 1980s. There, it was associated with certain outsider sensibilities and characteristics, which were also labelled as 'emerging', 'alternative', 'provocative' or 'underground' – a genre that consciously distanced creative outputs from those of the major companies or consumer trends. It was an artistic attitude that was grounded in the doctrines of deviance and anti-establishment protest, arising from the1970s youth subcultures such as punk, hardcore and New Wave. ▌ It is not surprising then that from the late 1970s Australian fashion was searching for another design language, one that faced head-on issues relating to derivation, lack of confidence in local product and a misplaced notion of national identity. This movement sought to respond to a rather tired definition of local dress culture, which was burdened with clichés regarding conservative nationalistic referencing and worth. There was an overriding preference for dress styles that blended in with the rest of the Western world, and a disheartening belief about inferior clothing examples produced locally to apparently emulate the superior imported ones. The expression 'independent designer', however, proposed another model – one of confidence, displaying a rebellious spirit, and an irreverence towards standard etiquette codes and predictable fashionable choices. This attitude potentially challenged the observation that Australia was a fashion wasteland. ▌ This essay identifies a series of 'moments', from the late 1970s to now, which witnessed the emergence of the independent designer. Exploring the growth of particular practices like freestyle or demi-couture, or alternative mechanisms for articulating fashion

ideas such as exhibitions, catwalk parades or a festival, we can see that Australian fashion has changed radically over the last 30 years. Fashion has evolved in response to the impact of globalism, which has altered the influence of design sources, and the speed of fabrication and offshore production has shifted the dynamics of industry. How do we now read Australian fashion, and is the independent designer perhaps a unique and defining aspect of our dress culture? ■ The headline in Italian *Vogue* December 1977,[1] announces: 'A fashion arrives from another hemisphere'. Over a six-page spread, the influential stylist Anna Piaggi enthuses about the latest Flamingo Park designs, the work of Linda Jackson (b.1950) and Jenny Kee (b.1947). She writes that theirs is 'one of the most inventive "free" collections we've seen in recent times'. Animated colour, gigantic pattern and idiosyncratic motifs, combined with the beginnings of unstructured dress forms, make a liberating style. It appears so very different from all the others, and the regimented sameness of boring chic trends is absent. Here is Australian-designed clothing revealing a rather brave amalgam of craft, theatrics and flamboyance, and inspired by an eclectic mixture of art and costume references from across the globe. Their exhaustive list of influences covers, simultaneously, the textiles of Sonia Delaunay, the revolutionary ballet costumes from Serge Diaghilev's Ballet Russes, the unique construction feats of twentieth-century couturiers such as Madeleine Vionnet, the traditional costumes of China and Japan, and the art and writings of the Australian artist Margaret Preston. ■ Flamingo Park (1973–82)[2] fashion was conversational, loud, highly irreverent and very entertaining. At the same time, it was confronting, drawing attention to the wearer by playing with the concept of a clichéd Australian identity and the image of the outsider. Distinctive aspects of popular culture titled and themed Flamingo Park collections: there was controversial architecture, the Opera House dress; an endearing character from children's literature, the Blinky Bill jumper; and the brilliant New South Wales floral emblem, the Red Waratah dress. It placed familiar things locally, and simultaneously introduced the exotic internationally. The Princess of Wales, for instance, was photographed wearing a Blinky Bill jumper through her first pregnancy, an image that was projected around the world (the jumper had been a gift from the New South Wales Premier's daughter).[3] Kee and Jackson consequently became known names in a highly competitive international market. Commentators labelled their fashion 'Australiana', or the first true Australian style, and Flamingo Park fast became an icon of independence, in line with the political agenda of the federal Whitlam Government (1972–75), the push for a republic and increased government spending to boost the arts.[4] 'Australiana' was symbolically charged, shifting the way that the arts, including fashion, were considered; however 'fast-forward 30 years and the thought of koalas on sweaters and the Sydney Opera House on dresses evokes an audible groan'.[5] ■ The fusion of original textile and fashion production eliminated issues surrounding availability of materials and monotony complicated by mass-produced design, and curbed the problem of a limited local manufacturing base, thereby forging a unique aesthetic. Kee and Jackson[6] either created original textiles for their collections or commissioned artists to work with them. Collaborations often resulted in some monumental cross-cultural fusions. Jenny Kee's Black Opal design

evocatively transposed the amazing prismatic colour effects of a cut opal onto fabric. This spectacular silk was contracted by Karl Lagerfeld and incorporated into his inaugural 1983 Chanel ready-to-wear collection, placing Kee's work on the most celebrated Parisian catwalk. ▌ Linda Jackson also instigated some remarkable synergies – she was inspired by the art of Aboriginal Australia since the 1970s, however it wasn't until 1980 that Jackson travelled to Aboriginal communities and worked collaboratively with various Indigenous communities, and embraced the use of original Indigenous textiles. Specialised art and craft classes introduced the resist-dyeing batik technique into the Utopia station community in the Northern Territory in late 1977,[7] and furnished the Indigenous women there with an extraordinary, abstract artform. These earliest expressions were translated by the Utopia batik artists onto T-shirts and wrap-around skirts of unparallel beauty. The late Emily Kngwarreye (Eastern Anmatyerr, c.1910–96), one of Australia's most respected visual artists, developed her distinctive painting style during these early batik excursions, where she represented quite lyrically her family's Yam and Emu Dreamings. Collaborations with designers like Linda Jackson allowed the Utopia batik fabric lengths to be incorporated into fashionable garments and consequently exposed to a larger audience. Although once the calibre of these compositions was recognised, the fabric lengths were soon sold individually as artworks, and their translation into fashion was halted. Fashion successfully acted as a conduit in making Kngwarreye's work more accessible; however, it also devalued the work outside a fine art context, where higher prices are achieved. ▌ Ironically, fashion aspires to be art to attain a certain status in a market and commodity-driven world. The fast turnover associated with fashion gives little time for contemplation outside the immediacy of wearability and the passing seasons. Through an exhibition, contemporary fashion can generate invaluable designer recognition and acknowledgement, albeit potentially making the medium available to closer scrutiny, and perhaps even ridicule, from substantial media and public attention. *Project 33 Art Clothes,*[8] assembled by the (then) Assistant Curator of Prints and Drawings, Jane De Teliga, opened at the Art Gallery of New South Wales on 20 December 1980. It was a seminal display, positioning local contemporary fashion in line with avant-garde art movements, and staged in the context of a contemporary art project housed in a state gallery that did not represent fashion in its permanent collection. *Project 33 Art Clothes* defined the clothing on display as 'wearable art objects', thereby vigorously placing the exhibits' functional design elements alongside the aesthetic concerns of art. Impressive garments including the *Ceremonial Coat for the Grand Diva of Paradise Garage* (1980), by Peter Tully (1947–94), proposed an example of urban tribal wear.[9] This wild assemblage of strips of vibrant plastic, dangling with everyday found objects, lined with luxurious fake fur, was Tully's fancy garb for the 'gay tribe' and nightclub outings. In keeping with the exploratory nature of many works, controversy prevailed. In particular, the reception received by *The Religious Cavalier* (1980) by Katie Pye (b.1952), which portrayed a deadly mix of religious and sexual imagery accessorised with two gun holsters carrying black crucifixes, caused a major incident when it was removed from display by a staff member

1 Linda Jackson, *Utopia costume*, 1982
Cotton, silk, batik.
Manufactured by Bush Couture, Australia
Photograph courtesy of National
Gallery of Victoria, Melbourne
2 Peter Tully, *Ceremonial Coat for
the Grand Diva of Paradise Garage*, 1980
Industrial vinyl and plastic.
1180 x 500mm
Photograph courtesy of National
Gallery of Victoria, Melbourne
3 Karl Lagerfeld for Chanel, *Suit*, 1983
Textiles designed by Jenny Kee
Silk, wool, metal.
Photograph Patrick Russell, presented by
Vogue, Australia, courtesy of National Gallery
of Victoria, Melbourne

as an act of voluntary censorship. It was later returned, but displayed in a manner that guaranteed the potentially offending aspects were obscured.[10] Pye's work found resonance in the music industry, where she was particularly successful designing for Shock Pop band Jimmy and The Boys, and the New Wave group Mi-Sex. ■ *Project 33 Art Clothes* was perceived as a milestone, gaining significant recognition for designers through the acquisition of their work by public art galleries and museums. A selection of 'wearable art objects' was purchased by the National Gallery of Australia, Canberra[11] and the Powerhouse Museum, Sydney, cultivating an ongoing public interface and a continuing critical analysis of these works. 'Art clothes' or 'wearable art objects' asserted a point of difference from the bland mass-produced item, and encouraged a resurgence in the handmade or crafted. The wild and whimsical renderings of many of these exhibits conveyed the unwarranted impression that they were unwearable, which was not the case at all. The idea of dressing up outrageously for clubbing was an underground fashion scene, where clothing was the most creative, experimental and sexually charged. Creativity was incited by the lush and provocative images presented in the cult London-based magazines *The Face* and *ID* (which were popular purchases, particularly the latest air-freighted edition), and spurred on by the activities of Leigh Bowery (1961–94),[12] who moved to London in the early 1980s in search of the glamorous nightclub scene of the romantic/blitz movement. In 1984 'The new glitterati' in *The Face*[13] enthusiastically documented Bowery's first collection – 'Pakis from outer-space'. It combined bright-blue all-over make-up, with a pastiche of a Hindu god, military splendour, Abba costuming and an asymmetrical cut. Bowery became the face of the Leicester Square Taboo nightclub, dressing performers such as Boy George and inspiring designers like John Galliano and Vivienne Westwood with his grotesque, exaggerated silhouettes, his kitsch-glam special effects and mind-blowing body and gender distortions. Australia's reputation for dressing up in an outrageous and unconventional manner was further liberated through the annual Sydney Gay and Lesbian Mardi Gras. Here the combination of oiled skin and politically charged fancy dress was a symbol of gay pride and recognition. ■ Australiana fashion, 'art clothes' and clubwear proclaimed a vociferous dress repertoire that emanated images of a striking and sophisticated artistic subculture. In Melbourne the Fashion Design Council of Australia (FDC) – a supportive body representing the rights of independent fashion designers, established in 1984 – eloquently preached the virtues of 'HIGH-RISK-DRESSING'.[14] Defiantly the FDC offered young designers an incitement to secede from the fashion industry's 'bland middle ground'[15] and to collectively support each other in such a seditious affiliation. Its manifesto stated a passionate commitment 'to the development of the art of fashion design, to the individualistic, the idiosyncratic, the experimental, the new and provocative, both in its wearable and unwearable form. It is critical of and sees itself separate to the conventions of mainstream and commercial fashion, the European tradition, the stranglehold of fashion houses'.[16] ■ This declaration articulated a stance that was progressive, potentially radical, and simultaneously disrespectful to most of the fashion industry, including retailers, buyers, the press and consumers. The FDC's encouragement of young people in becoming designers, making clothes

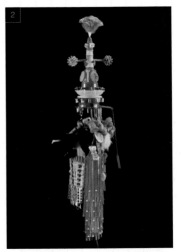

and engaging with fashion in whatever form they liked, attracted support from many quarters. The FDC, instigated by Kate Durham, Robert Buckingham and Robert Pearce, secured official sanction through state and federal authorities, with funding assistance provided by the Victorian state government along with further support from the Australia Council. Although based in Melbourne, the FDC's membership spread across Australia, and it was concerned with both creative and business issues, and researching the potential new export markets. Rejecting 'alternative', the FDA had selected and championed the term 'independent' as an important mechanism to acknowledge and profile a designer's reputation rather than the manufacturer's.[17] This issue drove many of its strategies, such as publishing designers' photographs in parade catalogues, in an ongoing attempt to pull the small-scale designer out of oblivion. Kate Durham recalls that the adoption of 'independent' positioned the freelance designer away from being controlled by the retailer who purchased goods upon consignment and often didn't acknowledge the designer. 'It was about stopping designers being ripped off and fighting for their independence.'[18] The FDC platform declared a desire to foster multiple forms of dress and appearance, to promote the status of fashion and cultivate an appreciation for these. Following this tactic, the FDC exposed fashion through illustration, photography, film, performance, installation and theoretical guises, and communicated and consumed via catwalk parades, diverse and thought-provoking exhibitions, a retail shop, particular events embedded in nightclub culture and the music scene, and business seminars. Hundreds of activities were orchestrated: from the dance performance, *No Fire Escape from Fashion*, staged by Leigh Bowery and Michael Clarke & Co, to *Tomorrow's forecast – raincoats of Melbourne*, where prominent Melbourne sculptures were dressed in raincoats, and extraordinary parades, starting with *Fashion 84 Heroic Fashion*. Over a nine-year period, the FDC (1984–93) was involved with a diverse array of artists and designers, architects, choreographers, musicians, hairdressers and make-up artists, among them Martin Grant, Kara Baker, Fiona Scanlan (formerly of Scanlan & Theodore), Leona Edmiston, Peter Morrissey (both formerly Morrissey & Edmiston), Alannah Hill, Bettina Liano, Gavin Brown, Rebecca Paterson, Dinosaur Designs, Rosslynd Piggott and Jenny Bannister, as just a small selection. Perhaps the real legacy of the FDC is in the ambitious infrastructure it pioneered, offering assistance to designers in both creative and business goals. Essentially, the FDC targeted the future, fostering emerging designers and offering its members an intricate support system and means for exposure. Aspects of the FDC's approach are reflected in the major changes that occurred in the 1990s, particularly in the introduction of incentives for young designers through the emergence of regular trade shows, and an annual fashion festival. The instigation of Mercedes Australian Fashion Week in Sydney in 1996 placed fashion in an arena that addressed sales, notably bringing buyers to Australia, and thereby opening up a vital, critical and commercial dialogue. The journalist Marion Hume became the infamous protagonist of the industry in the teething years, initially as a London correspondent for *The Independent* and *The Sunday Times*, and later in her role as the editor of Australian *Vogue*. An important part of Mercedes Australian Fashion Week was the New

1 Dinosaur Designs, *Agate shard necklace, Bowerbird necklace, Long Ball and Chain necklace, Sterling silver gem inlay ring, assorted resin and sterling silver bangles*, 2005
Resin, sterling silver, agate, leather.
Photograph Stephen Ward
2 Toni Maticevski, Runway image from Mercedes Australian Fashion Week, 2006 Spring Summer Collection
Photograph courtesy Toni Maticevski
3 Toni Maticevski, Runway image from Mercedes Australian Fashion Week, 2006 Spring Summer Collection
Photograph courtesy Toni Maticevski

Generation parade, where Hume found her only positive experience in the first year through the work of Akira Isogawa (b.1964) – his garments were purchased by the prestigious London store, Browns – while everyone else disappointed her. The following year she spoke of clothes that 'looked as if they were cut from Simplicity patterns, coded easy to sew. Let's not kid ourselves we know what the international buyers come here for, and it is rarely our frocks… .'[19] Isogawa's practice has generated a 'demonstration of cultural craftsmanship'.[20] No longer aligned to his Japanese origins, his ingredients are from the world: batik patterns, Indian embroidery, Japanese kimono silk, Italian wool or the iconic Bonds singlet. He has become a major drawcard at Mercedes Australian Fashion Week, although he chooses, like many others, to show collections in Paris. Launched by Isogawa in 2001, the Mercedes-Benz Start-up Program is an innovative and exciting national small business initiative that is specifically designed to seek excellence in design innovation and to enhance the future of the next generation of fashion designers. Winners receive a financial prize plus support, and are mentored within the industry and offered a place in the Mercedes Australian Fashion Week's New Generation parade. While Mercedes Australian Fashion Week is specifically for the trade, the annual Melbourne Fashion Festival, launched in 1997, curates a rich program of fashion events for the public, and also provides professional development for the industry through a substantial business seminar and a New Designer award. There is a concurrent public arts program promoting exhibitions, lectures and events, which further articulates connections between the applied arts, textile design, jewellery, film and photography. International guests are a feature of this week-long festival, and have included the commentators Ted Polhemus, Valerie Steele and Colin McDowell, and designers Philip Treacy, Walter Van Beirendonck, Bernard Wilhelm and Philippe Starck. The association of technical excellence with independent fashion is rarely discussed – more extreme designs are often considered poorly executed, although over the last decade this has changed dramatically. In fashion, the haute couture[21] exemplar symbolises the highest design level. This hallowed label implies very expensive, custom-made clothing produced from quality execution and materials, rigorous, time-consuming methods and meticulous crafting. This approach has a profound influence, and encourages aspirations for technical virtuosity and fabrication, original one-off designs, and the belief that fashion is an extraordinary aesthetic experience. Historically, 'haute couture' was the desired choice of many wealthy Australian women, expressing the ultimate in fashionability in being dressed from Paris. Public collections are testimony to the tastes of the local populace from the nineteenth century to now, with countless models by major French couture houses such as Molyneux, Patou, Chanel, Dior and Balenciaga in museum repositories bearing local provenances. A form of deluxe clothing production is suited to the market for small-scale independent design. The emergence of demi-couture practice since the 1990s has witnessed the appearance of designers who perhaps combine the detail of couture with the practicality of ready-to-wear. This can be particularly seen in the work of Toni Maticevski. After graduating from the fashion design degree at RMIT University, Melbourne, Maticevski has eschewed various chances to work under an experienced designer

like the American Donna Karan, or to perhaps attain a long-term apprenticeship in a major European house. Instead, Maticevski chooses to practice in Melbourne. He is drawn to an environment that encourages creative control and an appreciation for the aesthetics of his craft. Through exquisite detailing, and his subtle blending of materials, colour and shape, he achieves the essence of couture, and takes this to a more sophisticated level, where the breakdown of the garment's elements is transcended by the final result to evoke an emotional response from the experience of either wearing or viewing his fashions. Like a piece of love poetry or the uplifting effect achieved by a musical composition, this is the place where Maticevski takes us through the orchestration of his clothing designs. 'It's too easy to acquire ideas by opening up art books or fashion magazines. If you access your designs from the point of view of emotion, from the limitations you face, you can change what you know and what others see.'[22]   In contrast to Maticevski, Martin Grant, an original member of the FDC, left Melbourne and successfully established his practice in Paris. Grant is acutely aware of the heightened divergence in the fashion culture. In Paris, it is common practice for a young designer to work for an established fashion house for at least ten years, hoping they will eventually secure a financial backer, which will ultimately allow them to set up their own enterprise.[23] Grant, like Maticevski, is an independent, working proudly under the banner 'Martin Grant, Paris'.   The 'independent' Australian fashion designer is one unfettered by the grand traditions of historic fashion, the lineage associated with a particular fashion house, the burden of restrictive fashion protocols, or the commercial hysterics of an over-inflated market. Whether through the application of free style, humour, art clothes, the use of Australiana, the technical or emotive expressions of haute couture, or the formal structure of a trade show, Australian fashion is making plenty of noise.

1. L. Jackson, *Linda Jackson The Art of Fashion*, Fontana, Sydney, 1987, p. 14.
2. J. McPhee, *Linda Jackson and Jenny Kee Flamingo Park and Bush Couture*, exhibition brochure, Australian National Gallery, Canberra, 1985.
3. A. Joel, Best *Dressed 200 Years of Fashion in Australia*, William Collins Pty Ltd, Sydney, 1984, p. 202.
4. M. Maynard, *Out of Line Australian Women and Style*, University of New South Wales, Press Ltd, Sydney, 2001, p. 62.
5. S. Honnor, 'Australiana is back … ', *The Australian*, Murdoch Press, Sydney, 18 May, 2000, p. 5.
6. Jenny Kee and Linda Jackson worked together under the Flamingo Park label from 1977 to 1982, then Linda Jackson established her own label Bush Couture while Kee continued with Flamingo Park.
7. J. Green, 'Singing the Silk: Utopia batik', in *Raiki Wara Long Cloth from Aboriginal Australia and the Torres Strait*, National Gallery of Victoria, Melbourne, 1998, p. 40.
8. J. De Teliga, *Project 33 Art Clothes*, Art Gallery of New South Wales, Sydney, 1980.
9. Peter Tully was Director of the Sydney Gay and Lesbian Mardi Gras from 1981–87, and steered that event to create an opportunity for gay people to express themselves collectively.
10. A. Joel, 1984, op. cit, p. 204.
11. These were the first examples of Australian fashion to enter the National Gallery of Australia, acquired by the Gallery's Australian Decorative Arts Department.
12. *Take a Bowery: The art and (larger than) life of Leigh Bowery*, Museum of Contemporary Art, Sydney, 2003.
13. L. White, 'The new glitterati', *The Face*, no. 48, April 1984, p. 56.
14. *Fashion 84 Heroic Fashion*, Fashion Design Council of Australia, Melbourne, 1984, p. 2.
15. ibid.
16. C. Wood, 'The Fashion Design Council of Australia', *Design World*, no. 10, 1986, p. 21.
17. FDC Archive scrapbook 1, The Frances Burke Textile Resource Centre, RMIT University, City Campus, Melbourne.
18. Conversation between Robert Buckingham and Kate Durham, 11 April, 2006.
19. M. Hume, 'The verdict', *Vogue* Australia, July 1997, no. 7, p. 21.
20. Interview with Akira Isagawa by Maya Kanamori, Japan Cultural Centre, 1 November, 2003, www.craftculture.org/world/Isagawa1.htm.
21. The precise definition relates solely to the French fashion industry; the term 'haute couture' refers to custom-made clothes produced in Paris workshops, where the term is a protected appellation; however the popular interpretation relates to any form of high quality custom-made clothing.
22. Toni Maticevski designer profile, *Vogue* Australia, on-line www.vogue.com.au/fashion_central/people/fashion_designers/toni_maticevski
23. Miriam Cosic, 'Parisian life tailor-made for Melbourne boy', *The Age*, February 1998, p. 12.

1 Akira Isogawa, *Akira Silk Chiffon Ruffle Dress*, 2005
Automne Hiver 2005
(shown in Paris, March 2005)
Photograph Stephen Ward

What motivates and inspires the designers and makers who work in these particular fields? What shapes their various approaches to what they do? What makes them unique in their practice, yet, at the same time, what influences and connections might they share?

GRACE COCHRANE

A Material Approach: Ceramics, glass and jewellery

All set out to express their own ideas and meanings through the forms they make and the functions they might perform, and all have a sense of the different audiences and markets where their work finds its place. But underlying the breadth of these possibilities is a deep understanding of the materials and processes they use and the knowledge that their, and our, interaction with what they make and how they make it, also contributes to the meaning of their work. ▮ *When making my vessels and brooches, the soft organic forms are influenced by the process of chasing and texturing. The malleable, annealed metal surface gently 'moves' and 'shifts' as it is work-hardened with my small steel chasing tools.* Julie Blyfield. ▮ Within the decades of social and economic change following the close of World War II in 1945, most of these designers and makers are second or third-generation practitioners in the postwar crafts revival. They have inherited the example, experience, professional models and mentorship of practitioners in all fields, the education programs they developed and which have changed along the way, and the organisations and publications they set up. Then they have taken this legacy in their own different directions. ▮ Nearly all the practitioners in this loose category of *'Freestyle'* are the product of an education in art, rather than design, schools, and their emphasis remains largely on the personal expression of ideas and concepts, which are mixed with the pleasure of working with materials and the skills needed to make it happen. They are embedded in changing relationships with art and design: handcrafted objects contain elements of both, and there continue to be many interchanges of both adoption and rejection, in the swings and balances of value and influence

1 *Kathy Elliott finishing a piece in Edols Elliott workshop*
Photograph Nigel Noyes
2 *Oliver Smith planishing a copper vessel*
Photograph Ben Manson
3 *Janet DeBoos' work being slip poured in Huaguang China*, 2004
Photograph Janet DeBoos
4 *Ben Edols shaping a piece in Edols Elliott workshop*
Photograph Nigel Noyes

that take place between the two. The crafts retain a continuing role and identity in the making of beautiful or challenging objects for contemplation and pleasure. They also continue to be identified with serving functional purposes, where objects for use are enjoyed for an appearance and texture associated with working materials by hand: for wearing, for eating and drinking, for ceremonies and rituals, for sitting on, storing or covering. Currently these kinds of objects can be found both in galleries and fashion boutiques, and increasingly alongside manufactured wares in design showrooms. Audiences value both, and like to be able to recognise a name or a signature style that links the object to its maker. The separate stories and statements in this publication document career paths that explore the many interests, ideas and approaches of the practitioners represented here. Some give their entire attention to making unique pieces; some work solely in limited series. Others now extend to wider production runs using specialised manufacturing processes, sometimes outside the studio. A number cross confidently from one end of this spectrum to the other. Their experiences and ideals are shared with many who work in both fashion and textiles, and in furniture and lighting. Glass artists Benjamin Edols and Kathy Elliott, for example, make unique hand-blown and cold-worked glass, sometimes in limited series, while, working from his practical knowledge of blowing glass, Jonathan Baskett has developed a global production network to manufacture different stages of some of his glass vessels. An exemplary silversmith, Robert Foster has also established a well-known range of objects in aluminium and has developed production processes to make these in limited series, along with having work made in China and collaborating with a lighting company in Germany. Oliver Smith, also a skilled metalworker, has successfully developed a range of silver tableware into production in stainless steel. Interested in the images and materials of the urban environment and popular culture, Susan Cohn's handmade objects lend themselves to multiples, and her perforated aluminium *Cohncave* bowl has been manufactured by Alessi since 1992. Ceramic artists, long interested in making both individual works and limited series by hand, drawing on many cultural traditions, are now beginning to spend time developing prototypes for production in factories elsewhere. Bianca Looney, committed to a philosophical connection between her ceramic work and the land, has developed a tile system that may well find its form not only potentially in tile ceramic manufacture in Europe, but also in aluminium and perhaps timber in Australia. Both Janet DeBoos and Prue Venables have substantial international reputations for their one-off porcelain works, and have devoted their careers to exploring ideas based around hand-formed vessels and their meanings. Yet both have recently responded to the parallel challenge of designing for industrial production: DeBoos in Italy and China and Venables in Japan. *It was very exciting to work to a brief presented by a Japanese distributor, in combination with a production factory. The cultural differences with regards to both use and understanding of particular forms provided a multitude of questions and challenges … Ceramic objects for use are treated with such reverence … the development of the production prototypes called on all of my resources and experience gained through my other explorations of one-off exhibition work.* Prue Venables Jennifer Robertson, an experienced hand-weaver,

combines computer-aided design and programming with hand-weaving processes in Montreal, yet also makes complex jacquards on ancient looms in Florence and was invited to put her designs into (hand) production in Japan. Georgia Chapman, in Vixen, started her fashion and homewares range round her own hand-printed textiles. Easton Pearson has worked closely for many years with skilled beaders and embroiderers in Asia, as has Akira Isogawa, who also works at times with hand-printed textiles from the screen-printing workshop, Signature Prints. All these fashion designers expose the process and effects of construction, reflecting a spirit of 'the handmade'. ■ A number of events and experiences, pathways and people, cultures and circumstances have contributed as accumulating influences to this field in Australia, and on the people in this exhibition. The makers themselves reflect many different cultural backgrounds, and their experiences are equally varied. Indigenous Australian artists, like the Tiwi people and those from Maningrida in this exhibition, draw strongly on their traditions for their contemporary works, often now made in non-traditional media. The 200-year colonial presence brought a largely British heritage, overlaid by groups from Europe, who came in waves of later migration, and from Asia, especially in recent decades. Many identify with both an Australian heritage as well as that of another country of origin, sometimes generations earlier. Ari Athans' jewellery, which combines precious metals with gemstones, has grown out of her consciousness of being the child of Greek migrants who treasured the few possessions they brought with them, including jewellery, combined with her first training as a geologist. Ideas are also shaped by Australia's physical and cultural position in the South-East Asia-Pacific region, and most of these people have travelled widely or studied overseas as well as in Australia. Akira Isogawa's outfits are both international in their form and Japanese in their origins. Similarly, Chinese Malaysian-born Khai Liew successfully combines Asian influences with references to European furniture. A number see themselves as part of an international art or design continuum; others respond very directly to the environment where they live – city, beach, mountain, desert, farm or isolated community. If one seeks to recognise any single 'identity' here, it is clear that there are as many ways of looking out at the rest of the world as there are of looking in at Australians. ■ Relatively isolated from others geographically and, for most, not bounded by long national cultural traditions, Australians have always reached out to draw freely on ideas and experiences from elsewhere. From the early 1970s, the funding support from federal and state arts funding bodies for personal arts research, studio establishment, exhibition development and organisation infrastructure, encouraged a wider and freer flow of people, exhibitions and ideas around Australia and around the globe. Courses that had originally been in technical and teachers' colleges changed in status and location into firstly, colleges and institutes of advanced education in the 1970s, then universities in the 1980s, offering increasingly higher academic qualifications – today with often diminishing contact hours and hands-on experience. There are many options offered between art and design programs, with some acknowledged centres of excellence and specialisation. In recent years, both the need to finance tertiary education as well as a genuine desire to establish global networks have seen an extraordinary influx of foreign students into all

1 *Janet DeBoos with cups,* 2004
2 *Jennifer Robertson at loom,* 2005
Photograph Brian Parkes
3 *Julie Blyfield at Gray Street Workshop*
Photograph Grant Hancock
4 *Susan Cohn in her studio,*
Workshop 3000, 2005
Photograph Brian Parkes

programs, bringing different ideas and experiences. At the same time, there have been many opportunities for Australians to participate in exchanges and scholarships to other places.  While maintaining their own practices, many of the 'skilled craftspeople' in this exhibition have contributed to the wider development of their field. Janet DeBoos and Prue Venables both teach ceramics, and DeBoos has developed a major, distance education on-line course. Edols and Elliott have both maintained a constant program of teaching in summer schools, such as in the United States and Italy, and also offer employment and experience to other glass workers. The Gray Street jewellery workshop is an exemplary model of a cooperative workshop, where the partners have offered experience to many others over the years, while not only developing their own practices but also becoming individually involved at times in a range of external projects, such as public art commissions. Susan Cohn has consistently offered traineeships in her studio; and Robert Foster encourages collaboration with selected makers, like Oliver Smith, to develop new F!NK & Co. products. Smith, in turn, now also teaches and works collaboratively with makers in different fields on innovative projects.  *I look for opportunities where I can do what I do well and unite it with the strengths of another process, material or individual … the high level of skilled craft existing within industrial settings makes me seek opportunities where it could be given greater expression. Ultimately it is about making the whole greater than the sum of its parts. When this occurs the results inspire you to strive further.* Oliver Smith Most of those in this exhibition have been involved in one way or another with the specialist regional and national organisations that have evolved: among many others, the Potters Society of Australia (1956), Ausglass (1978) and the Jewellers and Metalsmiths Group of Australia (1980). Originally established to provide information, share experience, document events and hold exhibitions, a most significant continuing contribution remains their biennial conferences, journals, newsletters and websites. They continue to make information accessible and bring people and their ideas together. Cross-media organisations like Craft Australia and the state crafts and design organisations, like Object, all now have different characteristics and names, reflecting the audiences they serve, and the existence of other local infrastructures. New communication systems not only provide access on-line to information about people and their work, but also enable specialist or general audiences to enter into interactive conversations with each other.  Today, designers and makers work through galleries and other outlets in Australia, many of which have devoted decades to makers in their chosen fields, and usually have consistent gallery representation in other countries. Longstanding friendships and professional networks have benefited designers' and makers' practices and many have been concerned to open up similar opportunities for those who follow. As well as the longstanding representation in events like the annual ceramics exhibitions in Faenza, Italy, since the early 1990s there has also been constant representation in events such as SOFA (Sculptural Objects and Functional Art) in Chicago and New York, Talente in Munich, Germany, the Milan International Furniture Fair in Italy, Designers Block in Tokyo and more recently, at Collect in the United Kingdom. Venables, Blyfield, Liew and Foster were all represented at Collect in 2006. Jewellers

and metalsmiths, already influenced by the work of migrants from Scandinavia, Germany and the United Kingdom, maintain continuing exchanges through conferences, residencies and exhibitions in the United States and Asia. And glass artists Edols and Elliott have worked as far afield as Seattle and Portland in the United States and Murano in Italy.

The great benefit of overseas experience is the stimulation of visiting other artists, other studios and other countries – through conferences, workshops and exhibition openings – which are all terrific for reinvigorating our commitment to what we do. It provides that sometimes very necessary distance you need from your working life to get a fresh perspective on what you are involved in. Kathy Elliott Australia's museum collections also reflect stories of research and resource. Though waxing and waning at different times in their abilities to purchase important works as they are made, there are nonetheless highly significant reference collections of decorative arts, crafts and design in all state capitals. Some are integrated in exhibitions with wider collections and others stand alone, such as the recently opened permanent collection-based exhibition, *Inspired! Design Across Time*, at Sydney's Powerhouse Museum. Important regional specialisations are found, most notably, in Wagga Wagga for glass, Shepparton for ceramics, Hamilton for metalwork and Tamworth for textiles. Institutions, large and small, also mount temporary exhibitions that extend the experience of audiences to the parameters of this field, and work together as much as they can to share exhibitions across the country and, as with *Freestyle*, to send them to be viewed by new audiences elsewhere. Most of the people in this exhibition have their work represented in these collections, and themselves draw on the holdings, at times, for reference and inspiration. Apart from the decorative arts and design collections that provide a visual resource for most designers and makers, other collection sources are also researched. Sheridan Kennedy, for example, makes theatrical jewellery pieces based on what appear to be imaginary collections of specimens, sometimes using natural materials, taking us on voyages of imagination in attempting to trace their sources and identification.

Different approaches to designing and making are linked to different choices made for placing work in the marketplace. As well as seeking galleries to promote and exhibit the work as art objects, it is just as likely that some will be placed in a design showroom in the context of interior design or homewares, and in those promotional and critical journals. Most outlets now also promote their artists and designers on-line, and earlier objects find their way onto the market through internet sales as well as in auction houses. Some designers have set up businesses that have their own outlets. Significant here is Dinosaur Designs, a trio of designer-makers who started selling their jewellery in the local market in the 1980s and have developed an international reach for their jewellery and homewares, through their own outlets in Australia and elsewhere.

Opening an outlet in New York is great fun; the driving force is expanding our business so the world can see what we do. Chipping out a foothold in that city is an exciting thing to do. It is a world hub and so many people inevitably stumble across what we do. Having a showroom and retail outlet there opens things up for us. We like presenting ourselves there in our own way. Stephen Ormandy, Dinosaur Designs

1 Janet DeBoos, *Hand Beaker*
Photograph Greg Daly
2 Dinosaur Designs, *Sandblasted Glass Vase, Large Organic Oval Vase, Organic Boulder Dish*, 1998, *Organic Kidney Dish*, 1997
Resin, glass.
Photograph Petrina Tinslay
3 Robert Foster, *F!NK Bowls*, 1999
Manufactured by F!NK & Co., Australia
Anodised aluminium.
Largest: Ø.275mm

Australia does not have a large marketplace; for most people there is a challenge in identifying viable markets at home while also working out how to enter the specialist collector or larger design markets overseas. In fact, wider changes in the global patterns of manufacturing, where crafts-based, skilled industries are closing in the West and moving to the East, are opening up many new possibilities for production on a larger – and cheaper – scale. New technologies allow rapid prototyping, mass-customisation and design communication on-line, in factories that combine new technologies with centuries-old hand-skills. Jon Goulder makes his own furniture prototypes, then collaborates with factories in both Australia and China to develop production lines. Alex Lotersztain and Caroline Casey have both worked with skilled craftspeople in other countries to make their designs. They feel strongly about the value of the economic opportunities they provide, and trust their own processes of collaboration, but everywhere issues of economic independence versus exploitation, and copyright versus fair dealing, become part of global manufacturing language. And concerns for the world's forests, oil, mineral and water resources, as well as issues of global warming and population changes, become part of the discussion of the use of manmade and natural materials in consumer markets.

Australians are dealing intelligently with these changing times. Travel is cheaper; communication is more effective. Education is shorter, more expensive, more competitive. Glass and ceramic artists, jewellers and metalsmiths are able to combine old and new technologies and start experimenting with the new opportunities these juxtapositions offer. At the same time, many actively maintain independence in their one-off production, defending their enjoyment of the process, and the celebration of virtuosity of skill in the execution of a concept or idea, sometimes opting to make up-market pieces so complex that, in this time of global borrowing, no-one can copy them. Many criticise those who design

without understanding the habits and characteristics of materials; others enjoy the work of those who make challenging objects by not following any rules at all. New materials in timber, ceramics, fibres, metals and resins provide new opportunities for manufacture and finish, while simultaneously, and increasingly, designers and makers seek out small industries for contracted aspects of their work, where they value – as a form of personally researched intellectual property – the expertise of, and personal working relationships with, the highly skilled trade artisans, cutters, casters, sewers and embroiderers, who are themselves combining a lifetime of skilled knowledge with new technologies. The work of each of the people in this exhibition reflects their own personal paths through this set of circumstances, both into their chosen field, and in the way they choose to make it accessible to others. All have contributed to the ways in which Australia perceives its place in the world, through its designed and made objects, as well as providing insights for others in the ways they see people here, and what Australia might be.

Designer Profiles

After 12 years in practice, jeweller Ari Athans (b.1965) knows she's found the 'happy medium' in establishing a gallery workshop in the Brisbane suburb of New Farm. 'Opening the gallery was the best decision I ever made for my practice. It gave me the opportunity to meet the buyer and vice versa. It's a powerful experience on both sides.'

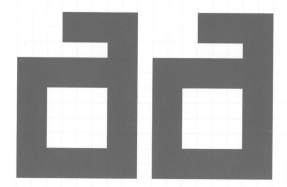

Ari Athans

The decision to move the practice into a commercial space came after spending 2003 in Melbourne, which she describes as 'retail heaven, but also retail overload'. With her son, Max, approaching school age, it was 'time to get the workshop out of the house', and return to the less frenetic pace of Brisbane. ■ The birth of her second child, Mia, forced Athans to consider employing other jewellers, which she'd never done before. 'I couldn't imagine another person creating my work. I've been so fortunate in employing two people with such different training. Kathy McLay is a fantastic technician who can make anything in my head. Anna Varendorff has an amazing aesthetic and does a lot of the production work. I sit somewhere in between.' ■ The long skinny space sits at the end of a strip of shops, fronting a charming Art Deco building. A white gallery occupies the front and the workshop behind opens onto a compact veranda with commanding views over the city to the north. 'It was the first place I looked at. The architectural divisions were perfect for what I wanted to do, and the vinyl floor at the back of the space was just screaming "workshop". People like the idea of visiting an artisan's workshop. It's something you don't really see anymore. It's amazing how drawn they are to the back of the space.' ■ While the space affords the discipline of working on production on a daily basis, Athans professes a 'random' approach to her work, getting easily sidetracked into different areas. 'It's a bad way of working, but enjoyable. I like to go with my first instincts about things. The ideas come constantly, but if I'm feeling stuck, I just get in there among the materials and have a play.' ■ The sheer materiality of the gemstones, minerals, silver and gold she uses has seductive

powers for Athans. Added to this passion is her academic understanding of their physical properties. Her first degree was in geology. She recalls the anomaly of joining a mostly white, mostly male student group at the University of Technology, Sydney, as an Australian Greek woman. 'Geology seems to attract white Aussie males. I was from the western suburbs, when everyone else seemed to be from the east.' Following graduation were two years of work in and around Mt Isa, where Athans was again in the minority in both gender and ethnicity. While they were happy times, it wasn't until she enrolled in a Diploma in Jewellery and Object Design at Randwick TAFE (now Enmore Design Centre), that Athans felt she was in the right place.

A technical understanding of the materials she works with has a huge bearing on Athans' designs. 'I don't overwork things, I try to let the materials speak first, so I keep paring back the design of the piece. I try to leave the materials untouched, and work with them rather than turning them into something else. I can't help but look at the stones in a scientific way. It's helpful to know their physical and optical properties, so I know how far I can push with them: their hardness, how much heat they can take, their chemistry, which influences how to drill, cut and polish them.' Apart from the scientific analysis, Athans is fascinated by the way jewels are 'loaded' with meaning and emotion. She enjoys the conceit that jewellery is charged with personal meaning at the same time as being such a public statement. Among her most vivid childhood memories are sessions spent with her two sisters and mother around her mother's jewellery box, and the enchanting tales her mother told to accompany each piece. She can still feel the power each jewel held. 'I love the mystery of jewellery. I grew up with things always attached to my clothes. Little pouches that Mum would put mysterious things in – like holy bread or charms to protect us from the evil eye. The Greeks call them *filakto*.' Athans' practice runs at a relentless pace and oscillates between an ever growing list of commissions and exhibitions, and the constant production work. Each area of practice balances and feeds off the others. 'All the elements come together here. I can conceptualise, create, exhibit and sell in the one place. Artists are often torn between the struggle to remain true to themselves while being commercially viable. Having the gallery workshop completes the circle for me.' *Margie Fraser*

1

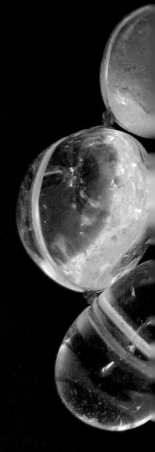

1 *Quartz Stumps*, 2002
Quartz crystals, linen.
240 x 60mm
2 *I'm lucky neckpiece*, 2006
Bone, freshwater pearls,
sterling silver, agate.
400 x 100mm
3 *Eklektika*, 2006
Hematite, serpentine, tourmaline,
labradorite, agate, quartz, onyx,
chalcedony, sterling silver.
1000 x 30mm
4 *Foolish Star*, 2005
Pyrite crystals, sterling silver.
70 x 60mm
5 *Tumbled bracelet*, 2002
Quartz, nylon.
145 x 20mm

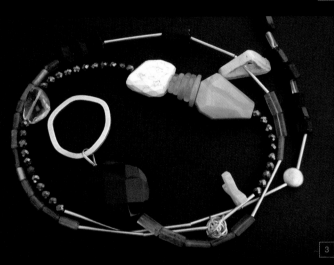

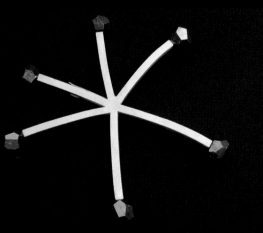

Jonathan Baskett (b.1969) is not preoccupied with the label of 'craftsman' or 'designer'. Both an experienced glass-blower and designer, Baskett is comfortable working with others in the fabrication of his designs.

Jonathan Baskett

'While, as a glass-blower, I am used to working with others to achieve an end goal, design is a different discipline. As a designer, one works with many other factors, such as market trends, manufacturing and market limitations, which can push the design in a new direction, often producing unpredictable and exciting results. Having an innate knowledge of the material allows one to push the bounds of what is possible. However, more and more, external designers are bringing some very interesting ideas to the table, and pushing the material further in unexpected directions.' After graduating from his undergraduate degree in 1996, Baskett worked for various companies throughout Europe in the fields of production, limited series and unique glassware. At the time, Michael Kramer owned and operated his own workshop in Bremen, Germany. 'I was inspired by his aesthetic and unique approach to marketing,' Baskett says. He was based in Germany for 18 months, working under Kramer but also exhibiting and developing his own glass ranges. 'I actually began to design and exhibit in Denmark and Germany, and it was strange to come back to Australia and start again.' In 2001, Baskett was introduced to Nouvel Studios, a medium-sized glass-making facility in Mexico, through Michael Kramer (who is now Nouvel Studios' director). Both Baskett and Kramer were students of the late Stephen Procter: Kramer at West Surrey College of Art and Design in the United Kingdom and Baskett at the Canberra School of Art. 'During my undergraduate degree, Stephen really encouraged me to investigate design and production glassware. He is still an inspiration to me today.' Baskett operates in a truly global market. His work is produced and marketed in Mexico, the United States, Europe and Asia.

He is now designing new pieces to add to the Nouvel range twice a year, sending the specifications electronically to the production team in Mexico. Development time is often very short, and the internet has been valuable in the development of ideas. 'Quite often an idea is bounced back and forth between the factory and my studio via e-mail, whether it is a computer rendering or just a simple photo.' He also travels to Mexico on a regular basis, developing ideas and prototypes at the factory. Glass is such an immediate material and allows the rapid development of an idea in a relatively short time. Being able to speak Spanish has given Baskett a good rapport with the makers at the factory, and he often works with them directly on the floor. ■ Having a manufacturing facility in Mexico has been beneficial for Baskett. **'There is no manufacturing base for glass in Australia and it is at present difficult to source manufacturers with flexibility in Asia,'** he explains. **'Nouvel works in small, medium and large production runs, and has a wide range of colour possibilities.** There are very few factories worldwide able to work in this manner ... Nouvel gives me access to a market that I could not access myself. We work towards the New York International Gift Fair, held in February and August each year. The company undertakes the marketing of my production, which is labelled "produced by Nouvel, designed by Jonathan Baskett".' ■ In addition to the steady supply of designs to Nouvel, Baskett regularly submits designs to German glass manufacturers such as Ritzenhoff, Rosenthal and Salviati. These companies have shown distinct interest in his work. He is confident that this kind of work will become part of his income stream in the future. 'If a design is accepted, one is usually paid on a royalty basis.' With these manufacturers, Baskett responds to a tightly defined and competitive brief that is sent to over 1,000 designers around the world twice a year. ■ For Baskett, the challenge is to design an object with clean lines and minimalist aesthetics, suitable for manufacture yet retaining a distinctive and individual flair. Knowing the properties of the material as he does, he can push the limits of what is possible with the manufacturer. Baskett imports the ranges made by Nouvel back into Australia and markets them himself through retail outlets, galleries and directly through his website. ■ With ongoing design projects scheduled for 2006 with Nouvel, a design residency in Berlin at the end of the year and his teaching commitments at the Fashion, Art and Design Department at Canberra Institute of Technology, Baskett's future seems sure to be busy and productive. ■ *Meredith Hinchliffe*

1

2

3 | 4

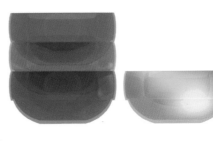
5 | 6

7

1 *Ogi egg cups*, 2003
Mould-blown and cut glass.
40mm x Ø.70mm
2 *Cafissimo latte glass*, 2003
Mould-blown borosilicate glass.
100 x 70 x 70mm
3 *Cafecito espresso glass*, 2003
Mould-blown borosilicate glass.
60 x 60 x 60mm
4 *Flower Pot Vase*, 2006
CAD Drawing.
5 *Bebol, green with fruit*, 2003
Mould-blown and enamelled glass.
Ø.180mm
6 *Caterpillar Bowls*, 2006
CAD Drawing.
7 *Utility Cup with Decanter*, 2006
CAD Drawing.

Photography Australian National University

Since establishing their partnership, bernabeifreeman, in 2002, Rina Bernabei (b.1968) and Kelly Freeman (b.1976) have designed almost entirely for fabrication in sheet metal. 'We went for the harshest, most masculine material you could tackle and tried to make it feminine,' says Bernabei.

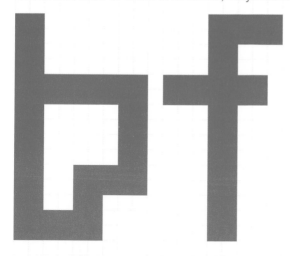

Rina Bernabei and Kelly Freeman

bernabeifreeman

'We decided straight away that we would look at technological textiles, play with manufacturing processes and explore how we could bring a craft sensibility into the industrial realm.' Freeman adds, 'It's been a challenge for us and for the manufacturers, because we're pushing the machines beyond what they were designed to do.' ▪ Bernabei and Freeman have distinguished themselves as pioneers of a design approach that reconciles two seeming opposites: the brute masculinity of industrial manufacture and the soft, tactile, decorative quality of traditional textile crafts. From this basis, they create unique and thoughtful lighting concepts. ▪ Often referring to their practice as 'storytelling', they interrogate what makes an object become a cherished part of somebody's life, perhaps an heirloom. They employ the notion of domesticity as a conceptual linchpin, believing that their tapping into the universal experience of the home is one of the reasons audiences and the marketplace continue to respond so well to their work. Bernabei explains, 'The domestic household is something that we all connect with. You can probably remember the smell of your grandmother's dressing gown.' ▪ In their work, bold simple forms are fabricated from sheet metal, which is powder-coated or anodised in neutral shades. The surfaces of these forms are laced with botanical or geometric patterns, which are created through a series of punched-out circular perforations – a technique that has become their signature. Lighting from within brings a warm glow to the perforated patterns, generating an atmosphere of texture, warmth, nostalgia. But theirs is a contemporised lace – embroidery with light itself. ▪ Both Bernabei and Freeman are, however, resolute that their practice resides within the realm of industrial design. The 'story' of the crafts

Kelly Freeman and Rina Bernabei

is not for them to tell, rather they relate a newer story founded in material technology and manufacturing techniques. 'There is a socialist aspect to it too,' comments Bernabei. 'Though we love textiles there is this other side that says you've got to mass produce this. You've got to take that story forward.' ▪ It is a challenge in Australia to make that happen.

Bernabei and Freeman have succeeded in assembling a group of like-minded manufacturers who are willing to devote the necessary energy to producing their work. They comment that these manufacturers are not really taking on this work for the money. Rather, they feel rewarded with a sense of pride in their craftsmanship and a better understanding of the potential of their technology. 'They do love to see the end result and have a connection with it,' says Freeman. 'They are punching out quite mundane things normally, so we get a really great response.'

▪ Perhaps it is true that, as women, they are better disposed to cultivating these relationships. 'But not just because we go in and bat our eyelashes, more because we've proven ourselves,' Freeman is quick to assert. 'I do the actual mechanical drawings for them. Usually that's the kind of thing they would do for a lot of other clients.' It is clear to the manufacturers, and others in their professional sphere, that Bernabei and Freeman are serious about what they are doing. ▪ In conversing with the two, their words and thoughts overlapping, there is a strong sense of the collaborative spirit that exists between them. Beyond the studio, as lecturing staff at the University of New South Wales, they continue to cross-pollinate one another's work. Bernabei observes that their design and academic lives are integrated and mutually beneficial: 'Writing about our work has made us understand what we've done and influences what we do next. We can justify what we do,' she explains. 'We go back to: what are our beliefs? What are we trying to say here? Where does this fit in the story of things?'

▪ *Emily Howes*

1

Photography (2) Penelope Clayton

4

Photography (1/3-4) Dieu Tan

1 *Lace Pendant*, 2005
Punched and rolled aluminium with
powder- coated finish, crossbar fabricated
from stainless steel.
300 x Ø.500mm
2 *Peony Floor Light*, 2004
Perforated anodised aluminium panels.
300 x 300 x 1500mm
3 *Cloth Table*, 2006
Punched and folded aluminium top/tray with
powder-coated finish, fabricated stainless
steel base with powder-coated finish.
400 x 400 x 500mm
4 *Ema Pendant*, 2006
Punched aluminium diffuser with
powder-coated finish, hand screen-
printed fabric.
380 x Ø.330mm

Caroline Casey (b.1964) is a multi-talented designer who effortlessly moves between interior, textiles and furniture design, although she is most recognised for her furniture in Australia and abroad. After completing a degree in fashion and textiles at Sydney College of the Arts in 1986, Casey spent four years directing her own sportswear and hand-printed textiles company, Caz Designs.

Caroline Casey

In 1990 she moved to New York to study interior design at Parsons School of Design. After the intensity of the fashion industry, Casey rediscovered her passion for creativity and entered into a new stage of professional development. Interiors gave her the opportunity to enhance her design sensibility and remarkable eye for detail. In 1992 Casey won the Palazzetti Design Showcase award in New York, which led to a series of furniture commissions for domestic settings. Casey's *Elliptical* folding screen and *Frank O'Neill* bookcase were the first in her range of meticulously designed furniture. In 1995 she returned to Sydney to focus on expanding this range. She also started doing interiors for her partner, Robert Brown, of Dawson Brown Architects. They had always worked from the same office and saw the benefits in combining talents for interior and architectural projects. The same year, 1995, Ute Rose, manager of one of Sydney's leading retailers, Anibou, recognised Casey's talent for furniture design and gained the exclusive rights to sell her work. Anibou was responsible for launching Casey's new works, and has continued to support her flourishing practice over the last decade. In 1998, Casey's work was featured in a solo exhibition at the Powerhouse Museum, Sydney, and it has also been collected by the San Francisco Museum of Modern Art, Victoria & Albert Museum, National Gallery of Australia, Powerhouse Museum and Art Gallery of South Australia. Her work now sells internationally through Aram in London and Studio Willmann in Nuernberg, Germany. Casey's furniture designs exude confidence and sophistication. She constantly challenges her practice, taking it in new directions by researching innovative technologies, discovering unique sources of inspiration and being playful with her ideas.

Her works are essentially sculptural, with each piece starting as an exploration into form and ending with a resolved functionality. 'My challenge is to find the trigger that drives the creative force … the conceptual content is vital,' she says. At the moment, Casey is focused on knotting, a recent springboard for new work. Her investigations into this ancient artform began after seeing rigging knots on a boat moored in front of her harbour-side house. Her mind considers the crafted technique, industrial implications and eventual domestic setting. ■ Once she has explored an idea, further development requires models, prototypes and sample testing. Casey works with a number of small-scale workshops in Australia and Germany. These highly skilled fabricators bring considerable knowledge and experience to the production of the works, and are dedicated to producing pieces of the highest quality. In Germany, every element of her timber furniture is hand-selected, worked and finished by third-generation furniture-makers. **The result is finely crafted objects that take on the aura of an artwork, 'objects that not only do something but say something', as Casey says**. ■ Coming full circle now, Casey is revisiting textile design. Intuitively, her background in textiles has always been present in her work, through pattern, repetition, texture and rhythm. Her *Woven Wall* storage units are a direct response to traditional craft techniques used in Indonesia. Casey's *Monstera* rugs are hand-woven in Tibet, and have a more obvious connection to textiles. Currently, she is working on a new sofa range for Anibou, which features hand-painted fabric furnishings and cushions.

Another recent endeavour, Casey Brown Architecture, formally establishes the long-term collaboration between Casey and Brown. Together they offer

1

an integrated design experience, which includes exteriors, interiors and furniture for new houses. Casey designs the interiors and furniture as a response to Brown's architectural housing projects. For Casey, these are long-term projects that may take up to three years to complete. Casey has now formed a clear path for her future designs. She has ongoing retail support from Anibou, international representation and a new partnership that will sustain lifelong work. She has a vital role in a thriving studio with Brown, working with model makers (doing architectural and furniture projects), industrial designers and others. Casey remains loyal to Australia, saying, 'I wanted to prove that you could do it here and create demand for works of the highest quality'. *Annabel Moir*

1 *Zella Daybed,* 1998
Woven seagrass, cane.
580 x 2020 x 950mm
2 *Flip* newspaper stand, 1998
Anodised aluminium.
460 x 450 x 540mm
3 *Tina* tables, 1997
Laminated hoop pine,
colour-lacquered MDF.
500 x Ø.450mm, 720 x Ø.900mm
4 Casey Brown Architecture,
James-Robertson House.
5 *Elliptical* folding screen, 1994
Rock maple, solid and
veneered plywood.
2000 x 1500 x 30mm fully extended
2000 x 325 x 180mm folded

Photography (4) Anthony Browell

Photography (1-3/5) Jonathan Rose

For Nicola Cerini (b.1969), designing textiles was an early career decision. Growing up in a creative environment in country Victoria, she developed a love for making things. After graduating from Royal Melbourne Institute of Technology (RMIT) with a Bachelor of Textile Design, Cerini decided to travel before getting drawn into the fast-paced fashion and design industry. 'I felt I needed to explore my own sense of design.'

Nicola Cerini

Influenced by her travels, including working at the Banff Centre for the Arts in Canada in 1993, the summer program at The Fabric Workshop in Philadelphia in 1995, and living in Japan for a time, Cerini returned to Melbourne and established her studio, Nicola Cerini Australia, in 1995. The company was set up to produce highly individual textiles for furnishing fabrics and homewares. With no business background, Cerini enrolled in the NEIS Program to learn about running a viable small business. In the first few years, this training was invaluable. Even so, there were times when all her efforts seemed unrewarded. Then Cerini experienced her first major breakthrough. ■ It was in the middle of the night when she came up with the idea to produce a bag with clear PVC covering over unique, printed fabrics held together with seat belt webbing. The bag now symbolises the turning point for Cerini's business and the start of her widespread following. In a short period these bags became the major selling range of the business, their success due to their practical, funky look and versatility. 'I wanted a bag for myself that I could wear 24 hours a day, that I didn't have to change when I went out at night, and I could ride my bike with it. It had to be durable, really durable, but also fun and elegant.' Now it is hard to walk more than a block in Melbourne without seeing one of Cerini's iconic bags slung over someone's shoulder. Including a wide range of print designs, the bags appeal to a diverse group of people. According to Cerini, 'it is women in their early twenties right through to my great aunt who is in her nineties!' ■ With production quantities increasing to around 15,000 a year, Cerini is still adamant about sustaining manufacture in Australia. 'It's pretty unique to be manufacturing bags in Australia, on this

scale'. But that is part of the charm and widening support for the bags. And Cerini still continues to expand her ranges of textile designs to be made into wearable fashion, accessories and domestic homewares. Her products are stocked in numerous retail stores in Australia and New Zealand, as well as in limited export to the United Kingdom, the United States and Canada. However, the local market is her main focus; people also come from far and wide to visit Cerini's studio, which is open once a month. ▪ Cerini's passion for the environment has given her another way of connecting with the wider community. In 2003, this passion began to inform her work, when she was invited to exhibit in the *Cecily and Colin Rigg Contemporary Design Award* at the National Gallery of Victoria. The designs she entered in the exhibition were inspired by rare and endangered plants from East Gippsland in Victoria. Since then, she has featured rare native plants in a series of collections, and a percentage of these sales are donated to the Tree Project, an organisation dedicated to revegetation of the Victorian countryside.

▪ **With a strong design philosophy and ongoing commitment to the Australian textile industry, there's nowhere Cerini would prefer to be based. Her strong community focus extends to her chosen methods of production. Issuing around ten new designs every season, Cerini's starting point is her textile designs. She produces her artwork from original drawings that she has developed digitally into repeat patterns**.

The designs are then exposed into screens, and sampled directly onto fabric in the studio. A final selection of colourways are then sent to a printer. With some lateral thinking, Cerini found a regional manufacturer after considering the types of fabrics required, pursuing an industrial manufacturer rather than handbag specialist. The lengths of fabrics are cut in-house according to pre-orders, and sent along with the other components – vinyl, seat belt webbing, straps and magnet closures – to be constructed into bags and distributed to her stockists. Three full-time studio staff assist Cerini with design, production coordination, sales and general duties. A number of fashion producers make the garments. Cerini's clothing range has been developing as a significant part of the business over the last three years, and there are plans for its continued growth. ▪ In 2006, Cerini was awarded a three-month Australia Council residency in Barcelona. This opportunity gives her time out of the day-to-day business to research and develop new designs. She has also begun negotiations with several companies to start licensing her designs. Soon we'll see her designs featured on a range of umbrellas, and there are plans for bedlinen, dinnerware, stationery and a whole host of other products. There really are no limits to where Cerini can go with her enchanting and eclectic designs, inspired by everyday life, fauna and native flora.

▪ *Annabel Moir*

1

Photography David McArthur

1 Detail of *Baw Baw Daisy*, 2003
Spring Summer Collection
Fabric
2 *Green Waratah Cushions*, 2006
Cotton, nylon, spandex, pigment,
feather, foam.
Largest 500 x 500 x 150mm
3 Detail of *Green Waratah fabric*, 2006
Cotton, nylon, spandex, pigment.
1090mm, 700mm repeat
4 *Waratah repeat artwork*, 2006
Original Illustrator file.
1500mm, 700mm repeat
5 *Plasto range*, 2006
Pink Waratah Mums Tote, Red Seed
Pod Long Tote, Red Cloud Joy Bag, Pink
Waratah Small Satchel, Red Cloud Purse.
Clear PVC, texturised polyester binding,
seat belt webbing, polyester, pigment.
Largest: 300 x 390 x 110mm

Drawing together their complimentary studies from the disciplines of landscape architecture, visual art and architecture, Lucas Chirnside (b.1976) and Bianca Looney (b.1977) operate a Melbourne-based studio that engages with research-intensive design projects ranging in scale from small, hand-crafted objects, to consumer products and urban design interventions.

Lucas Chirnside & Bianca Looney

The studio aims to deliver an engaging and rigorous design conversation to a diffused audience, by fully exploring the critical aspects of their practice and its relevance to society, contemporary design and culture. Prior to their founding of their studio, Chirnside and Looney, as partners, were already entwined in each other's work. While they were individually engaging with their own projects, ongoing conversations and observations had begun to capture moments where their independent projects intersected and revealed mutually stimulating insights. These observations, in turn, activated the growth of an intimate language that allowed both practitioners to trigger a blurring of scale, a widening of parameters, and a dissolving of project boundaries that ultimately allowed both to develop a unified distillation system for their design problems. In addition to this constantly evolving language of reference and awareness, other layers started to be revealed. By researching and interpreting each other's work over six years of exhibitions, competitions and propositions, both partners had nurtured their collaborative potential, bringing to the foreground the vivid language of their own platforms of understanding and respect. What still draws them together is a mutual intensity, an overwhelming sensitivity to an object's potential for meaning, and a common joy in realising projects through a lens focused on a moment in time and place. This intuitive working relationship has been forged over many long days travelling and working together, and has encouraged these designers to approach projects via a thorough background of development and research. Chirnside and Looney dissect and reassemble meaning in spaces, typography, objects, architecture and fashion. In developing new work they seek to engage

Lucas Chirnside and Bianca Looney

with intersections of potentials, as well as established problems, referencing global processes, geography, evolution and change. **In describing their process of design, they talk of throwing an idea between frames of reference, such as discourses of art, design and architecture. They refer to this process as a method of dissolving and recombining meaning in various different languages to find cracks and fissures. It is within these interstitial spaces that they can explore – these are their zones of reinterpretation.** Looney studied visual arts and landscape architecture, and is interested in testing the language of art as a functional device of design. The objects and environments she creates are as much products of their cultural context as they are cultural 'generators'. She discovers meaning as an added dimension of the object. She often works with materials that convey some of the conceptual grounds of the projects, for example, her topographic *Z-Series* tiles consciously relate to the earth through ceramics as a terrestrial material. Embracing technologies of craft and the digital, the *Z-series* explores the interpenetration

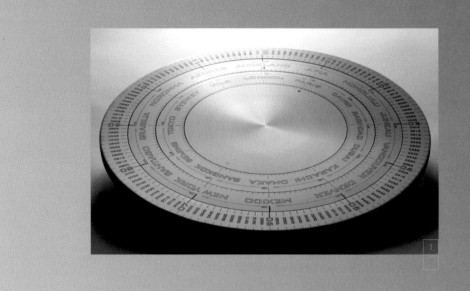

of process, material and concept, offering alternative ideas of 'landscape'. Looney is currently working on urban interventions in Melbourne, with a focus on product-scale artefacts that convey a contemporary sense of place. ■ Chirnside studied architecture, and has applied the structural program of the built environment within a global context, exploring conceptual problems through a new lens. His designs innovate on existing typologies, or invent new ways by bringing an inspiration to life through a practical application of materials and processes. Chirnside explores new technologies and adjacent design fields in order to harvest his required toolkit of parts. He then utilises these to construct intricate and exquisitely resolved products, ranging from lighting to furniture and architecture. ■ **He has recently been recognised as the recipient the 2005 *Bombay Sapphire Design Discovery Award* – Australia's richest product design award. Chirnside has built a reputation as a designer who works in fine detailing, addressing the minute while embedding it into a broader social or global conversation.** ■ His *Pi* world clock is a perfect example of the 'zooming' of scale from the intricacies of a working timepiece, capable of communicating the time in many locations simultaneously, connecting time zones within one framed form of reference. ■ Looney and Chirnside have both been recognised for their work as independent practitioners, receiving travelling scholarships and grants, and they have exhibited together at the Australian Centre for Contemporary Art and co-founded an occasional journal, *Geophil*, to inform and record their design process. These two designers look set to continue their personal and professional explorations – we can expect to see some interesting output from this well-grounded studio. ■ *Ewan McEoin*

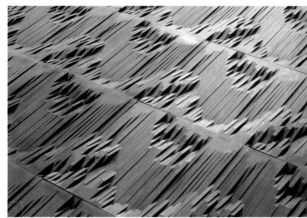

1 Lucas Chirnside, *Pi world time clock*, 2005
Laser-cut aluminium, anodising, acid etching,
copper ballast, clock mechanism.
Prototype
Ø.520 x 120mm
2 Lucas Chirnside, *Pi world time clock*, 2005
Laser-cut aluminium, anodising, acid etching,
copper ballast, clock mechanism.
Prototype
Ø.520 x 120mm
3 Bianca Looney, *Flatlanders (from Z-series)*,
2004
Glazed ceramic tiles.
Each tile 18 x 157 x 157mm
4 Bianca Looney, *Slipmap (from Z-series)*, 2004
Glazed ceramic tiles.
Each tile 18 x 65 x 65mm
5 Bianca Looney, *Terrain (from Z-series)*, 2003
Coloured concrete tiles.
Each tile 48 x 360 x 360mm
6 Lucas Chirnside, *smlwrld*, 2006
Milled aluminium, chrome electroplate, anodising,
copper ballast, laser etching, clock movement.
Ø.116 x 93mm

Julie Paterson (b.1963) moved to Australia in 1989. In the United Kingdom she had completed a degree in printed furnishing design at Trent University, as well as postgraduate study in design education at Goldsmiths College. Paterson had also worked as a senior designer for Anna French in London.

Julie Paterson

cloth

Before establishing cloth in 1997, with business partner Penny Simons, Paterson was working as a freelance designer for local homeware and fashion companies, providing new directions for textiles in the industry. She saw huge potential in the local market and started experimenting. The first public display of cloth fabrics was at the annual design fair, DesignEX, in 1997. There was an encouraging response to the fabrics and furnishings, so Paterson and Simons continued to release limited production designs under the cloth brand. ▓ cloth fabrics are made primarily from hemp, jute and linen, screen-printed by hand, and are designed for both residential and commercial interior markets. cloth has become synonymous with handmade homewares that are environmentally conscious and emotionally engaging. Interested in a sustainable practice, Paterson uses all of the fabric offcuts to make accessories, bags and fabric dolls. ▓ In 2000 Paterson took over the ownership of the company and opened a retail space in the beachside Sydney suburb of Clovelly. Paterson takes her own sketches and paintings as her starting point, translating them directly onto cloth's fabrics – she is intimately involved in the complete design process, from artwork ideas, to fabric production and product design. She set up her work table in the 'clothshop' to give customers an insight into her working practice. Customers became involved in the cloth story and, through their deeper understanding of the creative process, developed an appreciation for cloth textiles' unique and handmade qualities. ▓ Owning a design business in Sydney was an inspiring and refreshing move for Paterson. She felt she could be intuitive and explore new ways to create in a place with limited historical

baggage in textile design and therefore no strict rules to break. Responding to the distinctive Australian environment, Paterson developed a palette of raw ochre colours in her irregular designs on natural fibres. Her *Rough Rose* (2001) design was a response to the English floral textile tradition. With a series of bold, over-simplified shapes roughly overprinted she combines the delicate English rose with the harsh Australian landscape. Through her work at cloth, Paterson currently produces and sells a range of over 20 fabric designs, each in a variety of colourways. She is also about to launch a new range of fashion and accessories, including silver and wooden jewellery produced in collaboration with Warwick Edgington. cloth products are also stocked by key retailers in Sydney, Melbourne, Perth and Brisbane, and six of Paterson's designs are being distributed internationally through a licensing agreement with leading Australian textiles company, Woven Image. This new commercial expansion for cloth is an important evolution for the business, and there are other large-scale projects in development. In 2005 Paterson completed a fit-out at Lend Lease's Jacksons Landing building. She is also in the process of designing fabrics for sofas, beds and limited edition artworks for a Japanese ski resort. Her latest partnership involves cloth designs being scaled-up for production as woollen rugs by Designer Rugs. Since relocating the clothshop to the eastern Sydney suburb of Randwick in 2004, and then inner-city Surry Hills in 2006, Paterson has also reviewed her approach to the business. She has appointed new staff to assist with sales, marketing and distribution, and has built The Shed, a creative haven in the Blue Mountains, west of Sydney. This idyllic location allows her time for contemplation and the development of new ideas, such as her latest explorations into native Australian flora. Paterson lets her plethora of ideas incubate for extended periods before applying them to specific projects. She sketches and paints images and motifs onto blocks of wood, and cuts paper stencils or creates linocuts to develop the ideas before translating the patterns onto silk-screens for printing on fabric. The fabric prototypes are put in the clothshop for client feedback, a sign of Paterson's pragmatic approach to the marketplace and to the high cost of each fabric production. Working in short-batch production, she still has the freedom to respond easily to new ideas and alternative colourways. cloth has a strong art focus, reflecting Paterson's early dream of being a fine artist. She combines art and design with equal energy in her practice. Each element is part of her personal journey to grow the cloth business and to satisfy her own creative output. She regularly presents her work in exhibitions and design festival events, such as Tokyo Designers Block 2004, Sydney Esquisse 2005, and DesignEX 2006. Paterson recently received funding from the Australia Council to promote cloth overseas. The outlook is promising, with good media coverage in design and lifestyle magazines in the United States, the United Kingdom and Scandinavia. Over ten years, Paterson has established cloth's distinctive identity and clear direction in the local market – now she is ready to conquer further afield.

Annabel Moir

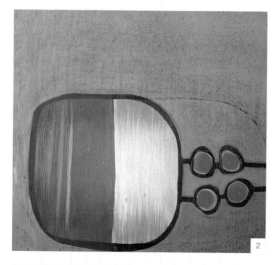

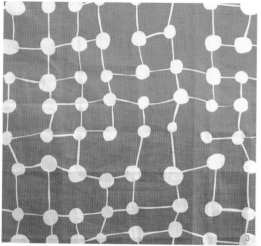

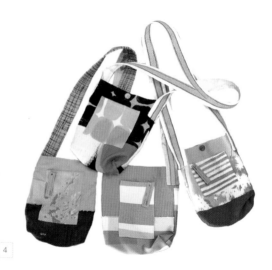

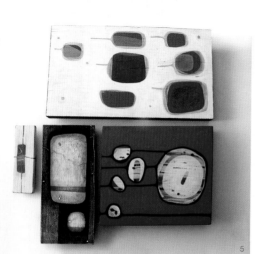

1 *Stuffed Olives burnt*, 2000
Screen-print on hemp.
2 *Roundabout painting*, 2003
Acrylic on pine.
3 *Spotcheck* (lino colourway) from
In The Shed collection, 2005
Screen-print on hemp.
4 *Patched shoulder bags*, 2004
Printed hemp and linen offcuts.
5 Paintings (clockwise):
Looking for Water, 2004; *Islands*, 2003;
Woy Woy wood, 2002; *Crossing A over E*,
2005
Acrylic and enamel on found wood.
Largest 240 x 120mm
6 *Groundwork rug* from *In The Shed*
collection, 2006
Felted wool.
Manufactured by Designer Rugs, Sydney
1500 x 1200mm

Photography Julie Paterson

Susan Cohn (b.1952) is one of the most influential designers working in Australia, and she steadfastly remains one of the least conventional. She is variously described – by herself and others – as a jeweller, a craf tsperson, an artist and a designer. She embraces each of these terms and refutes any hierarchical distinction between them.

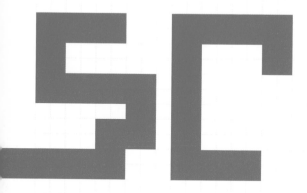

Susan Cohn

From 1971–77 Cohn trained and worked in the field of graphic design with Garry Emery, who has for many years been one of Australia's genuine design luminaries. Working in two dimensions proved too great a constraint for Cohn, however, and in 1980 she completed a Diploma in Gold and Silversmithing at RMIT and established Workshop 3000 in Kirks Lane, Melbourne with colleagues Marian Hosking and Harry Rowlands. In 1984 Cohn bought out the partnership, relocated to Flinders Lane in 1992, and continues to run it as a jewellery production workshop. Cohn admits to two main streams in her practice: exhibition work and the daily practice of the workshop (which, for Cohn, includes the hands-on fabrication of production work and private commissions, as well as occasional designs for industrial manufacturing). She says, 'One stream feeds the other. Work either starts out or ends up in an exhibition, and exhibition work will feed back into new production work. I find practicing in those two streams an interesting way of expanding and exploring ideas.'[1] And it is 'ideas' that are central to Cohn's practice. Much of her work involves transforming commonplace or industrial materials into valued jewellery objects, through the injection of meaning or emotion and her accomplished technical skill in handling the materials. Her *Doughnut* bracelets, which she has produced since the early 1980s – incorporating materials such as anodised aluminium and plastic – are a fine example. Work such as this enables Cohn to challenge notions of preciousness and value. Cohn is a prominent figure, within Melbourne's design community in particular, and has been an influential mentor and advocate within the industry. Many successful designer-makers have spent time learning from

...Cohn within her workshop over the last 20 years, including Miyuki Nakahara, Andrew Last, Blanche Tilden and Tiffany Parbs; even Marc Newson spent three months in the workshop early in his career. Her *disc earrings* (1982), which allow the wearer to change colours through simply swapping the anodised aluminium discs, have become an almost ubiquitous accessory and signifier for many influential women in Australia's art and design world. ■ Through Workshop 3000 Cohn has always been concerned with production and, by 1995, she was employing five staff to assist her with the output. She was then faced with a critical decision – to significantly expand the business to sustain growth, or reduce the scale and be more selective. In choosing the later, Cohn reflects, 'I realised that *what I was saying through the work* was more important to me.' ■ **Though she continues to make production work for a number of select galleries and retailers, the majority of Cohn's time in the workshop these days is devoted to producing provocative and experimental exhibition installations (always using jewellery objects) and completing numerous private commissions.** Her new work, *Design is …* (2006), developed specifically for the *Freestyle* exhibition, utilises the simple, industrially produced badge – possibly the most democratised jewellery adornment – and is both a provocation and an invitation. Cohn has asked hundreds of people to complete the sentence, 'Design is …', and has then presented their handwritten responses in the form of individual badges, simultaneously highlighting the difficulty in defining 'design' and encouraging thoughtful debate about it. ■ One of Cohn's best known works is the *Cohncave* bowl, which has been mass-produced by the Italian manufacturer Alessi since 1992. This elegant bowl, made from two sheets of pressed, perforated steel held together with a stainless steel rim, was the result of a successful collaborative process between designer and manufacturer. Cohn says, 'When I learned of the company's craft background, I felt like they understood what I was trying to achieve'. The Alessi company has been in existence since 1921, but the Alessi family has been traced back to 1633 in the Lake Orta region – they believe their forebears lived and worked in the Omegna area, where makers of metal household objects had craft workshops. The *Cohncave* continues to sell well and the designer receives regular royalty income from it and for her

design is
STARTING A NEW SENTENCE

design is

design is not
getting your hands dirty

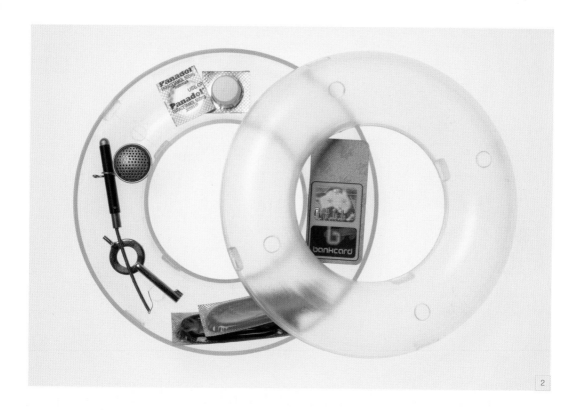

2

Cohndom box (1997), also produced by Alessi. ▉ Although the *Cohncave* is mass-produced, each is individually unique – the moiré pattern created by the two sheets of mesh is subtly different every time. Cohn has explored this idea of industrial processes creating individually unique objects in other works, such as the *Compressed brooch* series (1984–), in which small pieces of scrap aluminium are compressed into a bar-shape through a precise mechanical action. Several recent commissions have utilised this same basic idea, with pieces of keepsake jewellery embedded into the form, such as a parent's wedding ring, which resonate personal meaning for the individual client. ▉ Cohn's work has featured in well over 100 group and solo exhibitions in Australia, Asia, Europe and North America, and in 2000 a major retrospective exhibition of her work was organised and toured nationally by the National Gallery of Australia. ▉ *Brian Parkes*

1. Susan Cohn, quoted in *Belle*, December/January 2005-06, p. 41.

Photography (3) John Gollings

Photography (4) Greg Harris

Photography (1–2) Shannon McGrath

3

4

1 *Design is ... ,* 2006
Full panel badge work (detail), badge units
and mixed media on aluminium frame.
Badge unit Ø.56mm
2 *Survival doughnut bracelet,* 1995
Clear high-impact styrene, condom, Panadol,
credit card, key Bluetooth attachment in
anodised aluminium, 750 gold.
Ø.135mm
3 *Cohncave,* 1992
Powder-coated steel bowl, stainless steel edge.
Production bowl manufactured by Alessi
Ø.500mm
4 *Cohndom boxes,* 1995
Stainless steel.
Production condom boxes manufactured
by Alessi (from 1999)
62 x 62mm

Known for its bold marketing, functionally rational design and strident use of colour and pattern, Crumpler is an Australian brand of bags with its own retail outlets springing up all over the country and around the world. This Melbourne brand has consistently grown since its almost cult arrival in the early 1990s to become a common element within the urban landscape of Australia. Crumpler bags are notoriously practical, expressive, and just quirky enough to be a 'non-brand' success story.

Stuart Crumpler, Will Miller, Dave Roper

Crumpler

There is a subversive currency embedded within the product, appealing to skaters, bike riders and office commuters alike. This subversive quality is encapsulated within the dancing dreadlocked figure chosen as the icon for the label – an icon of freedom, movement and irreverence. Crumpler's is the non-design design story that we all like to hear, the story of some guys who needed something that they couldn't find in the shops, and so made it for themselves. As it happened, everyone loved what they did and wanted one. And so of course they made some more, at first just for their mates, then they made more for their mates' mates and so it continued, until a success story emerged, of a product that was more made than designed, a product that was born from necessity ... and the rest is bag history. Stuart Crumpler (b.1973), the designer behind Crumpler bags, tries to keep things simple. He claims to know nothing about design, he says he 'just makes bags'. While this may be true (it is refreshing to have such an uncomplicated perspective on one's work), Crumpler and his business partners, Dave Roper (b.1970) and Will Miller (b.1970), obviously have an instinct for what works, and what others can relate to (and will buy). They have developed a vast range of bags and accessories, captured imaginations through clever marketing, and made some very astute and strategic business moves – all placing Crumpler as a strong, design-led brand. Crumpler's bags are rare exceptions in the world of commercial production. The original product has allowed many new typologies into the range with the minimum of fuss, while allowing the products to remain faithful to their original intention: to provide robust, individualistic bags for people who have stuff to carry

Dave Roper, Will Miller and Stuart Crumpler

1

2

3 4 5

around. Stuart Crumpler originally worked as a bicycle courier (for a company owned by Roper and Miller) in Melbourne in the 1990s. At some point he was looking for a decent bag to carry his deliveries in, and couldn't buy what he wanted locally. Being a practical sort of a guy, he decided to make a bag. The first bag was called the *CD3* (seedy three) (1995), and was specifically 'designed' to be a comfortable bag for bicycle messengers to carry all day. Crumpler tested the bags and then sold and received continued requests for them. Crumpler, Roper and Miller set up a limited production system, which eventually enabled them to sell the bags in bike shops. Orders were filled as they were received, with bags being made locally in Melbourne by Crumpler himself and a small team of six machinists (four part-time). As the business grew, Crumpler had to make the significant commercial decision to source a manufacturer offshore. This sending of production offshore was a crucial factor in the success of the brand, as it allowed the company to produce consistently high quality products at a significantly reduced price, meaning that the product could be more competitive, distributed more widely, and freeing up the team in Australia to focus on marketing and developing new ideas and producing samples of new products to send to China for manufacture. Stuart Crumpler refers to exhibiting at international trade shows and getting their manufacturing right as two key early factors in their success. After watching the team make thousands of bags (and making many himself), it was a great day for all when the first container of finished products came in. Better quality within the product and increased efficiency in the production process have seen a steady growth of the business since. When it comes to a discussion on materials and design innovations, Stuart Crumpler admits a fascination with the processes available in their Chinese factories, such as vacuum formers and injection moulding machines; yet he resists a purely style-driven change in a product that 'is essentially still fine as it is'. The product has remained true to its early form and aesthetic, largely attributable to Crumpler's 'ain't broke so why fix it' attitude. With a new satellite office in New York and an ever expanding export market, there seems plenty of adventure yet for the team at Crumpler. Their ongoing success lies in their ability to remain focused on being inspired by the origins of their product, sticking to enjoying what they do best, exploring all the depth that their brand can deliver, and not going and getting themselves too carried away. *Ewan McEoin*

1 *Crumpler Complete Seed*, 2006
Nylon, polyester.
600 x 250 x 350mm
2 *The Barney Rustle Blanket*, 2006
Nylon, polyester.
500 x 350 x 200mm
3 *The Moderate Embarrassment*, 2006
Nylon, polyester.
450 x 350 x 200mm
4 *The King Single*, 2006
Polyester.
500 x 350 x 300mm
5 *The Thirsty Al*, 2006
Polyester, neoprene.
90 x 110 x 40mm

Janet DeBoos, (b.1948) whose practice spans 30 years, is known for her production work. 'The importance and relevance of the functional object and the mark of the hand has been central to my working life,' she said in 1995. 'I view my whole body of work as a conceptually single artwork which, when it is sold and used individually, fragments and relocates haphazardly.'

Janet DeBoos

DeBoos has always had strong feelings about the relationship between food and ceramics. 'I am interested in the theatre of eating and drinking, and those things which are a part of the drama of everyday life', she says. 'My main concern is the act of use.' However, in querying the generally accepted tenet that handmade is 'better', she wondered whether 'handmade could be just a look' and our attachment to it rooted in romance and nostalgia rather than reality. At the same time, 'design' was becoming the latest descriptor in the craft field, and there was a rush to embrace the new term. 'When you think of design, you are compelled to think of a certain sameness of outcomes in functional ceramics that use CAD programs, RAM pressing and industrial slip casting,' DeBoos says. DeBoos' work is grounded by a background in science, which has kept her inquiring into why things are the way they are. She was keen to test a hypothesis that there might be no real difference between studio-produced handmade objects and factory-produced objects that 'look' handmade. In 2003, Italian company Paola C Ceramics bought some of her works to use as models and the rights to produce them for five years. This was DeBoos' first chance to investigate her hypothesis. Could industrially-produced ware have the same qualities as the handmade? The initial results were unsatisfactory (they were not porcelain), and so the models were taken to a small-scale, quality porcelain factory. The resulting works were illustrated on the company's website and were taken to *Maison D'Objet* in Paris and the Milan design fairs, as well as being displayed in the company showrooms in Milan. They were far more expensive than most Italian ceramics, and this has contributed to them

being slow sellers. ■ 'The company principals were enthusiastic, but the public was not. They may also have looked "too handmade" in a current climate of sleek lines and formal simplicity in ceramics. However, the quality is excellent and colleagues who have seen and handled the ware often think they are part of my own production,' DeBoos noted. ■ In 2003, DeBoos was invited to work in a bone china factory in Zibo, Shandong Province, China. 'I did rough, scaled sketches of the work and plaster models were made. There were some minor changes and nine days after I arrived in the factory, the first pieces had been cast, fired and finished.' **DeBoos received an Australian National University Arts Faculty Research Grant to enable the Zibo project to go ahead, and for graduate students to have the opportunity to have their work turned into designs for mass production – 'something that is almost absent in Australia,' she points out.** ■ More recently, after discussion with the factory team at Huaguang Zibo Bone China, and assessment of the project, it was decided that the research into the transition of the handmade into industry is exciting and paramount, and so her emphasis will shift from production to research. 'Consequently, rather than using model makers for the next stage, I have been throwing scaled-up work from which moulds, then models, will be directly taken,' she says. 'I hope that this will correct the loss of liveliness when drawing, and then that model making intervenes between the handmade and the industrial.' It is the first time that tableware factories in China have worked directly from thrown work without creating models in between. This means that the moulds may have to become more complex, with more parts, causing the work to be considered more like sculpture because of the lack of concentricity in the original work. ■ Based on these two events, and assessing the mixed results of the opportunities they presented, she notes that ' … "makers" seem to make different ceramic designs from those produced by "designers". There is an understanding of the way materials behave during firing, how a cup will feel in the hand, how liquid leaves a spout, which seems to produce more seamlessly functional objects.' ■ Having always seen herself as a maker, DeBoos is now considering the possibility that she might be a designer. ■ The future for this kind of close collaboration is uncertain. Many well-established ceramic production companies have, in the past, had active artist studios within the industrial complexes, where 'one-offs', as well as designs for production, were made. This model is fast disappearing, although Arabia continues, but with much more of a 'designer' orientation, and Rosenthal is using established design 'names', such as Versace, to market its products. 'Perhaps that has lead to a dearth of real innovation. The establishment of a studio where factory experimentation and research can take place without the pressure of "delivery yesterday" is exciting,' DeBoos states. 'I think that time is necessary, and such a place and arrangement buys that time.'
■ *Meredith Hinchliffe*

1 *Solitary Pleasures*, 2002
Australian porcelain.
Ø.310mm
2 *Studio shot, pourer and tray*, 2002
Australian porcelain.
220 x Ø.85mm
3 *Huaguang bone china prototypes*, 2003
Chinese bone china.
Tallest 160mm
4 *Saladier, pourers, bowl and tray*, 2003
Australian porcelain.
Tallest: 240mm
5 *Leaving Home #1*, 2005
Australian porcelain.
Tallest 270mm

Photography (2/5) Janet DeBoos

Photography (1/3-4) Robert Little

Louise Olsen (b.1964), Stephen Ormandy (b.1964) and Liane Rossler (b.1965) formed Dinosaur Designs in 1985. Today, with around 60 staff, it is one of the most successful design-based businesses in Australia. Designing almost entirely for in-house production, the three designers continue to maintain a prolific output, with new ranges of products being developed every two to three months.

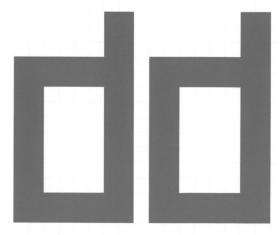

Louise Olsen, Stephen Ormandy and Liane Rossler

Dinosaur Designs

Made and finished almost entirely by hand, Dinosaur Designs' distinctive jewellery and homewares are sold through their own flagship stores in Sydney, Melbourne and New York, and through an extensive network of retailers in Australia and around the globe. ■ Despite Dinosaur Designs' success and the scale of their production, the three partners still feel honoured when people choose to buy their work. 'People treasure our products … there are some people for whom pieces of our jewellery are like an extension of their personality. They wouldn't leave the house without them – that's a very rewarding feeling.' ■ Olsen, Ormandy and Rossler met in 1983 while studying at what is now the College of Fine Arts, University of New South Wales. Each of them studied painting and drawing, and were drawn together through several shared interests, including the emerging contemporary Australian fashion scene (in particular the work of Linda Jackson and Jenny Kee). Eager to generate an income from their creative energies, they formed their partnership and began producing screen-printed fabrics and T-shirts to sell at the weekly Paddington markets. After a short time they added handmade jewellery to their range and this soon became the focus of their work. The designers invested every spare cent back into their new business and have maintained a similar strategy to this day, allowing them to grow steadily and within their means. ■ It was during these early market-stall days that the trio first began to use resin – a material that is now synonymous with Dinosaur Designs. They developed their own techniques and machinery to transform this non-precious industrial material into cherished pieces of contemporary jewellery. Casting in resin allowed them to retain the handmade qualities

Stephen Ormandy, Louise Olsen and Liane Rossler

they sought, while providing them with the means to produce in multiple. With the inexhaustible variety of colours and casting techniques they use, and the extensive hand-finishing required, no two pieces are ever the same. **By the end of the 1980s, with their first store just opened in Sydney's Strand Arcade, Dinosaur Designs had already established a significant national reputation. Various celebrities such as Kylie Minogue and Michael Hutchence were regularly wearing their work, and the designers were receiving significant exposure in the Australian fashion press.** In 1989 they were included in *Australian Fashion: The contemporary art*, a groundbreaking exhibition that toured to the Victoria & Albert Museum in London. With growing confidence, the 1990s saw Dinosaur Designs expand their product range to include resin homewares, glassware and silver jewellery. The early jewellery was highly figurative featuring robots, spaceships, mermaids and dinosaurs. This approach continued into the development of their homewares, with ranges of functional objects based on themes, such as the

apple-shaped lidded sugar bowl with its grub spoon from the *Garden of Eden* series (1991). The simple, organic shapes that characterise so much of their work today also began to emerge in the early 1990s and several of these items are still in production today, such as the *River Rock Beads* (1990), the *Gelato Cup* (1991) and the *Organic Bangle* (1992). The designers still use the idea of designing in series, but focus mostly on formal, technical and material connections. Exciting new works, such as the *Gem Boulder* series (2005), are fine examples of this. In 2002 a major survey exhibition of the work of Dinosaur Designs was organised and toured nationally by Object Gallery.

1 Assorted Homewares:
Oval Lidded Jar, 1996, *Square Tile Plate*, 1999, *Small Bamboo Vase*, 1998, *Organic Boulder Dish*, 1998, *Morandi Dish*, 2001, *Martini Cup*, 2001, *Medium Afro Bowl*, 1998, *Sandblasted Vase*, 1992, *Large Oval Lidded Jar*, 1996, *Cone Vase*, 1995, *Chopsticks*, 1995, *Round Sake Cup*, 1998, *Ball Jar*, 1997, *Large Oval Lidded Jar*, 1996, *Spot Vase*, 2001, *Stone Soy Dish*, 2001, *Medium Bamboo Vase*, 1998, *Oval Sugar Bowl*, 1997, *Small Bamboo Vase*, 1998, *Smoke Vase*, 2001, *Stem Cup*, 2001, *Morandi Dish*, 2001, *Art Tall Boulder Vase*, 1999, *Round Jug*, 2001, *Dot Entree Plates*, 2002, *Dot Dinner Plate*, 2002.
Resin, glass.
Tallest: 460mm

This exhibition highlighted the innovation and success of the company. 'It helped to cement a place for us within the Australian psyche … we're now featured in textbooks and studied in schools. That's such an amazing thing for us,' says Ormandy. An alternative version of the exhibition was also developed for Tokyo Designers Block 2003, and later toured to several countries in South-East Asia. Since then, the designers have been invited to design textiles for Woven Image, rugs for Designer Rugs and speculative concepts for electronics company BenQ. ■ 2002 also saw Dinosaur Designs open their first overseas store in the hip district of Nolita, New York. This store has given the Dinosaurs a significant international profile. Ongoing and sustained editorial coverage in some of the world's most influential magazines, such as US *Vogue* and *Harper's Bazaar*, has established Dinosaur Designs as a global brand. This, in turn, has had a significant impact on the perception of the company back in Australia. In the four years since opening the New York store, the company has virtually doubled in scale and the designers have produced some of their most innovative work to date. ■ *Brian Parkes*

Photography (1) Tim Richardson

2 *Assorted Resin, Wood Veneer and Brass Bangles*, 2005
Resin, wood veneer, brass.
3 *Spot Glass Vases*, 2001,
Large Organic Oval Vase, 1998,
Cocoon Vase, 2000, *Handle Up
Jug*, 2004, *Polished Belly Vase*,
2001, *Round Boulder Vase*, 2004,
Oval Boulder Vase, 2004, *Bulb
Vase*, 2005, *Stone Salt Dish*,
2001, *Bird Jug*, 2005, *Ball Jug*, 2004.
Resin, glass
Tallest: 440mm
4 *Gumball and Space Wabi Necklaces,
Assorted Resin Bangles, Spot Rings*, 2005
Resin, leather.
5 *Gem Boulder Necklaces, Gem Inlay Rings*,
2005
Resin, semi-precious stones, gems, leather.

3

Photography (2–5) Stephen Ward

Pamela Easton (b.1958) and Lydia Pearson (b.1957) are thankfully not given to management-speak or fashion jargon when they discuss their practice. Passion is, instead, the recurring theme, and the driving force behind their design and business decisions. They recount the Easton Pearson history with a down-to-earth warmth and candour not always associated with the fashion industry, especially among those who have enjoyed such a meteoric rise and stellar position.

Pamela Easton and Lydia Pearson

Easton Pearson

Life is hectic in the EP camp, although you wouldn't know it. When we meet in their Brisbane office in early autumn, they have just returned from their latest showing in Paris and are in serious catch-up mode. They sit calmly sipping green tea in a cool, quiet space above one of Fortitude Valley's busiest roads, surrounded by their trademark finery. ■ When Pearson describes the 'constant damage control' they endure, the time pressures, the punishing travel schedule and their heady juggling acts between suppliers and buyers, it's hard to align the sense of chaos with the two delicate and serene faces before me. It is only when the breadth and scale of their markets become apparent that comprehension starts to sink in. ■ Starting as a small operation in Brisbane over a decade ago, then spreading nationally, the label now sells in stores throughout Europe, Japan, Russia, the United States, Asia and the Middle East. The reach is not unusual for top fashion brands, but Easton Pearson arrives there via a demanding and complex production process. ■ The raw ingredients and, indeed, much of the inspiration for the garments are in their exquisite textiles and hand-stitched and embellished fabrics. Long before 'vintage' became *de rigueur*, these women were trawling the markets of Paris and building a sumptuous reference library of clothing samples. ■ 'It's like an op shop when you open some of these cupboards,' admits Pearson. 'Sometimes we collect things just because we admire something like a hook and eye detail. It's all very haphazard.' ■ The bulk of their fabrics is painstakingly sourced and commissioned from skilled craftspeople in India and Vietnam. Easton and Pearson make frequent trips to each of these countries, and have a deep-seated passion for their cultures and

Lydia Pearson and Pamela Easton

the welfare of the people there. Easton notes that 'so much of the culture and history is in the craft. We're interested in helping the people to maintain skills and continue to make a living.' Their longest-standing relationship is with India. While most of the work derives from Mumbai, they take regular side trips to villages and provinces to pursue a particular group of craftspeople or art form. **A recent trip to Benares uncovered some precious antique fabric. After much discussion with the weavers, it was decided that this fabric could be rewoven for Easton Pearson for the next collection.** Working with small cooperatives of craftspeople who aren't driven by deadlines is juggled with the strict delivery and showing schedules required by buying agents. The logistics are not always smooth. The women in Hanoi, for example, time their work to complement the farming seasons. If harvests come earlier or later than predicted, their stitching, knitting and crochet work is put on hold. The chain reaction is powerful. The flip side is the quiet times. Easton and Pearson feel a strong social responsibility to provide continuous supply to the workrooms in Mumbai. 'It's an onerous task,' says Easton. 'Our contact in Mumbai started 12 years ago with one man and two employees doing the hand-embroidering. Now that same man has up to 300 people working for him. We sometimes design things just to provide the work for them.' Garments are, in the main, constructed in Brisbane. Embroidery is frequently done to the size and shape of a garment – the paper patterns are sent to the embroidery workshops with the fabric, and the embroidered fabric is then returned to the Easton Pearson workroom in Brisbane. It is then hand-cut, one garment at a time, and assembled. A small percentage of construction occurs in Hong Kong, where there is a skill-base still lacking in Australia. Easton and Pearson are at a crossroad. Markets are growing exponentially, and the pair wishes to hold onto their intimate knowledge of their customers and their close control of distribution. **Easton Pearson has, ironically, never sought publicity or markets. All clients have approached them. In home-town Brisbane, Pearson notes that 'we know 90 per cent of our customers, they're our friends, they've grown with us and the business.'** The two feel blessed by their opportunities and richness of life, but are at the same time 'almost horrified by the scale of it all. We never imagined it would grow this big.' Whichever direction they take in the future, it is certain to be guided by integrity and beauty. 'We just want to remain true to ourselves.' *Margie Fraser*

Easton Pearson

1 Easton Pearson, Autumn/Winter
Collection Fashion Parade, 2006
2 Easton Pearson, Autumn/Winter
Collection Fashion Parade, 2006
3 Easton Pearson, Autumn/Winter
Collection Fashion Parade, 2006
4 Easton Pearson, Mercedes Australian
Fashion Week Parade, 2002

Benjamin Edols (b.1967) and Kathy Elliott (b.1964) travelled to the United States soon after graduating from the Canberra School of Art at the Australian National University (in 1991 and 1992 respectively). Their partnership, Edols Elliott, began in 1993 as a practical arrangement financing their travels, but has continued to be an enduring relationship in life and work. Thirteen years later, they are running a prolific studio in the northern Sydney suburb of Brookvale, producing elegant one-off and limited production glass vessels using traditional studio techniques.

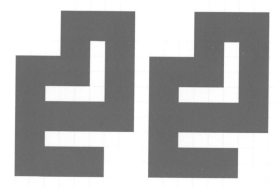

Benjamin Edols and Kathy Elliott

Edols Elliott

Their everyday work practice is heavily influenced by their former lecturer, the leading glass artist Klaus Moje. Originally from Germany, Moje taught Edols and Elliott the importance of keeping a global presence and international perspective. Their unique glass pieces have been exhibited extensively throughout Australia and internationally, including in major solo exhibitions in the United States. Their works are held in several major public collections and are highly sought after by private collectors around the world. Edols Elliott continues to have a strong presence at international craft fairs, such as Collect in London. Ben Edols also regularly conducts, or assists some of the world's foremost glass artists with, masterclasses in Australia, Japan and the United States. ■ Edols Elliott's first solo exhibition was held in 1993 at de Vera store in San Francisco. 'The style we were, and still are working in, is blown and cut glass,' Elliott says. 'At the time we were not aware of any other contemporary glass artists working in this style. It was a style from the mid-twentieth-century Italian aesthetic, and a genre we wanted to explore.' The exhibition gave Edols and Elliott their first opportunity to work together on a larger scale, spending more time on each piece and experimenting with form and texture. They still approach their work in the same way: testing, refining and evolving. The majority of their work is made specifically for sale through specialist galleries and retailers in Australia and abroad. They also undertake regular client commissions. ■ In 2000 Edols and Elliott established their impressive Brookvale studio. They run the studio as a long-term, sustainable small business, with the physical layout based on a traditional glass factory. The hot-shop work, involving the glass furnace,

is housed in one section of the studio, with cold working, grinding, cutting and polishing completed in another. Edols specialises in glass-blowing and creating the glass forms, and Elliott specialises in cold working, altering the surface of the glass. Through the collaborative process they respond to each other's work. At the beginning of each year, Edols and Elliott decide on the direction of their work together: which new techniques to explore and ideas to pursue. Working in a team environment with three full-time assistants, they make a range of work, from plant-like glass forms and cane-work vessels to blown goblets. **Constantly inspired by their environment, they create forms inspired by nature, such as the *Red in Tea 'Leaf'* vessel (2006). During the glass-blowing stage, Edols captures the deep colours within the transparent glass outer and, after cooling, Elliott painstakingly carves intricate and repetitive ridges into the surface.** They realise the importance of the handmade quality in their work, and potential for its uniqueness to differentiate them from industry standards. 'Glass moulds have never tempted us. They are quicker, but our work is process driven. It's a working life – part of a whole lifestyle,' says Edols. Despite their international success and the lure of overseas opportunities, Edols and Elliott would not want to base their business anywhere else. 'It is too beautiful to leave here! We are able to enjoy a wonderful quality of life supported by our families while we engage in our industry on an international level.' *Annabel Moir*

1

1 *Kamakura Group*, 2002
Blown and cut glass.
Tallest 670mm
2 *Red Foliage*, 2001
Blown and cut glass.
470 x 120 x 120mm
3 *Gold Fallen Leaf*, 2005
Hot formed and cut glass.
340 x 200 x 270mm
4 *Green Thorn*, 2002
Blown and cut glass.
410 x 270 x 130mm
5 *Red in Tea 'Leaf'*, 2002
Blown and cut glass.
520 x 250 x 130mm

Photography (3-5) Greg Piper

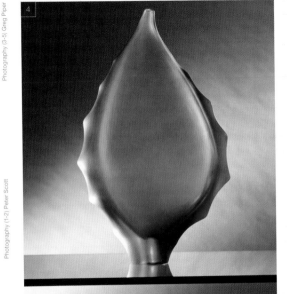

Photography (1-2) Peter Scott

Established in 1993 by acclaimed metalsmith and product designer, Robert Foster (b.1962), F!NK & Co. is a design and manufacturing company based just outside of Canberra in the New South Wales border-town of Queanbeyan.

Principal Designer Robert Foster

F!NK & Co.

Since 1997 the company has been jointly run by Foster and his partner Gretel Harrison (b.1968), who is responsible for the company's innovative marketing, sales and distribution. F!NK's products include trays, bowls, vases, wine coolers, cups, shot glasses, jewellery, containers, serving cutlery and lighting. Using bold colour and a distinctive formal language, F!NK aims to transform utilitarian items into objects of pure pleasure. Undoubtedly, the best known of their products is the sleek *F!NK Water Jug* (1993), which is used widely by many of the best restaurants throughout Australia and New Zealand, South-East Asia and the United States, and is often referred to as an icon of Australian design. F!NK is regularly commissioned by restaurants, corporate clients and design firms to produce both large and small runs of custom-designed objects. Currently the company employs six people and distributes to around 50 quality retailers around Australia, and to another dozen internationally in New Zealand, Denmark, Germany, Japan, the United Kingdom and the United States. Foster originally trained in gold and silversmithing at the Canberra School of Art. He studied with Ragnar Hansen and says that this relationship was fundamental to the development of his career: 'I started in 1981, the year that Ragnar started the course … he drove us like crazy and instilled in me a keen sense of aesthetics and balance and the drive to get every little nuance right. He encouraged us to make our own tools and to use our resourcefulness.' Hansen emigrated from Norway in 1972 (he also spent nine years teaching in Tasmania) with a rigorous craft training and an interest in the relationship between design and nature – both strong characteristics of twentieth-century Scandinavian

Robert Foster and Gretel Harrison

design and a strong influence on Foster. ■ Another key influence from Hansen was a wary suspicion of production. Despite Foster's interest and regular experiments with production processes, it took him until five years after leaving art school to embrace the notion of production, while also maintaining the integrity of his one-off works. Production also allowed Foster the financial support to progress his art practice. It could be argued that this original wariness has contributed to F!NK's demanding quality standards in manufacturing and design. Foster remains excited about the influence and interplay between his experimental hand-crafted exhibition works, which have been acquired by major museums and galleries around the world, and the F!NK production pieces. ■ Foster grew up in the Victorian mining town of Bendigo within a creative family that travelled regularly all around Australia. Despite the industrial and aerodynamic aesthetic that permeates his work, Foster draws much of his inspiration from the Australian landscape. He says, 'Many of the forms and contours in my work are derived from Australia's extraordinary natural environment – the unique flora and fauna and the weathered features of the landscape shaped by unrelenting elements'. Foster likens this later feature to the behaviour of the materials he uses as they undergo various physical and industrial processes. ■ **Foster's approach to design and manufacturing is shaped by a craftsman's deep knowledge of materials, backyard-shed resourcefulness and a mad-scientist-like obsession with risky experiments. Not surprisingly, F!NK has become renowned for innovative production methods.** Almost every product has involved some technical innovation, such as shaping an aluminium tube with explosives in a steel mould for the *F!NK Explosive Vase* (1999), or a new heat fusion process for joining a food-grade plastic to aluminium for the *F!NK Cream and Sugar Set* (2001). None of the F!NK products are mass-produced, and many of the experimental manufacturing processes have been developed to enable viable short-run production – achieving a predetermined price point without excessive tooling costs. Each product is produced in relatively small batches of 20 to 100 units at a time, and each object is individually hand-finished in the F!NK studio/workshop. ■ Foster has worked with some of the world's leading design houses, including Alessi (design and prototyping of teapots in 1996 and 2000) and Ingo Maurer (lighting prototypes in 2000), and has in turn played a key role in mentoring and supporting many young Australian designers. A key aim for F!NK from the outset was to produce and promote work by other Australian designers. Many products never get past the prototype stage and some are released and then abandoned if sales or quality control fail to meet expectations. Currently-available F!NK products have been designed (often in collaboration with Foster) by glass artist, Elizabeth Kelly; sculptor, Rachel Bowak; jeweller, Bronwyn Riddiford; and metalsmiths, Rohan Nicol, Oliver Smith and Sean Booth. ■ Harrison describes F!NK as a company that 'promotes manufacturing know-how with experience in coordinating projects from initial design liaison, to tooling, prototypes, manufacture, assembly, packaging and distribution'. F!NK has evolved as a unique hybrid within the Australian design industry, and is a stellar example of the entrepreneurial self-reliance that supports so much of Australia's most innovative design. ■ *Brian Parkes*

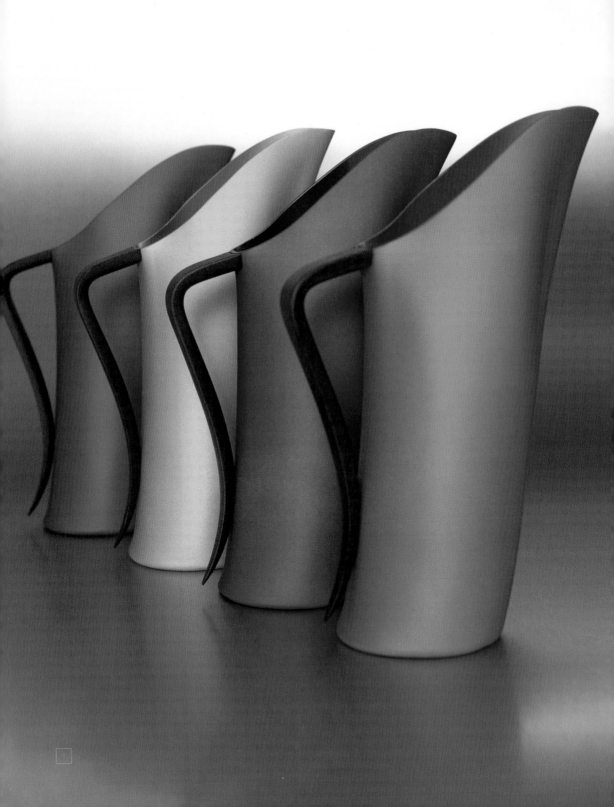

2

1 Robert Foster, *F!NK Water Jugs,* 1993
Manufactured by F!NK & Co., Australia
Anodised aluminium, powder-coated handle.
300 x 950 x 100mm

2 Robert Foster and Bronwen Riddiford, *F!NK Wine Chiller,* 2003
Manufactured by F!NK & Co., Australia
Laser-cut and pressed anodised aluminium, rotation-moulded plastic.
245 x 172 x 160mm

3 Robert Foster, *F!NK Wall Light – Morph 6 (red/blue),* 2005
Hand-hammered perforated anodised aluminium, anodised aluminium frame, fluorescent globe, acrylic diffuser.
400 x 400 x 100mm

4 Robert Foster, *Blue Ether Handbag,* 2001
Prototype
Water-formed anodised aluminium, plastic lined, rubber trimming.
280 x 320 x 110mm

5 Robert Foster, *F!NK Water Jug, Beakers and Tray,* 1993–95
Manufactured by F!NK & Co., Australia
Anodised aluminium, powder-coated aluminium handle.
Tallest: 950mm

Adam Goodrum (b.1972) is one of the rising stars of Australian product design. He completed a degree in industrial design at the University of Technology, Sydney, in 1993 and won the *Sydney Morning Herald Young Designer of the Year Award* in 1997.

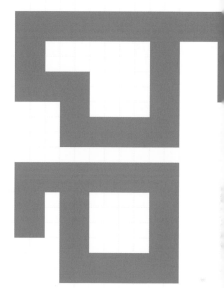

Adam Goodrum

However, it is since he returned to Australia in 2003, after a two-and-a-half-year stint in London – including a commission to design and create a large sculptural installation for a private collector in West London – that he has established a firm foothold in the national and international design arena.
The winning of another prize, the 2004 *Bombay Sapphire Design Discovery Award*, enabled him to go to the Milan International Furniture Fair for the first time as an exhibitor in 2005. Having attended the Fair twice before as a visitor, Goodrum knew what to expect and how best to prepare for it, and he has amassed an impressive folio of work, with designs ranging from an innovative, mass-producible plastic peg, to complex high-end furniture objects – most developed through to highly resolved, immaculately finished prototypes. Goodrum received positive interest from a number of leading Italian companies, including Sawaya and Moroni, B&B Italia and Draide. Many of these manufacturers were impressed with the innovation of the work and also with the fact that finished prototypes had been made. Goodrum attributes some of the positive responses to his being from Australia. 'These manufacturers see us as a bit exotic and very resourceful. In Australia we're less restricted by history … we tend to be risk-takers and have to be both good designers as well as good entrepreneurs.' Goodrum is proving to be both, and is currently having products developed by Cappellini and Whiteflax while also negotiating with a number of other companies. Many of these initiatives are the outcome of repeated contact over several years. 'The whole thing is about building up relationships,' he says. Goodrum often speaks of his passion for merging functionality with aesthetic beauty, and this is well illustrated in his *Eve seat* (2004), in which the complex curvilinear geometry and contrasting materials

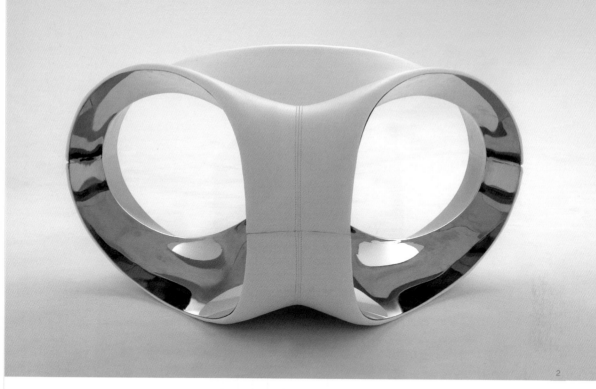

1 *Stitch Chair*, 1996–2005
Aluminium, stainless steel.
850 x 430 x 400mm
2 *Eve seat*, 2003
Stainless steel, leather.
900 x 750 x 450mm
3 *Folding House (and scale model)*, 2005
Cardboard coated in inert waterproof
paint, industrial tape.
3100 x 2800 x 2500mm
4 Graphic for *Folding House*.
5 *Tsunami Bowl*, 2003
Plastic chop sticks, stainless steel rod.
600 x 450 x 120mm
6 *Stitch Chair* (detail), 1996–2005
Aluminium, stainless steel.
850 x 430 x 400mm

1. Adam Goodrum, quoted in Geoff Piggott, 'Adam Goodrum form
& function', *Lino* magazine, Issue no. 13, 2006, Sydney.

of stainless steel and leather combine to create a beautiful sculptural object that comfortably cradles the seated figure. Another preoccupation for Goodrum is a playful fascination for folding systems. He designed his first folding chair while still studying in 1992, and has constantly revisited this theme. Works in this vein have included *Baby's High Chair* (1993), *Concertina Table* (2000) and the very clever *Tsunami Bowl* (2004), made from simply hinged plastic chopsticks. Perhaps the most striking of these investigations is his elegant *Stitch Chair* (1996, modified 2004), which folds, piano-accordion style, along its vertical axis to 15 millimetres, and was selected as one of the 'Best Designs in 2004' by United States' magazine *ID International Design Review*. ■

In 2005, Goodrum was able to take these folding concepts to a new level. In response to a brief based on functional design and quick fabrication – put out by the Canberra Architecture Biennale – he developed his extraordinary *Folding House* (2005). Goodrum had long had an interest in socially and ethically responsible design and, with the *Folding House*, he was able to create, and stick to, his own brief. He sought materials that were recycled, recyclable or in some other way sustainable, and developed a useful network of new contacts. After numerous experiments with different materials and hinging systems, Goodrum settled on a 20 millimetre-thick, lightweight corrugated cardboard; an inert, waterproof, non-flammable sealer produced by B-Earth (new Australian product); and an industrial tape called Smart Seal by 3M. This final ingredient fastened the panels together, capped off the end-grain of the cardboard, and allowed the whole structure to fold with the same simple action as the original scale models. Conceived of as an easily transportable (flat-pack), rapid assembly shelter for use in refugee and disaster relief situations, Goodrum's *Folding House* is currently being reviewed by a number of American organisations. ■ Goodrum currently supplements his various design activities with lecturing in furniture design two days a week at the University of Technology, Sydney. The environment provides him with stimulation and dialogue about design, as well as access to some state-of-the-art facilities. He aims to instil some of his own personal philosophy into his students. 'Design should stimulate and help,' he says. 'I create some pieces with a very strong sculptural element, but I also design pieces to solve problems. Our world already has too much stuff. A product should be of worth and made to last.'[1] ■ *Brian Parkes*

5

6

Photography (1-2/5-6) Blue Murder Studios

Jon Goulder (b.1970) is an impressive and pragmatic furniture designer, and a major contributor to the current momentum of Australian design. In 1992 he completed an apprenticeship in upholstery and furniture-making to become a fourth-generation craftsman. Goulder began his professional design career in 1994, designing soft furnishings for large commercial retailers, before moving to Canberra in 1996. He completed a Diploma in Art, Craft and Design in the Wood Workshop at the Canberra School of Art in 1999. Since then his work has featured in several important exhibitions and publications in Australia and overseas.

Jon Goulder

Goulder was the inaugural winner of the *Bombay Sapphire Design Discovery Award* in 2003 and was winner of the *City of Hobart Art Prize* (which focused on furniture design) in 2004. His elegant *Leda seat* (2003) was acquired for the permanent collection of the Powerhouse Museum in 2005. Despite Goulder's history in furniture and his significant success over the past five years, he still considers himself to be at the beginning of a lifelong journey in design. This grounding, long-term view enables him to patiently sort out the many details at each of the stages of taking a design idea through to a highly resolved, commercially-produced product. Much of the furniture surrounding Goulder in his youth was antique, and though he was encouraged to appreciate the various styles, none of them appealed to his aesthetic. He describes his clean-lined design sensibility as something of a reaction against this. During his time at the Canberra School of Art, Goulder was greatly influenced by the late George Ingham, who placed particular emphasis on craft skills within the course. 'George was instrumental in the way I work because of his refinement and his philosophy on how to make things ... to appreciate the process as you go, rather than rushing to see the finished article,' says Goulder. In 2000, Goulder's work was taken on by Anibou – one of the leading design showrooms in Australia and the exclusive importer of classic brands such as Artec and Breuer. He says that this representation was critical for him in establishing a profile, and adds that the loyalty and friendship of Anibou's director Ute Rose has been a powerful influence in his career. Rose is highly respected in the architecture and design community, and she has always provided Goulder with 'straight answers and honest criticism'. His skills as a maker allow

him to design through creating three-dimensional models rather than drawing on a computer. Starting with rough sketches and several months of thinking time, Goulder produces several, full-scale mock-ups to test the form for comfort, making considered adjustments with each prototype. These skills have also enabled him to undertake his own batch production. However, after making 150 of his innovative, multi-purpose *STAK stools* (2000) by hand, and being frustrated by the inability to have it manufactured cost-effectively in Australia, Goulder became interested in the possibilities presented by China. ■ Through an industry colleague, who had been having office furniture made in China in significant volume, Goulder was introduced to a number of factories. Eighteen months and several visits later – with Goulder having invested significant time and funds in helping the factories develop specific skills and equipment – the first batches meeting Goulder's high quality demands were produced in early 2006. The first of these new China-produced *STAK stools* are now being sold in Australia, and he expects to proceed with higher volume production for global export by early 2007. Through the process, Goulder has also developed several other pieces (employing the same techniques and aesthetic as *STAK*), including a bench/shelf and a table, which are also scheduled for production. ■

1

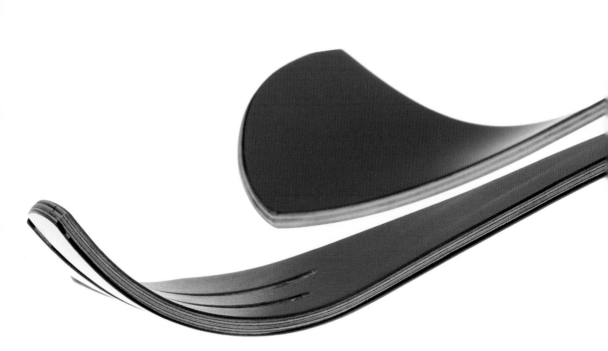

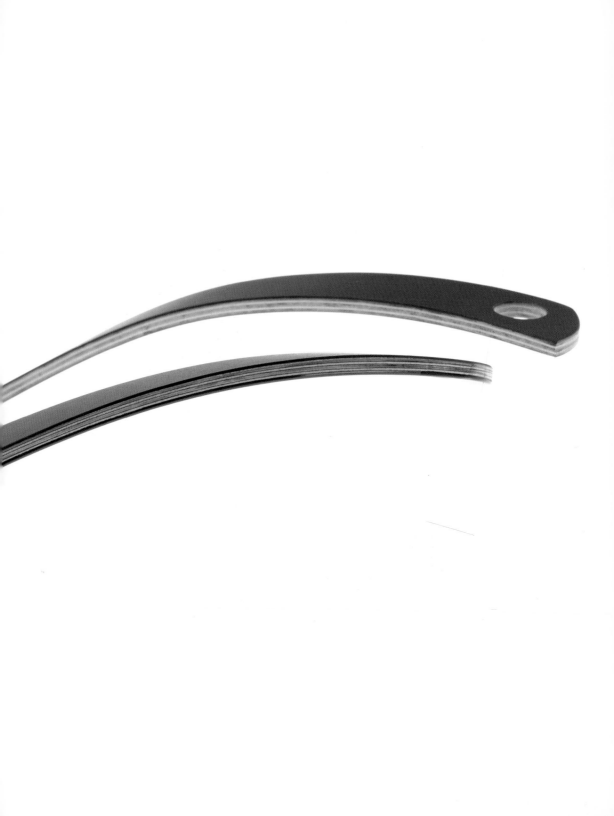

2

Not one to put all of his eggs in one basket, Goulder has also pursued opportunities for manufacturing in Australia. **Initially keen to take his _Leda seat_ to several prominent Italian companies – with whom he still hopes to work in the future – Goulder took the advice of fellow designer, Berto Pandolfo, and approached the Australian company, Woodmark International. He loaded up his ute with the award-winning prototype and all of the jigs and tooling he had developed. Almost instantly, Woodmark's managing director, Arne Christiansen, agreed to put _Leda_ into production.** After 12 months of research and development, the first units went on sale in October 2005. Goulder says, 'it took five trips up to the factory to get everything right … there was no way I could have taken five trips to Italy!' With a natural aptitude for teaching and five years of part-time lecturing at the University of Technology, Sydney, Goulder agreed to take up an exciting opportunity coordinating a new training program in Western Australia in mid-2006. A joint initiative of FORM Contemporary Craft and Design and Curtin University in Perth, this program will see Goulder working closely with Marina Lommerse and a committed team aiming to significantly develop the creative capacity and fresh new design industry that is emerging within the unique geographic and social context of Western Australia. ■ _Brian Parkes_

Digital Render (4) Tim Bird

Photography (2-3) Blue Murder Studios

Photography (1) Benjamin Healley

3

1 *Salad servers*, 2006
Plywood, Laminex.
Manufactured by Jon Goulder, China
Length: 305mm
2 *Leda seat,* 2003
Plywood and aluminium.
Manufactured by Woodmark International,
Australia.
740 x 1760 x 940mm
3 *STAK* stackable stool/table/shelving unit, 2001
Plywood.
Manufactured by Jon Goulder, China.
450 x 600 x 600mm
4 *Fruit Bowl,* 2005
CAD Drawing

4

Lorinda Grant (b.1974) is responsive to her immediate environment. Whether in her home town of rural Bendigo or the fast and furious world of fashion, Grant has simultaneously woven into her work a strong sense of ethics and aesthetics.

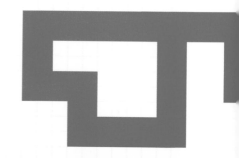

Lorinda Grant

The daughter of fourth-generation wool-growers, Grant has lived in regional Victoria most of her life. As a child she was constantly knitting and sewing as a form of play. Now in her early thirties, Grant is best known for her signature use of wool in creating felted and knitted garments. Maintaining comfort and flexibility within garments is a key element in her design process. Felted dresses, skirts, trousers, coats and wraps are designed to wrap and drape effortlessly from the body. While working in Melbourne's bridal industry, Grant dreamed of creating her own label. Her inspiration was to design using traditional hand-knitting techniques with pure wool that had minimum chemical treatments. From 1998–99 she commuted from Bendigo to study at night at the Melbourne School of Fashion, and began to develop a strategic business plan. In 1999 she was a finalist in *Australian Gown of the Year*, but it was in 2000 that the potential and talents of this young designer came to public attention. The success of her Craft Victoria solo exhibition, *A Thread and Two Sticks*, provided Grant with the confidence to market her designs commercially. That same year, Grant began to wholesale into the retail outlets of Andrea Gold, Perugia, T.L. Wood and Zambesi. She also met Akira Isogawa at this time, which was the start of a mutually beneficial relationship that has seen Grant produce a series of pieces for Akira Isogawa. A participant in Mercedes Australian Fashion Week since 2001, Grant has continued the dual lines of exhibition and production works with much success. In 2002 Isogawa curated the exhibition, *Following Lorinda*, for the Bendigo Art Gallery; in 2003 Grant was an exhibitor in *Un Wrapped*, which toured internationally; and in 2004, her participation in the National Gallery of

Victoria's exhibition, *Pins & Needles*, resulted in her exhibited work being purchased for the collection. Such acknowledgements have positioned Grant firmly in the Australian fashion design industry by exposing her work to a broad national and international audience. **Grant finds inspiration from her surrounds. The texture of a landscape viewed on a drive through the country can easily be translated into a new garment range. She developed a unique felting technique in 2001 that resulted in a seamless garment design. The versatile qualities of wool combined with her design skills have enabled Grant's designs to be worn inside-out and upside-down, with your head in an arm-hole or an arm through a head-hole.** For Grant, it is a dream come true. Owning her label, Eternal U, has provided a sense of freedom both in design and in manufacturing. Working almost exclusively in hand-spun dyed wool and unspun/undyed yarn, she maintains strong ties to her country roots and sources fine merino wool from local suppliers, including from the farm that once belonged to her grandfather. Grant has most recently begun experimenting with machine knits, using a semi-industrial machine to make cardigans and sleeves. This shift from needle to machine has allowed her to design shapes that are edgier, and to continue to produce exhibition pieces, while still earning a living. The legacy of taking wool from the sheep's back is an intrinsic part of Grant's philosophy. She believes there is great innovation in regional Australia to be nurtured. The reality is, of course, that there are also challenges to country life, including isolation. Small-scale fashion production also needs to meet the demands of orders. To assist her with this, Grant has employed the skills of her family. Along with a few local wool suppliers, Grant's mother manages a dedicated team of some 70 part-time knitters, while her father makes her signature pins. While Grant is considered shy, it is the future of the wool industry that keeps her talking. She talks directly to local farmers about fleeces, the mills about yarns and new techniques for wool processing. Grant's environmental concerns continue to determine her future. *Sarah Bond*

1

2

3

5

Photography Simone Stabb

1 *Hand-knitted and felted shawl, 2002*
Merino wool.
Machine-knitted and laddered top, 2005
Wool, silk.
Machine-knitted, laddered and felted apron,
2005
Wool, silk.
2 *Hand-knitted string jumper, 1995*
Linen, cotton.
Felt skirt, 2000
Wool.
3 *Hand-knitted and laddered vest, 2006*
Hand-dyed Merino wool.
Hand-knitted scoop neck top, 2005
Merino wool.
Machine-knitted and laddered skirt/poncho, 2005
Wool, silk.
4 *Hand-knitted jacket, 2005*
Merino wool.
Machine-knitted, laddered and felted tunic, 2005
Merino wool, cotton.
Machine-knitted skirt, 2005
Merino wool.
5 *Machine-knitted and laddered dress, 2005*
Colana Red Merino wool, cotton.
Machine-knitted and laddered skirt, 2004
Wool, silk.

In August 2005 the partners of Gray Street Workshop – at the time, Julie Blyfield (b.1957), Sue Lorraine, Leslie Matthews (b.1964) and Catherine Truman (b.1957) – commemorated their twentieth anniversary with an exhibition at galerie ra in Amsterdam.

Julie Blyfield, Leslie Matthews, Catherine Truman

Gray Street Workshop

Signs taken for wonders highlighted not only a sense of cohesion – of the interconnectedness that has been apparent from the outset – but also the evolution over that period of each artist's preoccupations; and the emergence, too, of distinct points of difference. ■ 'My starting point,' says Truman, 'has always been the body, either as a canvas, a subject in itself or a metaphor.' Utilising a Netsuke carving technique discovered during a 1990 residency in Japan, Truman realised that the bold, curvilinear line work of her carved limewood pieces, and the rhythmical red striations coloured with red *shu niku* ('red meat') ink – for example in *Red Seas* (1994) – created an uncanny resemblance to human flesh and muscle. This recognition, literally of 'the flesh of her work', led her into extensive research of many significant anatomical collections in Europe. In recent years she has been profoundly influenced by her first-hand experience of major collections of anatomical waxes produced at La Specola Museum in Florence during the eighteenth century, as well as her viewing of original sixteenth-century anatomical figurative sheets at the Wellcome Trust Centre for the History of Medicine in London. Three of Truman's carved, paraffin-wax portraits were included in the National Gallery of Victoria's national survey of contemporary art, *2004: Australian culture now*. ■ Consistent with Blyfield's abiding interest in botanical forms, an early twentieth-century album of Indigenous Australian pressed plants provided the impetus for the *Pressed Desert Plant* (2005) series of brooches and neckpieces. Remarkable for its unprecedented foray into colour – ochre, faded green, rusty red – the series consolidated a shift to a more sculptural form of making,

Leslie Matthews, Catherine Truman, Julie Blyfield

exemplified by her pivotal 2003 *Flourish* body of work. Blyfield says she had felt a compulsion 'to invest significant time and care in the making of an object', and four outstanding series of work were the outcome of an intense period (2003–06) of experimentation. Revealing a heightened sensitivity to the compositional possibilities of an ensemble mode of presentation, *Flourish's* exquisite assemblage of raised silver, seed-pod or gourd-like objects – in which the surfaces were intricately worked using Blyfield's preferred chasing technique – was exhibited in London in 2006. Like its 2003 counterpart, the series was underpinned by extensive research into botanical and pressed plant specimens, housed in Australia and the United Kingdom. The surfaces of Matthews' silver vessels and body ornaments were once intensively decorated using the ancient hammering technique of repoussé, but increasingly she has softened surface embellishment in order to foreground a fluid purity of form. Recent series, such as *The gentle wash of memory* (2002), exhibited in London in 2005, present abstracted, yet allusive, skeletal forms that are imbued with intimations of mortality. Employing only white or black oxidised finishes, her poetic silver pieces possess a delicate smoothness – reminiscent of time-weathered bones – which is the product of an exacting process of hammering and forming, sanding and refining. Titles are characteristically drawn from literature, and in the latest body of work, *When it comes, the landscape listens, shadows hold their breath* (2005), earlier curvaceous, closed forms have been unfurled, in an apparent reference to the possibility of transformation or rebirth. 'I have explored the concept of the narrative through personal experiences,' Matthews says, 'creating artworks that respond on a universal level to an inner understanding of our surroundings.' At the 2005 anniversary exhibition, the fluid sensuality of Matthews' pieces provided a perfect foil for the reductive logic and edginess of Lorraine's uncompromisingly austere, matte-black assemblage of laser-cut, mild-steel moth brooches. Since 1999, Lorraine (for 20 years the fourth partner) had balanced her position as Creative Director of the metal design studio at Adelaide's JamFactory Contemporary Craft and Design centre with a continuing commitment to Gray Street Workshop, but in late 2005 she made a pragmatic decision to leave the collective. **Typically, production pieces are scaled-down, simplified (or simply wearable) versions of the partners' labour intensive work for exhibition, but they frequently also afford the opportunity for greater spontaneity and for experimentation.** Beyond the supportive workshop environment, Gray Street Workshop's range of activities has developed to encompass involvement – either individually or collectively – in numerous public artworks, national and international residencies and lectures, teaching in tertiary institutions, mentorship schemes and so on. It is through the far-sighted decision to offer access workshop facilities, however, that the influence of the Workshop has been most effective and far reaching. To date, more than 60 jeweller-tenants – who have stayed for unspecified periods, lasting from a few weeks to five years – have benefited from continuous exposure to the partners' professionalism, commitment and intellectual rigour. Moreover, Blyfield, Matthews and Truman retain the sort of undiminished intellectual curiosity that ensures the continuing vitality and validity of Gray Street Workshop. *Wendy Walker*

4

5

Photography Grant Hancock

6

7

8

1 Julie Blyfield, *Pressed desert plant brooch series*, 2005
Oxidised sterling silver, enamel paint, wax.
Average 65 x 60 x 20mm
2 Leslie Matthews, *When it comes, the landscape listens, shadows hold their breath (group)*, 2005
Title from a poem by Emily Dickinson, 1862.
Sterling silver patinated black.
3 Leslie Matthews, *When it comes, the landscape listens, shadows hold their breath*, 2005
Title from a poem by Emily Dickinson, 1862.
Sterling silver.
4 Catherine Truman, *1:5 Model without portrait #8*, 2005
Carved English limewood, paint, graphite.
110 x 140 x 60mm
5 Catherine Truman, *1:5 Model without portrait #6*, 2005
Carved English limewood, paint, burnt surface.
145 x 160 x 45mm
6 Catherine Truman, *1:5 Model without portrait #7*, 2005
Carved English limewood, paraffin wax, *shu niku* ink, paint.
115 x 130 x 65mm
7 Catherine Truman, *Fugitive portraits brooches*, 2005
Carved English limewood, paint, graphite, ink.
Largest 90mm
8 Julie Blyfield, *Flourish*, 2005–06
Oxidised copper, wax, pure silver.
Average 160 x 110 x 110mm

Akira Isogawa (b.1964) is arguably Australia's most critically acclaimed fashion designer. He has forged this reputation through constant inventiveness and an uncompromising dedication to quality.

Akira Isogawa

Since opening his first boutique in Sydney in 1993 in Queen Street, Woollahra, Isogawa has steadily expanded his business. He now has two additional stores: one in Melbourne's GPO (opened 2005), and the latest in Sydney's Strand Arcade (opened 2006). His clothes are also sold though David Jones stores nationally and through around 50 influential stockists overseas, with exports accounting for almost 70 per cent of the overall business. ■ Since 1999 Isogawa has been showing his seasonal collections twice a year in Paris and three times a year in Australia. With each collection commencing development about five months in advance, it is a gruelling schedule, and he now employs a team of around 20 dedicated staff. From both a commercial and a creative point of view, showing in Paris has become vital for Isogawa. 'The Australian market is quite conservative … when designing for Paris, I can take more risks creatively,' he says. He does acknowledge, however, that the Australian market is growing rapidly and becoming increasingly sophisticated. The combination of designing for European markets, while being based in Australia, and having come from Japan, is part of what makes Isogawa's work so distinctive. ■ Having grown up in Kyoto, Isogawa was fascinated with the space and mystery of Australia and moved to Sydney (following a working holiday in Australia the previous year) in 1986. The city of Kyoto was founded on the ancient silk trade. It is the traditional home of the kimono, and Isogawa remembers his mother and grandmother regularly wearing them. His early work was a literal fusion of Japanese traditions with Western sensibilities – often re-using pieces of beautifully detailed kimono fabrics.

Today his textiles and influences are drawn from a much wider variety of countries and cultural contexts, and are integrated through his deft touch into sophisticated and expressive hybrid forms. ■ Following his studies at East Sydney Technical College, and with various part-time jobs to support himself, Isogawa began designing and making clothing in his own tiny apartment to sell into a handful of Sydney boutiques before eventually opening his own. It was not until his second showing at Mercedes Australian Fashion Week in 1997 that things really started to take off. His Spring/Summer 1997–98 collection, *Satori*, received favourable reviews in prominent national and international media, and was purchased by the highly influential London fashion boutique Browns. He was the Australian fashion industry's Designer of the Year in 1999 and has been the subject of two significant solo exhibitions; one organised by Object Gallery for the 2002 Sydney Festival and the other developed by the National Gallery of Victoria in 2005. ■ **Isogawa is committed to the process of collaboration. Within the industry he has teamed up with others to achieve new possibilities within his collections. He has sought out skilled traditional textile producers in places such as Bali, Hong Kong, India and Vietnam to develop experimental textiles.**

For example, he recently negotiated with Chinese embroiderers to dramatically loosen and scale up their work to create the embellishments on the *Akira Embroidered Silk Organza Wedding Bird Layered Dress* (2006). He has collaborated for several years with Australian screen-printing company Signature Prints, interpreting and utilising their archive of designs by the late Florence Broadhurst, an Australian designer who travelled extensively through Asia in the 1920s. He has a fruitful ongoing relationship with iconic Australian clothing company Bonds, which began with Isogawa customising readymade singlet tops, and has evolved to creating a distinct range of more economically priced Akira garments using Bonds fabrics. Collaboration in other fields has led Isogawa to create costumes for Sydney Dance Company and the Australian Chamber Orchestra; develop furniture prototypes with Edward Wong; design rugs for Designer Rugs; and produce soft furnishings for the Sydney retailer Orson & Blake. ■ Isogawa's design is driven by the texture of fabrics and the almost infinite structural possibilities of garments. Rather than designing through sketching and drawing, he works by physically draping fabrics or paper over the figure; building up, stripping back, manipulating the form – always considering the very different shapes and needs of the women he designs for. Of his recent fascination for plaiting, knotting, folding and gathering, such as in the *Akira Embroidered Wool Gauze Flower Crane Plait Jacket* (2006), he says, 'In the past I was embellishing by adding another element to the textile, like in the form of embroidery or sequins, and what I'm really up to now is embellishing within the textile itself'. Each collection has a new starting point – a strongly defined concept, of which he says, 'I treat the concept as if it was home – a point to return to. When I feel a bit lost I always return to the concept.'[1] ■ *Brian Parkes*

1. Akira Isogawa, quoted in Katie Somerville, *Printemps-été: Akira Isogawa*, National Gallery of Victoria, Melbourne, 2005.

1

2

1 *Akira Kimono Velvet Gathered Shawl, Kimono Velvet Lined Long Skirt*, 2005
Automne Hiver (shown in Paris, March 2005).
2 *Akira Embroidered Silk Organza Wedding Bird Layered Dress*, 2006
Automne Hiver (shown in Paris, March 2006).
3 *Akira Red Silk Georgette Origami Tank, Akira Bonds Silk Organza with Cotton Jersey Origami Skirt, Akira Bonds Wool Jersey Leggings, Akira Bonds Wool Jersey Plait Belt* (worn as necklace), 2006
Automne Hiver (shown in Paris, March 2006).
4 *Akira Silk Georgette Ruffle Dress*, 2006
Printemps Été (shown in Paris, October 2005)
5 *Akira Embroidered Wool Gauze Flower Crane Plait Jacket, Plain Silk Organza Vest, Embroidered Wool Gauze Multi Floral Skirt, Plain Wool Jersey Tights*, 2006
Automne Hiver (shown in Paris, March 2006).
6 *Akira Layered Silk Gauze Ruffle Jacket, Embroidered Silk Organza Gradation Layered Dress*, 2006
Autome Hiver (shown in Paris, March 2006).

As a contemporary jeweller, Sheridan Kennedy (b.1964) responds to her diverse experiences, interests and imaginings. She creates objects of wonder, combining lush decadence and playfulness in equal measures. Her jewellery is meticulously made by hand to be admired and treasured for a lifetime.

Sheridan Kennedy

Individual pieces may feature articulating joints, kinetic complexities, coral clusters or feathery frivolity. There is a strong sense of transformation and theatrics in Kennedy's creations. Since establishing her jewellery practice in 1985, Kennedy has become well known for creating highly original works, which blur boundaries between art, craft and design. First drawn to gold and silversmithing because it conjured up visions of lost worlds and ancient cities, Kennedy continues to explore ideas of this nature. 'Romanticism lies at the heart of my work,' she says. After completing a Bachelor of Arts (majoring in jewellery) at the Queensland College of Art in 1987, Kennedy was mentored by established jeweller Barbara Heath before travelling to Europe and Egypt. The Renaissance extravagance she encountered in Italy inspired her foray into fashion, attracted by its ability to make big statements and express excessive individuality. More recent travels have taken Kennedy to Barcelona (1991) and New York (2003) for Australia Council studio recidencies, and to the United Kingdom (2003) to participate in the *Here and There (HAT)* exchange program. Growing up on a sheep and cattle station outside the remote town of Winton, Queensland, Kennedy developed a fascination for the way machinery works. Tractor motors, generators and old equipment lying about the property became sources of inspiration. This began her investigations into jewellery's potential to act as a tool or active instrument on the body. Mechanics and interactivity are now an integral part of her practice. In 2000, Kennedy was asked to create a large-scale, site-specific work at the Brisbane Powerhouse Centre for the Arts. Responding to the building's history as an electricity station, Kennedy chose to focus on the machine

age and its initial reliance on manpower. To interact with Kennedy's installation, *Optogemel*, visitors are invited to turn a handle, which causes a large disk to spin on two simple axes in a fluid motion. This simple device, or 'gimble', is also used in many of Kennedy smaller works to explore how the body utilises kinetic energy.

As well as major installations, exhibitions and commissions, Kennedy has undertaken successful collaborations with fashion designers, including Justine Taylor (2001), Michelle Jank (2001) and Akira Isogawa (1998, 2002). Her collaborations with these designers for Mercedes Australian Fashion Week were sponsored by Autore South Sea Pearls, and resulted in a major design commission to produce a range of jewellery for Autore under licence. For this project, Kennedy worked to a specific design brief, with numerous consultations before the product was manufactured in Hong Kong. This differs greatly from her usual approach to making, which is more spontaneous and responsive to new ideas and experimentation. *Specious* is an experimental collection of work that has evolved and grown significantly over the last five years. First exhibited at Object Gallery in 2001, *Specious* plays on the conception of jewellery as adornment – something captivating that draws the gaze. In this series, Kennedy makes reference to museological classification and European 'discovery' voyages, with her intricate insect and botany inspired jewellery. The fascination and intensity of Kennedy's practice stems from her active mind and high level of technical aptitude. Currently completing a PhD at Sydney College of the Arts, she is pushing current conceptions of jewellery, researching the complexities of the body's relationship to jewellery. Her jeweller's bench is surrounded by a multitude of silver latches, catches, hammers, feathers, beads, tiny drill bits, sketches, CAD renderings: evidence of her trade. Supported by wholesale sales, commissions, scholarships and grants, Kennedy enjoys the freedom of not running her own retail business. Having the space and time to develop new ranges of work, she sells to fashion stores and design galleries across Australia and overseas, predominantly in London and Los Angeles. Travel is still an important catalyst for new work, but she enjoys being based in Australia. 'I like the hybrid cultures here. We are not confined by traditions. There is an openness and interest in new things.' She has recently begun to consider setting up her own fantasy salon, selling couture jewellery – a place where customers could come to feel indulged. Employing the frivolity of fashion and costume, Kennedy would be right at home in such an excessive environment.

Annabel Moir

Photography (3–5) JJ&K

Photography (2) Alex Zotos

1 *Arachnid brooches and earrings*, 2002
Emu feathers, sterling silver and jet crystal.
Art Direction/Styling: Marian Simms
Make up: Rae Morris Model: Rose at Chic
2 *Tarantula earpiece* for Michelle Jank
and Autore South Sea Pearls, MAFW, 2001
Created with assistance from Kass Warner.
South Sea pearls, sterling silver, 9k gold, glass.
3 *Leaf Cloud Thorn rings*, 2005
Sterling silver.
Average: 60 x 30 x 15mm
4 *Elegant Feathered Dandyfly*,
(from the *Specious Voyages*), 2005
Pheasant feathers, sterling silver, rhyolite,
hematite, stainless steel, quartz crystal.
200 x 200 x 230mm
5 *Mandibulae earrings*, 2005
Sterling silver and coral.
Prototype
95 x 20 x 10mm
6 *Feather Berry necklace*, 2002
Emu feathers, jet crystal, sterling silver, steel.
Art Direction/Styling: Marian Simms
Make up: Rae Morris Model: Rose at Chic

Photography (1)(6) Ivan de Petrovsky

6

korban/flaubert is a design and production partnership between Janos Korban (b.1961) and Stefanie Flaubert (b.1965). After completing degrees at Adelaide University in 1988 (Korban in arts, majoring in psychology and genetics, Flaubert in architecture), the couple left Australia in 1990 to travel overseas.

Janos Korban and Stefanie Flaubert

korban/flaubert

Flaubert worked for four years with German architect Günter Behnisch, known for his specialisation in lightweight structures. During this time Korban developed advanced metalworking skills, within the innovative architectural metal workshop K.M. Hardwork. He also worked collaboratively on exhibition and theatre design and his own sculptural work, concentrating on experimental metal fabrication techniques. The two established korban/flaubert in Stuttgart in 1993, focusing on collaborative research and formal investigations into materials, structure and spatial relationships. They continue to articulate their unique interests through exhibitions, commissions and experimental design work. The pair returned to Australia in 1995, and responded to their close proximity to nature, which is a fundamental source of inspiration for their work. Re-establishing their business in Sydney, they continued to produce experimental work as well as simpler, more pragmatic furniture and lighting products, such as the *block* table (1999) and *bongo* stool (1999). These small-scale objects started to take over from their architectural and interior projects, and allowed more direct experimentation. In 2001 Korban and Flaubert set up their current studio/workshop/showroom in Alexandria. Maintaining their experimental methodology, they describe the workshop as 'a laboratory of form', in which they playfully explore the cross-over between geometry and nature. Their fascination with mathematics – pattern, rhythm and resonance – leads them on different trajectories of exploration, with no preconceived function in mind. The final outcomes are either functional or purely sculptural forms. Practical applications may emerge after intensive processes of analysis, model making and prototyping.

Janos Korban and Stefanie Flaubert

Ironically, by not actively designing products, korban/flaubert has successfully produced some of Australia's most iconic and celebrated designs. The partnership's critically acclaimed *cellscreen* (2003) began as a series of simple, geometric experiments with a single line-length and a repeated, five-way joint. The resulting object's potential use as a decorative screen or room divider was only revealed once it was scaled up to a certain size. Similarly, *array* (2005) is based on a simple mathematical growth pattern found in nature, and is now produced as a screen and can be seen in numerous corporate interior environments.

korban/flaubert has had significant commercial success with its elegant range of rotomoulded polyethylene forms, including the *bubble*, *bongo* and *pod* stools. Australian design company Schiavello has also licensed their *Tom* stool design. Involvement in the commercial market has enabled ongoing research and development, allowing korban/flaubert to expand and diversify its practice, pursuing innovative ideas and putting new work into production. Distributing the majority of its products through the korban/flaubert showroom gives the partners direct contact with their clients, and they have developed important relationships with architects, interior designers and international media. **korban/flaubert's work concentrates on furniture and lighting product development, commissioned pieces and ambiguous structural forms.** The designers also maintain an active practice developing site-specific projects. These large-scale installations respond to their respective backgrounds and early-stage collaborations. Major interior installations include *Tetra-Five*, at the Melbourne Docklands, and *Arterial* at King Street in Sydney. They have also been invited to create temporary installations, such as *Siren* for Sydney's *Sculpture by the Sea* and *Adventure* for Object Gallery. In these projects, korban/flaubert aims to explore ideas about object perception and push the scale of its experimental themes. korban/flaubert has gained significant international exposure through exhibitions at Designers Block in London and Tokyo, designmai in Germany and the Milan International Furniture Fair, Italy. In conjunction with London Designers Block 2002, korban/flaubert was invited to create an installation in Selfridges department store windows. *Sway with Me* featured multiples of their *Swaylamp*, and entranced vast audiences with its moving illuminated form. Their involvement in key design fairs around the world has led to productive

1

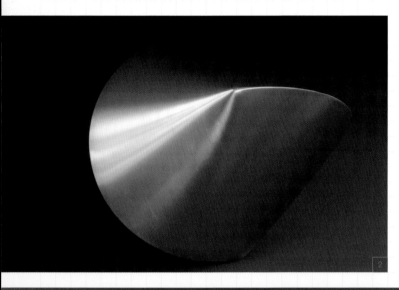

1 *bubble stool*, 2005
Rotomoulded polyethylene.
460 x 380mm
2 *tetrasphere*, 2002
Stainless steel.
600 x 480 x 450mm
3 *array screen*, 2005
Stainless steel.
1950 x 1950 x 60mm
4 *Adventure* installation
at Object Gallery, 2005
PVC, flourescent tubes, acrylic.
12000 x 12000 x 5000mm
5 *burst light*, 2006
Anodised aluminium.
1000 x 800 x 360mm
6 *split block*, 2002
Stainless steel, acrylic,
flourescent light source.
1800 x 750 x 600mm

4

5

Photography (4) Andy Stevens

6

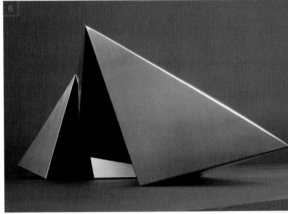

associations with international manufacturers and retailers and established important clients in Europe, the United States, Asia and Australia. ■ Korban and Flaubert describe their organic approach to design as 'a process of discovery'. From transparent chaises longues to burst lights and coffee tables in hi-tech metal meshes, they 'try to generate something fundamental by understanding basic effects of materials, volume and action'. The end product may be decorative, meditative, hypnotic or therapeutic. The application is found in the form, 'the idea falls out of life, the form falls out of the idea'. ■ *Annabel Moir*

Photography (1-3/5-6) Sherrin Rees

It is wonderfully difficult to define Simone LeAmon's practice. LeAmon (b.1971) may be best described as an interdisciplinary artist and designer, whose role shifts among those of artist, designer, craftsperson, performer, curator, publicist, businesswoman and teacher as each particular project or idea demands.

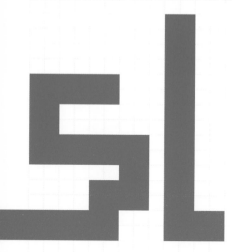

Simone LeAmon

LeAmon works as an artist individually across a variety of media including drawing, sculpture, performance and digital media, and often initiates collaborations to develop conceptually informed design projects. She states, 'My practice is essentially a by-product of the dialogues found between the creative disciplines and the corporate sectors'. She sees art objects and functional objects as intrinsically linked in their ambition to seduce and incite desire. LeAmon has designed, or developed design proposals for projects as varied as jewellery, graphics, lighting, public art, and even a women's motorcycle racing suit. She recently signed a contract to develop designs for esteemed Italian lighting company, Oluce, in Milan, and has exhibited in Australia, Italy, Japan and the United States. LeAmon completed a Bachelor of Fine Art in 1993, majoring in sculpture, from the Victorian College of Arts. Since then her work has increasingly engaged with notions of function, consumption and desire. She completed a masters degree in industrial design in 2004, however exhibitions and performances remain important vehicles for LeAmon in her pursuit of inverse and unorthodox design methodologies. In 1996–97, she worked part-time with Susan Cohn as an assistant in Workshop 3000. Cohn's influence and encouragement are highlighted in LeAmon's healthy interdisciplinary attitude and interest in the transgressive potential of design. 'One morning in the workshop, Cohn asked me to procure sponsorship for several hundred condoms. I remember thinking "cool, here's an opportunity to speak about sex, protection, design and craft to a CEO".' From 1999 to 2003, LeAmon was a partner in n+1 equals, an interdisciplinary studio that she established in Melbourne with artist Charles Anderson. n+1 equals engaged in a broad range of activity, from

projects within the built environment to fashion and accessories design. The best known project from this venture is the *Bowling Arm* bangles (2001), in which an industrial waste product (the offcut leather rings created in the manufacturing of cricket balls) is re-formed, or rather re-presented in multiple, as desirable contemporary jewellery. Available until recently in red, yellow and white versions (with the white sold exclusively through Japanese fashion house, Issey Miyake, in 2001) the bangles are now only being produced in yellow by LeAmon's new studio O.S Initiative – sadly the iconic red Australian cricket ball is now made offshore. **In 2001 LeAmon was a recipient of an Australia Council studio residency in Milan. This opportunity enabled her to build and strengthen networks within the Italian design and manufacturing industry, and to participate in the *Salone del Mobile* during the Milan International Furniture Fair that year.** Her project involved a kind of game or performance, where visitors were invited to play with a series of what she referred to as *Conceptual Models* with interlocking parts that could be pulled apart and reconfigured in innumerable ways; the players were then asked to define what their new configurations represented: a sofa, a house, a spaceship, etc. This work formed part of LeAmon's ongoing investigation into how the end-user plays an active role in defining the function of an object. LeAmon has subsequently exhibited in Milan during the Furniture Fair in 2003 and 2005. In 2005 she showed with fellow Australians, Marc Pascal and Matthew Butler, as part of *Anytime Soon*, curated by Via Farini for *Salone del Mobile*. LeAmon's presentation, titled *A Supersystem Concept for 5 Products: Post object confessions*, consisted of digitally-rendered images of new designs for a light, a kettle, a timepiece, a purse and a day bed, with an accompanying narrative text and video-documented performance for each. She says the work 'explores the notion of lifestyle products in the company of general human affections such as desire, comfort, disappointment and love'. LeAmon makes a point of acknowledging her collaborators, and collaboration is very much a part of her modus operandi. *Bodywork* (2003), the women's motorcycle racing suit mentioned earlier, is a poignant example: working with digital effects director Daryl Munton (who also worked on the *Supersystem Products*) and architect David Morison, LeAmon used her own body as a model for creating the virtual one-piece leather suit. Juggling multiple art and design projects, LeAmon is also currently lecturing across the university departments of industrial design, new media and visual arts at RMIT University, Swinburne University and Box Hill Institute, Melbourne. In late 2006 LeAmon will relocate to Milan to establish her own interdisciplinary office there in order to better leverage her contract with Oluce. Let's hope she returns in the near future to be a protagonist for further improvement in the relationship between the corporate and creative industries in this country.

Brian Parkes

1

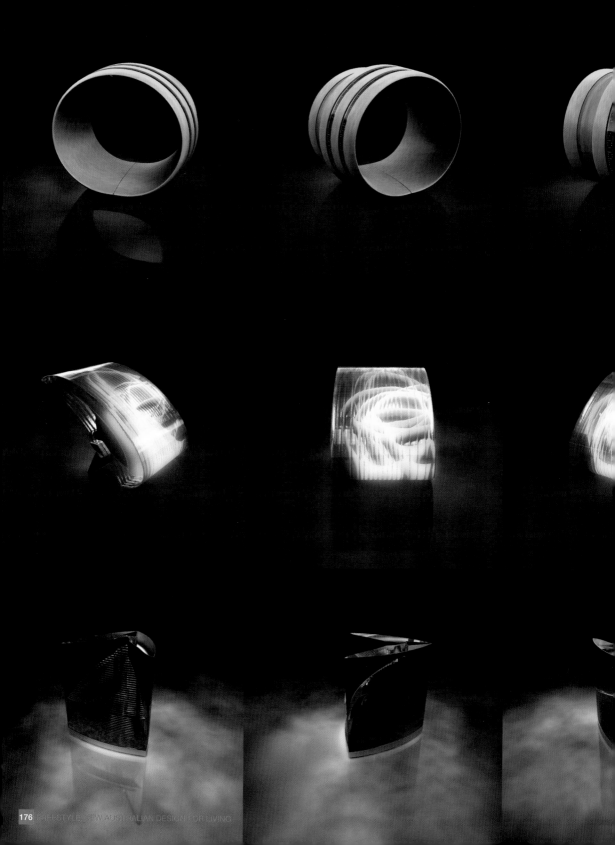

1 *Super Sofas: Furnishings for body play and rest,* 2003
Flocked polyurethane.
2 *Cuff,* 2005
3D Computer-generated models.
Daryl Munton (digital collaborator)
3 *Headlight,* 2005
3D Computer-generated model.
Daryl Munton (digital collaborator)
4 *Little Kettle,* 2005
3D Computer-generated model.
Daryl Munton (digital collaborator)

Stefan Lie's (b.1968) ambition has always been to be a designer, and he is now on the edge of soaring success. Over the last ten years he has gained significant local support and elevated his designs onto an international platform.

Stefan Lie

In his formative years, Lie trained and worked as a toolmaker in Switzerland, and developed sound problem-solving skills during the eight years he spent in Europe specialising in injection mould manufacturing. He then returned to Australia in 1994 to study industrial design at the University of Technology, Sydney (UTS). Now, Lie's approach to design is distinctly Australian. He has overcome the limited manufacturing opportunities here by producing many of his works himself, as well as the tooling components. This 'can do' attitude has given Lie the freedom to pursue a broad range of design projects. ■ While studying, he decided he wanted to design consumer products, and started a furniture design elective. Realising the sculptural possibilities, he 'became interested in objects that have an individual aesthetic'. In his third year of university, Lie was assigned to design a piece of furniture based on the idea of interactivity. He designed the *Ribs* bench (1996), which responded to the brief and also proved to be his first major design hit. After a friend's offer to buy one, five other people put deposits down and this continued to have roll-on effect. Leading retailer, de de ce, launched the product, attracting the attention of staff in Decorative Arts and Design at the Powerhouse Museum, Sydney. In 1998, the Powerhouse purchased *Ribs* for its permanent collection, and in the same year Lie won the award for the most outstanding graduate in Object Gallery's annual graduate exhibition *new design*. ■ With funds from the Australia Council, Lie went on to produce the *Swell* sofa (1997) in response to the tidal swell of the ocean, and *Thong* stool (2002) inspired by a g-string displayed on a hoop in a Kings Cross shop window. The natural and constructed environment is a strong influence on the conceptual basis

of Lie's work. His works are of a high quality, made to last for a lifetime. His pared back aesthetic optimises simple, repeating shapes, with a strong emphasis on form. Although function is often secondary, Lie is firmly pragmatic about what he does. █ An ongoing and supportive relationship with de de ce has led Lie to develop works in direct response to retail demand. Stephen Cassidy, manager at de de ce, approached Lie about his need for an inexpensive room divider. The result, Lie's *Strip* screen (2002), is a clever system of narrow pre-cut strips that lower the overall cost. Other opportunities, such as Lie's inclusion in *workshopped 03* and *05*, held at the Strand Arcade during Sydney Design Week, and Object's *Sydney Style* exhibition presented at the Sydney Opera House,

1

produced a sculptural version of the *Strip* screen, a *Ribs* bench in aluminium and new monumental *Pila* seat (2004). ■ **Lie's latest ventures have involved jewellery and product design. Working on a smaller scale, he continues to explore form in the same way. He has modelled eight simple, yet emotive shapes for his range of rings that are sold through fashion boutiques. Lie has also designed a tea-set made with rapid prototyping technology.** As a finalist in the 2005 *Bombay Sapphire Design Discovery Award*, Lie's *Genie* teapot was the featured design. Eventually the set will be put into production, either by Lie or a commercial manufacturer. Lie's aim is to start focusing on concept creation and design for manufacturers. ■ In 2006, he is involved in the *Rendez-vous Project* in Japan, facilitating product development collaborations between designers and regional Japanese manufacturers. With Object's support, Spiral Art Centre in Tokyo has matched Lie with a traditional Japanese manufacturer in Shizuoka (near Mount Fuji). This has given Lie the opportunity to develop new products, which will be released into the vast Japanese market. ■ Lie also wants to stay focused on Australia. He has established important relationships with retailers and 'will continue to work with them in symbiosis,' he says. As a former student and teacher, Lie received patronage from UTS – this connection has given him further exposure, and prompted his involvement in exhibitions at UTS and other off-site projects, along with giving him access to vital studio space when required. ■ Being based in Australia has been a conscious decision for Lie. Europe's close proximity to the major design centres does make it more possible to be seen and heard on the international stage, but he acknowledges that it takes time to be recognised anywhere. 'Often I've been asked if it would be easier to be a designer somewhere else,' he says, 'but with *Ribs* as an example, I found it easier to make myself known here and to maintain a strong identity.' ■ *Annabel Moir*

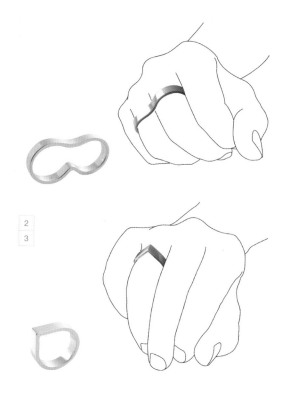

2
3

1 *Genie* teapot, 2005
Prototype
Slip-cast fine bone china
with clear glaze.
273 x 105 x 107mm
2 *Loop Ring,* 2004
Polished tarnish-resistant
sterling silver.
25 x 50 x 5mm
3 *Tear Ring,* 2004
Polished tarnish-resistant
sterling silver.
30 x 25 x 5mm
4 *Ribs* bench, 1998
Laminated MDF, Rock
Maple veneer, aluminium.
350 x 1500 x 750mm
5 *Strip* screen, 2002
Thermo-formed plastic,
plastic, extruded aluminium.
1850 x 2700mm

Photography (1) Stefan Lie

4

5

Photography (4/5) Robert Young

Rigorous in both concept and execution, the designs of Chinese-Malaysian Khai Liew (b.1952) are distinguished by a reductive, Donald Judd-like purity of form, a meticulousness of finish and an emphatically natural, sometimes opulent and even metaphorical use of materials. The (auspicious) colour red aside, Liew adheres to a restricted palette of muted natural hues, preferring to foreground form.

Khai Liew

Integral to his design rhetoric – a refined synthesis of multiple historical and cultural influences – is a highly considered interplay of light and shade, void and mass. There is also an abiding interest in texture and, in particular, woven materials (leather, grass, metal, wood), such as the woven-leather seat of the *Jess* chair (1997). ▪ Compelled to leave Malaysia in the wake of the disastrous (anti-Chinese) race riots of May 1969, Liew moved to Adelaide in South Australia, where a practical decision to sell early Australian furniture (in order to support himself, while studying for an economics degree), led to the opening of his first antique shop in 1974. In the course of the ensuing decades he has become a valuer, conservator and consultant, supplying private collectors, state and national public institutions with finer examples of furniture and other forms of material culture for their permanent collections. ▪
A shift of focus to mid-twentieth-century Danish furniture was prompted in the early 1990s by the sharply escalating prices of nineteenth-century Australian furniture. Drawn to its spare aesthetic and 'exquisitely resolved economy of construction', Liew was surprised to discover that classical – and, in particular, Chinese and Japanese techniques – were frequently integral to the construction of these Danish pieces. 'Years of taking furniture apart in the restoration process has enabled me to examine and study the techniques of furniture construction from various countries and cultures, from different artistic movements and centuries,' he claims. 'This has been the principal factor in the formation and development of my design vocabulary, and has greatly shaped the way I assess what good design is and how I apply this assessment to my own work.'[1]

1

In 2000 Liew received his second Design Institute of Australia award for the *Deloraine* armchair (1998), one of several designs that reveal a (modernist[2]) celebration of both the classical and the vernacular.[3] In Liew's contemporary interpretation of the structurally ingenious Jimmy Possum chair – which recalls a Ming scholar's chair, as well as the more familiar spindle-back Windsor chair – it is given an altogether more squared-off, severely geometric form. With this design, there also emerges for the first time a distinctly Rietveldian influence, which resonates in Liew's work to the present day – most notably in the seven (similarly award-winning) *Jeannie* outdoor bench seats (2000) for the Southbank riverside promenade, which overlooks the banks of the River Torrens. Central to the design – intended to emulate a line of birds with outstretched wings, their plumage shimmering as they skim across the water – was the bird as a universal symbol of peace. The angularity of the sculptural forms is tempered with soft grey, glass mosaic tiles, and the aluminium/steel sunshades – necessitated by the exposed north-facing site – are fashioned from curved, interlocking metallic sections. Liew reiterates an atypically curved form, which first appeared in the sunshade structures, in the woven elements of a walnut light shade that complements his *Love Cube* (2004): a walnut table and chairs, designed as the centrepiece for a wine cellar that is also lavishly lined with customised walnut shelving.

With narrow horizontal penetrations into dense mass that allude to Islamic architecture, the *Love Cube* is unequivocally Liew's most solid design – an effective counterpoint to the *Wanda* slatted bench (2000). Whereas the already pale, silver ash *Wanda* bench was further lightened with a limed finish, and its potentially ponderous mass cunningly dissolved with the strategic use of timber battens, the *Love Cube* is unapologetically dark, anchored, heavy, contained. It is 'an altar', says Liew 'to wine'.

In the period since the formation in 1997 of Khai Liew Design – a retail showroom and workshop with a small scale of production, carried out by a network of skilled artisans – Liew has established a discerning national and international clientele for work that is almost entirely site-specific or purpose-built. Current commissions include the design of the exhibition space at Adelaide's Museum of Economic Botany, the design and interior fit-out of a seaside house, the refurbishment of a bar in North Adelaide's Melbourne Street and a collection of contemporary furniture in rich and exotic materials for a private client. Interestingly, these latest furniture designs include an intriguing indicator of potential new directions. Interpreted in rich timber veneers, a cabinet on a stand will feature stylised chrysanthemum and maple leaf decoration, adapted and abstracted from a nineteenth-century Japanese watercolour design for an *obi* sash to be worn with a kimono. *Wendy Walker*

1. Khai Liew, 'Double happiness' paper presented at *Shifting Foundations – Designing Futures Forum*, Perth, Western Australia, 16–18 August, 2002. 2. There is also a non-modernist incorporation of narrative and luxury materials, and a concealment of the means of construction – in particular Liew's favoured sixteenth-century Chinese mitre joint. 3. Jimmy Possum chairs were Indigenous to the Deloraine region in Tasmania.

1 *Deloraine armchair*, 1998
Walnut.
945 x 620 x 520mm
2 *Remi*, 2000
Limewood cabinet on stand
with slatted handle, finished
in red paint.
1300 x 1300 x 450mm
3 *Lamp light shade*, 2004
Walnut.
380 x 500 x 500mm
4 *Andrea hall table*, 2003
American oak with cross-banded
veneer.
780 x 510 x 2000mm
5 *Jeannie outdoor bench*, 2000
Painted jarrah.
1000 x 2400 x 1500mm
6 *Love Cube table and chairs*, 2004
Walnut.
152 x 120 x 140mm

Photography (1-2/5) Grant Hancock

Photography (3/6) Stephen Gray

Photography (4) Sarah Long

Alexander Lotersztain (b.1977) is a designer who seems to carry his world with him. He holds most of his meetings in cafes and is rarely ever without his portable design factory of laptop, mobile phone and a satchel of sketchbooks.

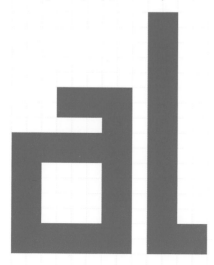

Alexander Lotersztain

There's nothing cumbersome about it – just a few, slim, over-the-shoulder accessories suitable for breezing in and out of town at will. He has mastered the art of being a global nomad. ■ 'I watch people a lot – my office is the street,' admits Lotersztain. Attracted to the human spectacle, he is irrepressible in his minute and constant observations of people: where they rest their elbows on the tables, how different heights of chairs influence their postures, how they hold their cutlery or sip at a cup in a certain way. It's all part of how he approaches design solutions to what he refers to as the 'unconscious mysteries' of life. ■ Splitting his time between studios in Brisbane and Barcelona also affords the enrichment of contrasts between European and Australian cultures. 'I feel privileged that I can work in two places at the same time. I walk down the street from my studio in Barcelona to my favourite cafe, listen to the Catalan, Italian and German around me, eat a fantastic prosciutto sandwich and all those things. Europe is very fast moving. When I arrive in Australia I can hit the stop button and regenerate and refocus. Here the weather is beautiful. The surf is beautiful. I take my laptop and books down to Byron Bay when I want. It's a unique lifestyle.' ■ Lotersztain's first big break came when he met with the Japanese design luminary, Teruo Kurosaki. Kurosaki invited the young designer to be part of his team designing products for Idée and Sputnik. This opportunity enabled Lotersztain to visit trade fairs and manufacturers around the globe and to meet with many of the world's leading designers. The most successful products he developed for Idée were the *Soft Sofa* (2002) and the *Skid* seats (2001). ■ Travelling and working in different countries is the lifeblood of Lotersztain's innovations.

It is not surprising that he can dance between lighting, interior and tableware design, while also authoring projects in urban renewal, or re-inventing the cane chair. He thrives on a high octane mix of energy and passion that propels him through his constant migrations. His friends stereotype him as Latin in temperament, but there's much of Old Europe in his gentle bearing and refined manners to counter the claim, and a seriousness and maturity that belies his 28 years. Lotersztain was born in Argentina to Polish parents, who then toted him around much of the world before the age of 15. These early travels were rich in experiences of different cultures and levels of poverty. Designing for everyday needs is a driving passion, and goes hand-in-hand with a commitment to sustainability. **'Seeing poverty first hand makes you aware of your position of privilege. Most of my work tries to suggest ways to improve people's quality of life.'** Heading InAfrica Community Foundation's design team is a recent role that sees Lotersztain regularly visiting various regional centres in Africa – designing products that can be made by local artisans with locally available materials that have broad appeal in export markets. The project is one from which he draws enormous satisfaction. Working with impoverished communities to help them become self-sustaining is close to his heart. Collaborating as a designer with local craftspeople has broadened his own knowledge and techniques immeasurably.

'I believe I can learn as much from these people as they can from me. I'm grateful for the opportunity of gaining from 3,000 years of craftsmen's knowledge. Some people approached the job with patronage in mind … it doesn't work that way.' He admits to a pet hate of designers who put style above social responsibility.

Lotersztain can now officially call Australia home since the granting of his Distinguished Talent visa. With only 100 granted annually, he falls into the unique category of being the first designer to gain one.

'I think Australia, as a country, is in a prime phase of design. It's exciting to be part of what's going on. I think it's important to be here, lobbying and putting pressure on government and generating networks.' His words mark a new era in his work, which is seeing more time spent consulting, motivating colleagues and lobbying in the halls of power. Change, he's learned, must come from above as well as from the grassroots.

Margie Fraser

1 *Solitaire workstation*, 2005
Plywood.
Prototype
900 x 500 x 740mm
2 *Crusoe Sofa*, 2002
Stainless steel, inflatable rubber boat fenders.
1300 x 700 x 700 x 400mm
3 *Stone*, 2001
CAD drawing.
4 *Skid double seater*, 2001
Wicker/rattan on steel frame.
5 *Coral light installations*, 2004
Polythylene.
Each Unit: 400mm

2

3

4

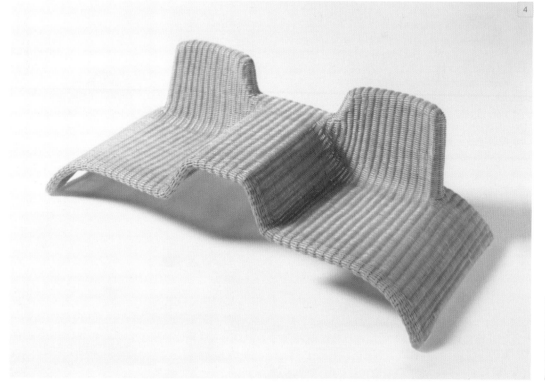

Maningrida Arts & Culture is one of Australia's largest Aboriginal artists' cooperatives. It is one of around 50 Aboriginal-owned arts centres in remote and regional Australia that affirm and promote the value of local culture and aim to maximise financial returns to artists. It focuses on sales, marketing and supporting the production of bark paintings, carved wooden sculpture, fibre craft, prints, necklaces and items of material culture.

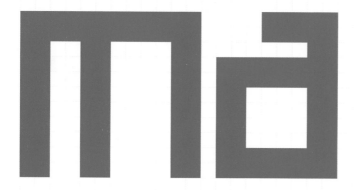

Maningrida Arts & Culture

Located in the north-central Arnhem Land settlement township of Maningrida (approximately 360 kilometres east of Darwin), Maningrida Arts & Culture represents around 700 artists from both the township and the surrounding 34 outstations in a region covering almost 10,000 square kilometres. ■ The Arts Centre itself is a busy repository for the work produced by the artists. With around ten full-time and casual staff, it is the beating heart of a substantial and complex commercial operation. All of the finished pieces are catalogued as they come in, and most are packed and shipped off to around 40 commercial galleries and specialist retailers in Australia and overseas, as well as to private collectors all over the world (many having purchased items on-line, via the Centre's impressive website). Works are also sold directly to the dedicated stream of visitors who make the effort to fly into Maningrida. Since 2004, Maningrida Arts & Culture has also owned and operated its own successful retail outlet in Darwin, further highlighting the organisation's savvy entrepreneurialism. ■ Another of the Centre's key activities is the organisation (often in partnership with other organisations and galleries) of exhibitions of work by Maningrida artists – showcasing their stories, culture and technical accomplishment to audiences around the world. Works by many artists from the Maningrida region are held in major public galleries and museums all over the world, including a major collection of over 600 works held in trust by the Museum of Contemporary Art, Sydney. ■ The township of Maningrida was established as a trading post in 1949 and hand-woven mats and baskets were regularly exchanged for supplies. The trade and sale of works by local people was greatly encouraged by the Methodist missionary Reverend Gowan Armstrong in the 1960s. A permanent craft shop was set up in 1967, and this facility has evolved into the Centre as it is today. ■ Although bark paintings depicting traditional stories are the most prominent and economically

valued art form from the region, woven fibre objects – baskets, bags, fishing traps and mats made predominantly by women – have also become highly regarded, and are acquired in various art and design contexts: as works of art, as decorative objects for the interior, or simply as functional everyday items. Of course, many of these items are also made for local use in hunting and gathering, and in some cases for specialised ceremonial purposes.

The Maningrida region has been described as one of the world's most multilingual communities, with more than eight distinct language groups (in addition to English). Most Aboriginal people in the area speak three, four or five of these Indigenous languages and there are strong ceremonial and cultural links between the groups. This lively cultural diversity is evidenced by the number of different religious ceremonies and the multitude of artistic forms in design, music and dance throughout the region.

As in Aboriginal communities throughout Australia, the many artists making fibre works in Maningrida are constantly reinventing traditional forms, functions and patterns, and experimenting with materials and new techniques. In this way the artists maintain strong links to the past, while producing vibrant innovative items that appeal to an ever-increasing market of consumers seeking goods that convey a sense of connection to specific places and cultures. Most of the fibre works from Maningrida are made from pandanus palm fibre, such as Agnes Djunguwana's (b.1945) striking circular mat (2005), or Lorna Jin-gubarrangunyja's (b.1952) dome-shaped dilly bag (2006). The leaves of the pandanus palm are harvested, dried, split, and then soaked (often in dyes made from the roots, leaves or bark of local plants), before being twined, coiled or knotted into the desired form. It is a laborious and time-consuming process. So too is the method for making hand-spun string from bark and other plant fibres, as in Nellie Nambayana's (b.1934) delicate string bag (2006). Over countless generations, the artists have acquired detailed knowledge of the properties of the various materials used for weaving and dying, and of how, when and from where in their land to obtain them. In considering the breadth and vitality of contemporary Australian design, it is crucial to look at the material culture of Indigenous Australia, its influence on the vernacular and visual language, its dynamic intertwining of tradition and innovation and its significant contribution to the creative economy. The work from Maningrida is only one of many fine examples.

Brian Parkes

4   5

1 Agnes Djunguwana, *Mat,* 2005
Dyed pandanus.
940mm
2 Lorna Jin-gubarrangunyja,
Necklace (detail), 2006
Seeds, shells.
Length: 420mm
3 Mabel Mayangal, *Dilly bag,* 2006
Dyed pandanus.
450 x 250 x 250mm
4 Alice Djulman Dalman,
Coil basket, 2006
Dyed pandanus.
320 x 320 x 540mm
5 Nellie Nambayana,
String bag, 2006
Kurrajong fibre.
260 x 350mm
6 Lorna Jin-gubarrangunyja,
Dilly bag, 2006
Dyed pandanus.
320 x 150 x 150mm

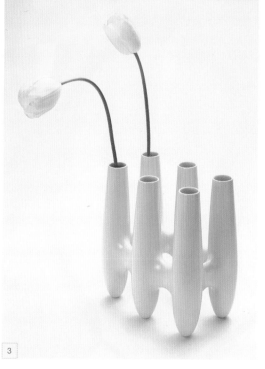

2

3

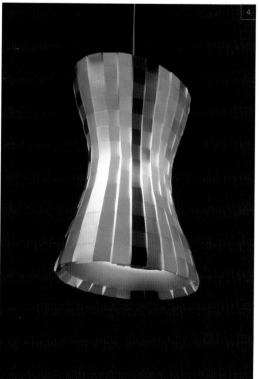

4

1 Woven form, 2006
Raytraced from Rhino program.
2 *Vovo with one flower*, 2001
Porcelainous stoneware.
375 x 140 x 270mm
3 *Vasse with one flower*, 1996
Porcelainous stoneware, satin white finish.
240 x 160 x 270mm
4 *Worvo brown pendant*, 1996 and 2002
Polycarbonate, polyethylene, hand-dyed.
300 x 200 x 480mm
5 *Eyoi Yoi* Table light, 2005
Polycarbonate, stainless steel wire, dyeing,
polyurethene rubber, Forton gypsum,
Hydro-stone.
1000 x 900mm

A childhood obsession with shoes combined with a belief in unlimited design potential gave birth to the remarkable Preston Zly. After initially meeting in 1988, it wasn't until 1993 that Johanna Preston (b.1967) and Petr Zly's (b.1961) first shoe samples were conceived and produced.

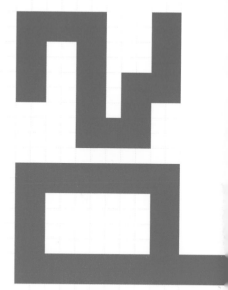

Johanna Preston and Petr Zly

Preston Zly

An innocent remark from Zly to his partner Preston suggesting she learn how to make shoes to relieve the anxiety of paying for ill-fitting shoes is definitely paying off. ▢ It was not a lack of ideas or passion, but the intricate process of learning the ancient craft of shoemaking that delayed the beginnings of Preston and Zly's shoemaking partnership. In 1993, Preston was studying part-time at Fitzroy TAFE (which later became part of RMIT) and during this time fortuitously met a master shoemaker whose mission it had become to pass on his dying craft. Zly, who was a sculptor, joined Preston in a series of intensive summer schools and both came away with a few hand tools and a sound knowledge of shoe construction. Along with these encounters came the realisation that their future was in establishing a small business, so for the next few years each found a way to earn a salary while planning for the Preston Zly brand. After nearly ten years, it is a brand now considered as one of Australia's most innovative producers of high-fashion, high-quality and highly unusual hand-tooled shoes. ▢ The signature style for Preston Zly is unmistakable, consisting of bold colour combinations in leather, sculptural heels and architectural toe shapes. Past ranges have also incorporated fabric, metal, straw and Swarovski crystals. Preston Zly design different shoes for different people. Preston has said that 'they are shoes for sophisticated people who understand the subtle design references we adopt'. Their most recognisable designs include the *Gaucho* boot, complete with a tribute to R.M. Williams in their elastic sides but produced in safety-yellow leather; the sexy *Derby & Gator* boot that literally wraps itself around the foot; and the more playful *Dorothy* and *Casablanca* that provide obvious references

Petr Zly and Johanna Preston

1

for the wearer. ■ 'We were complete novices in terms of fashion when we started … in the long run it was a good thing, as you learn along the way,' confirms Preston, who believes that a little is learned through doing, and everything by making mistakes. In the beginning, Preston Zly worked on custom-made orders and some orthopaedic work, and started to form relationships with local fashion designers like S!X, Dixon, Victoria Loftes and T.L. Wood through making shoes for their parades. These relationships provided a sense of design liberation – for the first time Preston and Zly did not have to comply with direct customer orders. The experience of working with Loftes and Wood initiated the idea of wholesaling. ■ Producing anywhere between 600 to 700 pairs of shoes per year, and supplying around ten outlets (local, national and international), these small production runs have created a competitive strength for Preston Zly, and helped maintain interest from niche markets hungry for something different. ■ With a few seasons now behind the duo, risk taking has become a thing of the past. Preston Zly currently employs 11 part-time staff, and has adopted an intimate artisan approach, from concept development, to production, through to wholesaling. According to Preston, too many things can go wrong and, as a result, most production now happens in the Fitzroy studio. While this can be limiting in terms of time away from the bench, this style ofself-representation has been fundamental to the partnership not only in their control of production, but also helping them to maintain trusting relationships (with suppliers, retailers and individuals) while affording

the designers an opportunity to directly respond to client needs. This process varies from face-to-face client meetings to international and interstate buyers ordering from images without spying samples of shoes. Establishing and maintaining a high profile is a priority. Participating in selected gallery exhibitions offers an alternative outlet for Preston Zly, while also providing the opportunity to experiment with design ideas and display concepts. As semi-regular participants in the Melbourne Fashion Festival and Mercedes Australian Fashion Week, the reality of running a small fashion house is that such events are often expensive and exhausting. In 2004 the Australian Embassy in Paris and Austrade invited Preston Zly to participate in Paris Fashion Week 2004 with *Gang of Five* (featuring works by Akira Isogawa, Mad Cortes,

Sarina Suriano, Camilla and Marc, Coussinet and Claude Maus). The show was acclaimed by retailers from all over the world and continues to provide a point of introduction. The future of Preston Zly is sharply focused on continuing to create directional designs and building up a business profile. The potential to expand retail operations both locally and internationally is also on the radar, and their recently opened salon store in their Fitzroy studio continues to attract loyal clientele. Preston Zly continues to work actively in exploring the language and potential of shoes and the finely crafted object. Future designs will continue to flit between Hollywood glamour, Art Deco interpretations, and the back-alley sex appeal of long leather boots mixed with the innocence of the Russian ballet shoe. *Sarah Bond*

4

Photography Petr Zly

1 *Josephine*, 2001
Leather, polyurethane, resin.
290 x 95 x 65mm
2 *Carnivale*, 2003
Leather, polyurethane,
EVA rubber, resin.
230 x 90 x 105mm
3 *Vatican lace-up*, 2004
Leather, resin, polyurethane,
gros grain ribbon.
270 x 95 x 90mm
4 *Casablanca*, 2005
Screen-printed leather, leather,
polyurethane, rubber.
250 x 90 x 145mm

Nick Rennie (b.1974) is a classic example of much that is good about design in Australia. Both his practice and his projects encapsulate a laconic humour underpinned by a technically adept and prolific output of well-resolved and memorable pieces.

Nick Rennie

Rennie first 'arrived' on the Australian design scene in 2000 as a fresh-faced graduate of Melbourne's RMIT University – his teacher and mentor Kjell Grant had facilitated a group show in Milan at *Salone del Mobile*, in which Rennie presented his *Sol light* (2000). This early project, realised with the raw enthusiasm of a student unperturbed by the commercial viability of a floating, helium-filled balloon lamp, gained Rennie instant notoriety both at home and abroad. *Sol* had articulated an emotional gesture though its weightless exuberance. The piece was irresistible, and while it did not ultimately go into production, it served as a perfect debut for the young designer. This project acted as a precursor for Rennie, a hint of things to come, illustrating his interest in childlike simplicity, emotional purity, and the uncomplicated, unpretentious and unusual. This set of characteristics plays across Rennie's body of work, expressed through movement, irreverence and a surprisingly minimalist eye for detail. ▪ From the outset Rennie has produced consistently 'publishable' work, which has meant that his international exposure was often such that prototype pieces were accepted as manufactured ones; this only served to fuel Rennie's passion to explore the realms of international production. His sights were set at an early stage on the United States and Europe, an orientation that he is only now placing into a regional perspective as he gears himself to work more closely with Japanese and other Asian manufacturers. ▪ By establishing his own independent studio in 2002, entitled 'Happy Finish Design', Rennie cemented his intention to harness his early international recognition as a furniture and product designer and turn it into commercial success. To achieve this, he committed to the continued production of groups of prototype products, most of which were handmade by Rennie or resolved within the local Melbourne manufacturing base. Local manufacturing capability is a resource that Rennie is keen to champion, stating that Melbourne holds an as yet unrealised resource within its

surprisingly rich manufacturing base, including multitudes of small facilities with skills that have been noticed by European design houses via Rennie's prototypes. Rennie took these product families on tour and has exhibited three times in Milan, in London and in Singapore, Tokyo, Seoul, and throughout Australia.  Rennie's work is primarily oriented around products of a domestic scale. **He explores the potential to find new meaning in common objects through playfulness and movement, through oblique references to traditional designs, or through references to cultural icons, toys and the like.** His projects often aim to utilise new manufacturing technologies, and serve to communicate the sophisticated material palette that Rennie places at his own disposal. There is a sense of discovery with each new project, with Rennie easily swapping from ceramics to rotationally-moulded plastics. He teaches on materials at RMIT University and is a strong proponent of innovation in materials, in the potency of mass production and the formal and commercial opportunities it can offer a designer. Through this preoccupation, though, he has set himself within a mode that can only find its ultimate expression through mass production, which, in Australia, can be a risk. Yet accepting this risk also creates a parameter within which Rennie is happy to explore materiality, form and commercial viability, prior to taking projects out onto the international market. Through exhibiting consistently in both Europe and Asia, Rennie has made some inroads with manufacturers, which adds promise to his consistently (and quintessentially Australian) self-effacing personal style. Much of his work is now prototyped in Japan, where several products are being developed commercially. Over the years, Rennie has illustrated an immense understanding of the commitment, investment and toil that are required to perform as a product designer within an international context. His projects range from his *Dimple bottles* (2005), with their grippable form, to his *Mushroom lamp* (2002), which wants to be pushed around (as it will always rebound to an upright position); other works include the *Groove* bowl and jug series (2006), the *System X* table (2006) and *Mori* shelving system (2006). Rennie's portfolio is both intelligent and impressive – he is not afraid to tackle a product well-catered for by other designs, relishing the idea that someone might gain joy from his playful reinterpretations. *Ewan McEoin*

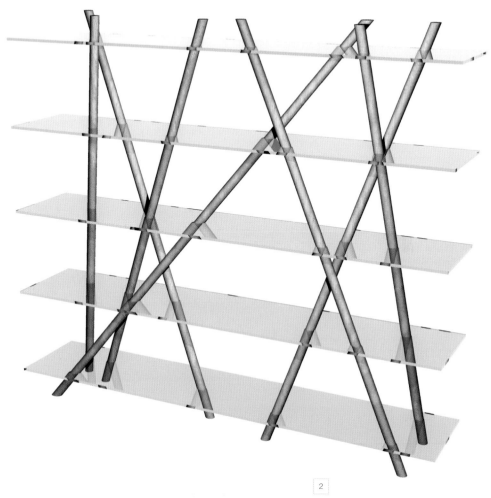

2

3

4

1 *Spoon*, 2004
Upholstered daybed.
1650mm x 300mm
2 *Mori* shelving system, 2006
CAD Drawing.
3 *Dimple Cup*, 2005
CAD Drawing.
4 *Mushroom lamps*, 2002
Pet plastic, metal base,
electronic components.
Ø.300mm x 450mm
5 *Daffy* table light, 2003
Aluminium, LED lights, batteries,
electrical components.
300 x 60 x 30mm

5

Jennifer Robertson (b.1962) is a Canberra-based textile artist and designer specialising in woven fabrics. She is fascinated by the adventurous period of weaving history – between the draw loom of the fifteenth century and the development and use of the Jacquard loom in the early nineteenth century.

Jennifer Robertson

Having undertaken considerable research in cut-silk velvet at the Victoria & Albert Museum in London and the Musée Historique des Tissus in Lyons, and working at the Fondazione Arte della Seta Lisio in Florence, Robertson is now considered a world specialist in the field. She also contributes to the sector as a lecturer at the School of Art, Faculty of Arts at the Australian National University. The Historic Houses Trust of New South Wales, which manages Government House in Sydney, commissioned Robertson to design a velvet upholstery fabric for a suite of gilt chairs (c.1867), as part of its refurbishment project of the state rooms, to showcase contemporary Australian craft and design. 'I prepared the patterns and point paper that will go to the production loom for weaving the fabric. The design is based on a waratah, the New South Wales floral emblem, which features throughout the building.' In May 2006 she took a third trip to the Fondazione to work with both historical looms that are used solely for hand-weaving as well as contemporary computerised looms, blending the techniques. Robertson uses small, repetitive images to create a language that is symbolic of the Australian flora and landscape. 'I want to build a pictorial language, not necessarily one that is literal but that is a representation in a different form. There is room for interpretation and ambiguity.' She undertook research into plant life in Australia, tracing right back to Gondwana-era fossilised plants, and also looked at seeds, pods, leaves, small plants with roots, flowers and berries that are found in the Australian bush. 'I am working with a contemporary Australian visual vocabulary in a very non-European way, but using a traditional European weaving technique. I want the surface to look soft and natural, even though it is

1

highly complex.' The textural quality of plants, such as the soft, smooth, velvet-like surface of banksias, inspires her weaving processes. Robertson is developing a new range of soft cloth that is closer to a furnishing weight than the fine wool double and triple cloths she exhibited in 2004 and 2005. 'This reversible cloth has a flexible application as scarves, rugs and wraps, and I am working towards three-dimensional upholstery fabric.' Combining different weights and scale of threads, and using a double silk and felting wool warp and different wefts, she creates a contrast of weaving structures. 'I want to create three-dimensional sculptural work, using the inherent qualities and characteristics of the materials and two-dimensional techniques,' she said. Robertson represents a bridge between hand-weavers and industry. She has a clear, long-term vision of a contemporary, cutting-edge woven textile practice. To achieve this, she and her husband Christopher Robertson designed and built a 32-shaft, semi-automated dobby loom to facilitate the complex, multi-layered weaving techniques and woven figurative images she

specialises in. The loom allows sampling, experimentation and small production runs. 'I can produce up to 50 x 2 metre pieces for each set up, and these can vary individually in colour, image, weft yarns and length. This is ideally suited to premium, value-added product development,' Robertson said. The loom enables her to have a production practice while maintaining the 'feel' of hand-weaving. **In 1994 Robertson began a professional relationship with NUNO Corporation in Tokyo – one of the world's leading textile companies, and known for its innovative approach to fabrics and research. NUNO undertakes the whole range of textile techniques, including weaving, felting and printing.** The company was initially established to supply textiles to the Japanese market only, but it quickly extended its reach into export markets and has a strong international reputation in the design and production of outstanding fabrics.

Designers at NUNO were very impressed when they saw Robertson's double and triple woven fabric lengths. The company licensed her work and consulted a specialist technician to work out how the off-set edges – a feature they had not previously seen – could be produced on a commercial loom. They produced the fabrics in three different colourways, acknowledging Robertson as the designer – this was both a compliment and honour, as it was the first time the company had put the work of a non-Japanese designer into production. Part of the agreement was her stipulation that the lengths be woven in Australian merino wool. Robertson works in different ways with NUNO and the Fondazione. She is hoping to develop a market in Italy, working with different companies and having exhibitions. She is interested in the breadth of ways designers and craftspeople can work in Australia. 'I want to keep developing a range of different contexts in which to work, including industry, and I have invested time, energy and funds into this. I want to make the business more sustainable, but also keep the door open for unexpected benefits and results.' *Meredith Hinchliffe*

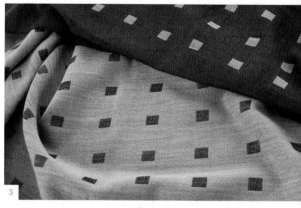

1 *Fraser Range 2*, 2006
Australian fine Merino wool triplecloth.
520 x 1850mm
2 *Basket Weave* (detail), 2006
Australian fine Merino wool and silk doublecloth.
3 *Jennifer Robertson for NUNO* (detail), 2001
Australian fine Merino wool, offset doublecloth.
Manufacture NUNO Corp. Tokyo, Japan.
4 *Banksia Paludosa*, 2005
Australian fine Merino wool doublecloth.
5 *Plait triplecloth*, 2006
Australian fine Merino wool.
560 x 1800mm

Denise Sprynskyj (b.1960) and Peter Boyd's (b.1971) enthusiasm for fashion is infectious. Candid and generous in nature, the duo that makes up the Melbourne-based design company S!X talks a lot about giving back to an industry that can sometimes be a one-sided love affair.

Denise Sprynskyj and Peter Boyd

S!X

Meeting at RMIT University and graduating with Bachelors of Arts (Fashion) in 1992, Sprynskyj and Boyd became friends through their shared passion for design and fierce competitive streak. Trained in traditional European methods of fashion construction, each became increasingly frustrated by these rigid systems of construction. Australian fashion, particularly in the early 1990s, was not considered among the best in the world, and leading designers of the time (Prue Acton, Trent Nathan) were ignored in favour of European labels. Sprynskyj and Boyd set up a collaborative studio and established their partnership design label, S!X, in 1994. When they started out, money for fabrics was limited, and led to S!X discovering the design process of deconstruction. According to Sprynskyj, it also came at a time when a lot of other things were happening in the fashion world with references to vintage and recycled clothing. ▓ Early design inspirations include traditional Japanese textile techniques and contemporary designers such as Issey Miyake, the classic styles of Dior and the basic principles of tailoring and construction. The duo began cutting and tearing existing garments apart, and then putting them back together. The clothes became one-off garments, but the response was uncertain, with only a handful of clients purchasing their unique pieces. This forced them to re-design their processes, and the recycled garment became the prototype that could be translated into a flat pattern and recreated in new fabrics. This early method of construction quickly become the signature style of S!X. ▓ Boyd's philosophy that nothing is sacred is obvious. There are so many parts of the S!X production process, that no one machinist will see a garment from beginning to end. The nature of fashion is that it requires

assistance, and many aspects, including printing, are outsourced.
A signature S!X item is a calico and nylon blend shirt, which is cut into, leaving a skeleton frame that is then screen-printed. S!X's fabrics are everyday materials that are often discarded prematurely from the wardrobe. ■ Sprynskyj believes that 'skill' and 'craft' are seen by some people as almost dirty words, yet without this combination sometimes great ideas remain just that: great ideas without means of execution. S!X has re-established a relationship between the wearer and the designer by placing value on the mark of the maker, however fleeting the experience may be. With an unconventional approach to designer promotion, their names are omitted from the label. Instead they choose a number for the label, which in itself is designed to wash off the garment. ■ Regular participation at Mercedes Australian Fashion Week and the L'Oreal Melbourne Fashion Festival is important for these designers. The demands of producing two complete bodies of work twice a year for parades, while maintaining a production range, are high. Putting the collection together is a complete process, from concept to production to the catwalk. Sprynskyj and Boyd are anxious not to become suitcase designers who send off catwalk shows but never see the whole production. Their design process also involves them in everything from how garments will be viewed within the venue and on the catwalk, to the lighting and the models' hair and make-up. ■ Currently wholesaling in Australia, Singapore and New Zealand, S!X is in no rush to commit to a broader international market. After years in the industry, the partnership has seen too many small fashion companies fail because of the urgency to market overseas. Both consider Australia and, in particular, Melbourne, as great places to be based because of the vibrant arts and design community. ■ Owning the company, and working collaboratively and also independently have provided a sense of freedom that continues to inspire this partnership. The concept of collaborative practices and the philosophy of mentoring is strong with each designer, and teaching is one way to fulfil this philosophy. Sprynskyj and Boyd see what they do commercially as very valid to their academic practice, as each teaches directly through their experiences as designers. By not being solely driven by the industry and its wants, they have enabled themselves not only to design but also to teach creatively.
■ S!X maintains a successful exhibition practice alongside its fashion design. Freelance curator Robyn Healy, one of their supporters and sources of inspiration, has invited the designers to participate in major exhibitions including *Male Order* (1999) and *Nobel Rot* (2006). The idea that fashion placed within an exhibition context, or public space, is more accessible than most retail spaces is of great interest for this duo, but that is another story. ■ Driven by original ideas along with a vast knowledge of traditional techniques, and a sense for the practical application of modern technology, S!X successfully disrupts the design process to create avant-garde, 'recycled' pieces that maintain a strong sense of tailoring and the iconic S!X style. ■ *Sarah Bond*

1 Hand-dyed Shibori cardigan, worn with
flying panel petticoat skirt, 2005
'This is not a collection' Winter 2005
Wool, polyester, nylon, silk.
2 Tulle Foil Swinging Panel Skirt and Tulle
Top with Gold Zip, 2006
'The Gold Room' Collection
Nylon, metal.
3 Skirt inserted into jacket, 2005
'This is not a collection' Winter 2005
Wool, Polyester, cotton, nylon.
4 Trousers worn either as a pant of halter
neck top, hand cut Molar top underneath,
2005
'This is not a collection' Winter 2005
Wool, polyester.
5 Mirror Vest and Bell Skirt, 2006
'The Gold Room' Collection
Wool, polyester, nylon, foil.

Marc Schamburg (b.1965) and Michael Alvisse (b.1963) met in the late 1980s, working within an architectural practice as an interior designer and an architect, respectively. Years later, it was Schamburg who conceived of the 'mad' idea of starting a furniture company together. Alvisse reflects: 'I thought: "What a pie in the sky dreamer you are. Let's do it".'

Marc Schamburg and Michael Alvisse

Schamburg + Alvisse

After years of struggle and limited resources, it started happening. Having built a momentum based on a good understanding of their market, a dedication to solid design principles and a sense of ethics, their company Schamburg + Alvisse has now been in business for nearly ten years.

Theirs is a complementary partnership, with Schamburg overseeing the production and development, Alvisse taking care of relationships, sales and marketing, and both contributing to the design. But, as Alvisse says, 'It's not the Marc and Michael show', with a team of nine staff, including designers, helping to bring the dream to fruition. 'Marc and I can be considered the "art directors". We've got a great crew on board to develop those ideas and explore our creative directions.' Ensconced in a Surry Hills warehouse, the inner-city Sydney suburb seemingly crammed with creative businesses, their studio doubles as a showroom. Their furniture is typically refined, elegant and exquisitely crafted, with an emphasis on seating and tables, and often with an expressive, individual flavour. Partially because it is impossible to compete with cheap, Chinese-manufactured furniture, and partially also because they don't want to do so, Schamburg + Alvisse directs its practice towards a dedicated niche at the premium end of the market. This allows for a high level of craftsmanship in their work – something difficult to achieve in mass production. Their decision to manufacture in Australia challenged conventional wisdom. 'Australia has not traditionally been a manufacturer of premium furniture,' says Alvisse, 'so it's very rewarding that we get regular sales enquiries from clients in Italy, Japan and the USA. To achieve this level of quality, we've needed to build very strong relationships with craftsmen who love their work.

We need to be available to those people who are actually crafting our pieces. We also deliberately set out to create a business where we value-add in Australia, rather than moving overseas and effectively exporting those job opportunities.' ▮ Schamburg's and Alvisse's professional backgrounds have assisted them in understanding their clients' needs all the better, and a substantial part of their support is from interior designers, architects, specifiers and corporate clients, although individuals also come to them to find furnishings for their homes. But as entrepreneurial furniture designers, Schamburg + Alvisse enjoys certain freedoms not previously afforded to

1

them, namely the rare satisfaction of being able to choose what they work on. As such, they are able to step outside the 'bread and butter' commercial ranges to explore other design works that are more experimental. █ They also distinguish themselves in their dedication to ecologically sensitive design and production, paving the way for best-practice processes. **'In the early days, the main criterion would be that it had to look gorgeous,' Schamburg reflects. 'Today we see those first designs differently: they didn't respond to a lot of issues that are hidden. Today, our ecodesign philosophy is about enriching the experience, by looking beyond the surface to ask: what are the consequences of creating this object?'** █ Recognising that their work operates as part of larger systems, they extend the theme into the societal realm. 'There's a movement towards the erosion of connection between individuals, of community,' explains Alvisse. 'It is probably the first time in history this is happening on such a large scale. So just as an item of furniture does not operate in isolation, individual people are also not self-contained entities … We need engagement with a community in order to flourish.' █ In response, Schamburg + Alvisse also consciously explores the capacity for design to stimulate interaction between diverse members of the community. One example is their recent *Stop Playing with Yourself* (2005), a giant version of a 'diagonal star' puzzle. In the classic sense, the 'diagonal star' is played in solitaire, the aim being to assemble the collection of faceted wooden pieces into a three-dimensional star or burr shape. Schamburg + Alvisse's upscaled pieces become benches, which also assemble to form a star the size of a small car. Because of the pieces' size and weight, however, a single person cannot create the star alone. In this way, the solo game is transformed into a team activity, and the passive object into a dynamic participant in people's lives. Gutsy and inventive, projects such as this illustrate the spirit that has allowed this niche company to survive in the perilous Australian design terrain.

█ *Emily Howes*

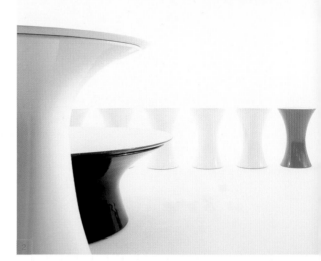

Photography (3/4) Schamburg + Alvisse

Photography (2) Alister Clarke

Photography (1) John Webber

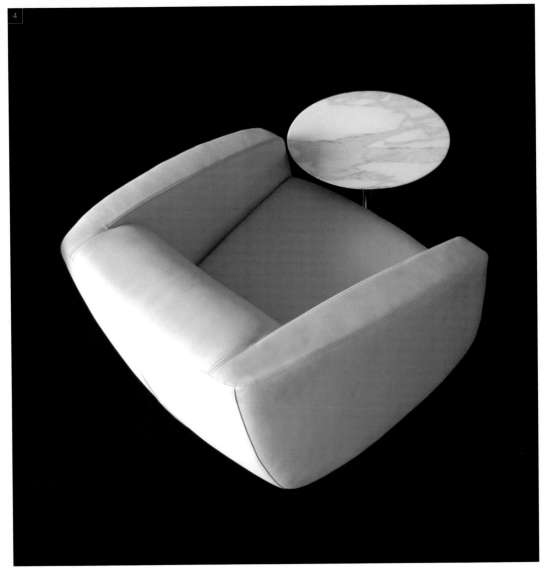

1 *Stop Playing With Yourself (SPWY)
interactive seating,* 2005
Flexible polyurethane foam, wool upholstery.
Star form: 1400mm
Modules: 1230 x 450 x 450mm
2 *Stretch tables,* 1995
Painted moulded resin, polyolefine floor pad
or chromed levelling feet
Tallest: 500mm
3 *Miss Molly Side Sled Chair,* 2004
Manufactured by Schamburg + Alvisse,
Australia
Eco-certified plywood shell, stainless steel,
polyethylene stacking bumper, upholstery.
555 x 555 x 785mm
4 *Smooth armchair,* 1999
Hardwood frame, CFC-free HR (high
resilience) foam, webbing, stainless steel.
850 x 820 x 720mm

After obtaining his Bachelor of Visual Arts in 1995, Oliver Smith (b.1974) worked with a number of leading gold and silversmiths around the world. 'When I graduated from Sydney College of the Arts, I worked with Hendrik Forster in Metung, Victoria, which was a valuable experience of sitting at the bench and honing my skills through repetitive making.'

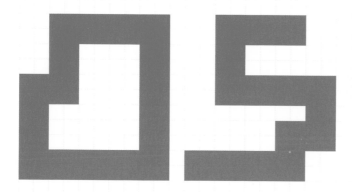

Oliver Smith

'I then travelled and worked overseas for four years in the tradition of the European journeyman, working with Warwick Freeman in New Zealand, in a coppersmithing workshop in Mexico and in the workshops of Howard Fenn and Alfred Pain in the United Kingdom,' Smith said. 'The opportunity of working with these craftspeople complemented the skills I learned as an undergraduate. I participated in a diverse range of approaches to making and running a craft practice, and saw the rewards of teamwork and collaboration.' When Smith returned to Australia he began to synthesise all he had learnt. 'I had a great deal of knowledge of different techniques, a wealth of ideas, and I needed to fit them all together.' He moved to Canberra to further his studies at the Canberra School of Art. 'Through further study I unravelled the variety of influences, and in doing so I began to understand my strengths and specific areas of interest. This led me to focus on the dining table and to find inspiration in the conviviality of the communal meal.' His passion for the technique of hot forging steered him towards making flatware, or cutlery. 'For me, handmaking is the beginning of the design process,' Smith says. In 2003 he received funding from artsACT to develop production methods that were compatible with handmaking skills. Smith approached John Kell, Managing Director of Hycast Metals in Sydney (a company specialising in ceramic-shell stainless-steel casting), and found they shared an enthusiasm for problem solving. 'John saw the worth of linking craft with industrial production, and he had always seen the potential for making cast cutlery. He was happy for me to work with his expert team. My knowledge of material and process was the

1

common language with those managing production and those directly producing the goods – craft gave me the insight.' A simple yet powerful idea grew in Smith's mind: 'The best of craft and industry became my maxim.' ■ This collaboration resulted in a series of stainless steel utensils produced in multiples through the ceramic-shell casting process, based on one-off hand-forged silver prototypes or patterns. 'The final range – "Generation I" – consisted of a serving utensil (*Sail*), a cheese knife (*Arc*), and a pair of condiment spoons (*Sweet and Treat*). Launched at Craft ACT late in 2004, the public response surpassed all my expectations. This was hugely encouraging,' Smith said. ■ Building on this success, Smith received one

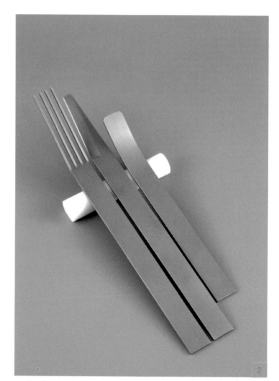

of three inaugural MMM grants (Maker to Manufacturer to Market) from the Australia Council. 'This provided sufficient capital to continue to develop my production work, resulting in "Generation II". These were a direct response to the results of Generation I, and I added hand-finishing as a refinement, rather than as a necessity.'

Respecting the creative thinking of others, Smith began his postgraduate research into flatware with a view to collaboration with chefs, and developed a dialogue with Tim Pak Poy, from Sydney, and ceramicist and restaurateur Anders Ousback. 'We met and discussed ways of increasing the synergy between our crafts and the evolving culture of the table. It was an exciting exchange of ideas, with prototypes and experimental objects tested alongside new dishes.' One outcome of this project was a contribution to a fundraising event at the Art Gallery of South Australia. Ten diners savoured Tim Pak Poy's cooking, presented on Patsy Hely's ceramic bowls and Peter Giles' wooden plates and eaten with Smith's silver cutlery. Both in terms of collaboration and support, Smith's Canberra location has been beneficial. He acknowledges the Australian National Capital Artists studios (where he shares a studio), and the supportive network of other artists in the region, such as Robert Foster, with whom he worked closely on the design and production of the *F!NK Fatware:* a pair of hard-anodised cheese knives with a polyethylene cheese board. Underlying Smith's work is his detailed knowledge of and interest in the materials he uses and the processes of making. 'I am fascinated by the process of forging, and the way the metal moves influences my sense of form. My awareness of different methods of production, from craft-based techniques through to industrial processes, with his philosophy of working with other creators, guides his multi-layered craft and design practice. 'I see myself operating on a number of levels – making one-off handmade objects, experimental exhibition pieces, commissions, collaborations and designs for semi-mass production. As a craftsperson and as a designer, I want the best of both worlds!'

Meredith Hinchliffe

Photography (4) Ben Manson

Photography (1-2/5-6) Sean Booth

1 *Serving Utensils, #1–5*, 2001
.925 silver.
Length 160–260mm
2 *Spartan Cutlery* (knife, fork, spoon
and rest), 2004
Titanium, teflon wire-cut prototypes
for production.
3 Oliver Smith and Robert Foster, *F!NK Fatware*
(black and white version), 2005
Hand anodised aluminium, polythylene, nylon.
Board 300 x 260 x 12mm, blades 170mm
4 *OSP Generation II**, 2006
*Oliver Smith Products. *Arc Cheese Knife*
and *Dorsal Serving Blade*.
Original prototypes hand-forged in silver
by Oliver Smith, manufactured in stainless
steel by Hycast Metals, industrially rumbled
by Mass Finish and hand-finished by
Oliver Smith.
316 Stainless steel (marine grade).
Length 230mm
5 *Fondue Set*, 2002
.950 silver, .925 silver, monel, stainless steel,
teflon, silicon fibre.
200 x 210 x 230mm
6 *Serving Utensil #3*, 2001
.925 silver
230 x 60 x 50mm

Brian Steendyk's (b.1970) conversation is peppered with words that could easily hark from the world of science rather than design. He speaks frequently of problem solving, logistics, rationale and discipline. Perhaps it's no surprise that this architect, urban designer, interior, landscape, furniture and product designer is also contemplating embarking on a PhD in the mathematics of architecture.

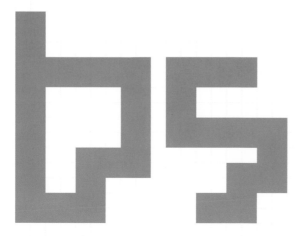

Brian Steendyk

It is a fine mind that can skip happily between such disciplines with an ear to history for reference and guidance. Running practices in all, and overseeing construction, production and marketing in several countries requires yet another level of skills and dedication. █ Steendyk operates his multi-disciplinary design studio from Brisbane. You get the feeling that solitude suits his quiet and thoughtful demeanour, and dedicated hours of labour. The formula of designing and prototyping in Australia, and frequent trips to European manufacturers and exhibitions in Milan and Tokyo, is working well. █ 'It affords me the best of both worlds, and allows me to escape the European winters. It also frees my mind to stroll down the larrikin Australian path unencumbered by staunch European tradition.' █ A three-month residency in Milan in 2005, sponsored by the Australia Council, afforded a hands-on knowledge of Italian design and production, and allowed for immersion in the country's richly layered design culture. His formative years, however, were spent in the architectural mecca, Chicago. There, Steendyk studied under the guidance of Myron Goldsmith, a former design director of Skidmore Owings and Merrill, and project architect for Mies van der Rohe's Farnsworth House. █ After Chicago, Steendyk worked with Van Berkel & Bos Architekt Bureau (now UN Studio) in Amsterdam, which was something of an affirmation of his family roots. His Dutch father migrated to Australia from the Netherlands in the 1950s. 'With a Dutch family name I feel a certain burden to uphold and respond to the Dutch design tradition. I needed to look into that side of me.' █ Steendyk often refers to memorable architectural moments and details when discussing his work. He speaks of the joyous quality of light emitted

through Frank Lloyd Wright's Prairie house windows, and of the material delights and sculptural qualities of Peter Zumthor's baths in Switzerland. In his own designs each element is chosen with a view to finding a similar 'sense of joy' at its encounter. ■ Through his architectural training Steendyk has developed the ability to simultaneously solve problems on a structural, tectonic and aesthetic level. His ideas emerge out of an objective analysis of contemporary problems, and he approaches his designs with the rigour of the perfectionist. His *Wave coat hanger* (2003) emerged after a year of 'playing around with ideas which culminated in a simple line drawing. Then I knew I had it ... its spirit.' ■ 'The hardest thing in design is to strip back and reduce a problem to its essence. Functionality is fundamental, but to imbue a piece with an artistic or sculptural quality, while not diminishing its functional aspects, takes careful consideration.'

1

2

1 *Cero and Wave Table,* 2004–05
Rotation-moulded plastic, compact laminate,
cast aluminium, stainless steel.
Tallest: 450mm
2 *Cero chair,* 2004
Rotation-moulded plastic.
420 x 575 x 450mm
3 *Wave coat hanger,* 2003
Digital rendering.
440 x 210mm
4 *Scoot (Uomo),* 2005
Digital rendering.
450 x 450 x 450mm
5 *Shift,* stool/table/planter/storage, 2006
Digital rendering of four units.
450 x 450 x 450mm

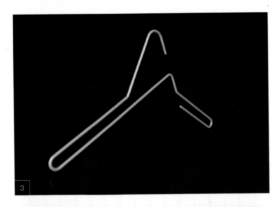

3

4

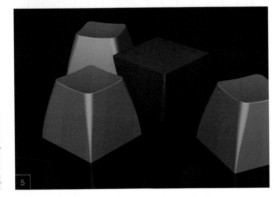

5

Photography (1-2) Erik Williamson

Digital rendering Shaun Crossman

Beyond the rigours of practice, Steendyk's chief satisfaction stems from the ability of good design to 'bring joy and a sense of quality to people's lives'.

'I love to see products like the coat hanger used on an everyday basis. For this to impact upon the broader community, price point and mass production need to be considered.' **While he admits mass production carries a stigma with it, he employs the Bauhaus philosophy that good design need not cost more than bad. He is critical of designers who create beautiful pieces but do not consider production techniques and, ultimately, the end price point.**

The idea of surfaces and materiality prevalent in his architectural work also has a bearing in his product design. His *Cero chair* (2002) is now produced in fibreglass, concrete and moulded plastic, each requiring a different production process and design resolution.

'You have to work hard to get the manufacturing process efficient enough to achieve a certain aesthetic finish and price point. Before the *Cero chair*, I hadn't worked with fibreglass. I went to the manufacturer's factory, and discovered the process first hand, and the techniques and limitations involved, to then fully consider and resolve my design.' A recent foray into rug design for Interior Equipment is again combining his appreciation of materiality with an implicit understanding of tectonics. 'I like the process of turning a two-dimensional, rectilinear shape into a three-dimensional object by utilising the inherent qualities of texture and light found in wool and wool blends. For me, the discipline is in the proportions of the rectilinear shape, and the counterpoint to this is the organic patterns employed in the designs.' Steendyk's method is one of refinement and purification, of stripping back to bare and beautiful forms, rather than tacking on the decorative. Creating the simple is a complex process.

Margie Fraser

Tiwi Design Aboriginal Corporation is one of the oldest and most diverse Indigenous arts enterprises in Australia. It is a dynamic arts and crafts centre that incorporates a carvers' shelter, pottery studio, screen-printing studio, painting studio, administrative office and retail gallery.

Tiwi Design

Tiwi Design was established in 1969 and is located in the remote island township of Nguiu on Bathurst Island, about 80 kilometres north of Darwin. Nguiu has a population of around 1,500 residents. Bathurst Island and its near neighbour, Melville Island, have been home to the Tiwi people for thousands of years. Tiwi Design's purpose is 'to preserve, promote and enrich Tiwi culture'. It represents around 100 artists working in traditional and contemporary media including wood carving, bronze and ceramic sculpture, textile design and printing, pottery, bark and fibre art, painting, print-making and jewellery. The centre supports and facilitates art and design practice and is responsible for sales and marketing of the work. Items are either sold wholesale to around 20 galleries and specialist retailers around Australia and to others in Europe and North America, or sold directly through the centre's retail gallery or via its website. ▪ The work of Tiwi artists is highly distinctive, and works by many of the community's leading artists – such as Declan Apuatimi (1930–1985), Eddie Puruntatameri (1948–1995), Bede Tungatalum (b.1955) and Jean Baptiste Apuatimi (b.c.1940) – are represented in major public galleries and museums around the world, including the National Gallery of Australia, the National Gallery of Victoria, Sammlung Essl Museum in Austria, the Museum of Ethnography in Geneva and the Seattle Art Museum in the United States. Since the early 1970s, Tiwi Design has become particularly well known for its distinctive range of hand screen-printed textiles. These textiles – including silks, linens and commercial grade upholstery fabrics – are used regularly by fashion and interior designers throughout Australia. ▪ In 1968, a young Bede Tungatalum and his friend, the late Giovanni Tipungwuti (1953–Year unknown)

worked with Madeline Clear, the art teacher from the local Catholic school (who later became a full-time art advisor at Tiwi Design), to produce woodblock prints depicting totemic Tiwi imagery. Woodblock printing was introduced to the artists because of its natural links to the traditional wood carving techniques of the area. By the time Tiwi Design was established in 1969, Tungatalum and Tipungwuti had begun to transfer their designs onto silk screens and the design and production of printed textiles quickly became a significant activity for many Tiwi Design artists. Since winning the Industrial Design Council of Australia's *Good Design Award* for a set of six linen place-mats in 1970, Tiwi Design has participated in many exhibitions and received numerous awards and commissions for its textiles. The most recent of these was the *Memento Indigenous Design Award* (2005). Osmond Kantilla received first prize for the hand-printed sarong on chantung silk he created by using the *Yilinga* (carpet snake), designed by Declan Apuatimi in (c.1984), overlaid with *Muputi* (fish), designed by Angelo Munkara. ■ Until the beginning of the twentieth century, the Tiwi people had very limited contact with outsiders, and their deeply valued traditions continued uninterrupted in their relative isolation. They have always practiced the art of body painting – *jilamara* – for ceremonies. The same decorative patterns, painted in ochres, were also used on *Pukumani* poles (burial poles) and *tungas* (baskets made from folded and dried sheets of bark). The emphasis in most of these bold, vibrant and geometric patterns is in the graphic strength of the designs, rather than any specific narrative. However, narrative elements are important within Tiwi design, and they usually relate to the Tiwi creation story or the two major ceremony cycles: the *Kulama* initiation ritual, which celebrates life, and the unique and complex *Pukumani* funeral ceremony, which affects the behaviour and activities of all those connected with the deceased, ensuring proper respect in their passing. The contemporary textiles of Tiwi Design are deeply rooted in these traditions and are a living, evolving expression of Tiwi culture. ■ The printing workshop at Tiwi Design houses three, 13-metre-long tables for screen-printing textiles. The workshop is run by Osmond Kantilla, who has been printing textiles at Tiwi Design for more than 20 years. Kantilla has designed some of the patterns within the range, including *Pandanus* (c.1990), and he also supervises the translation of original artwork onto silk screens and plays a critical role in determining colours and specifications for the production of most of the existing designs. A genuine testament to the enduring quality of the Tiwi textile designs is the fact that many of the original patterns from the early 1970s are still in demand and being produced today. ■ *Brian Parkes*

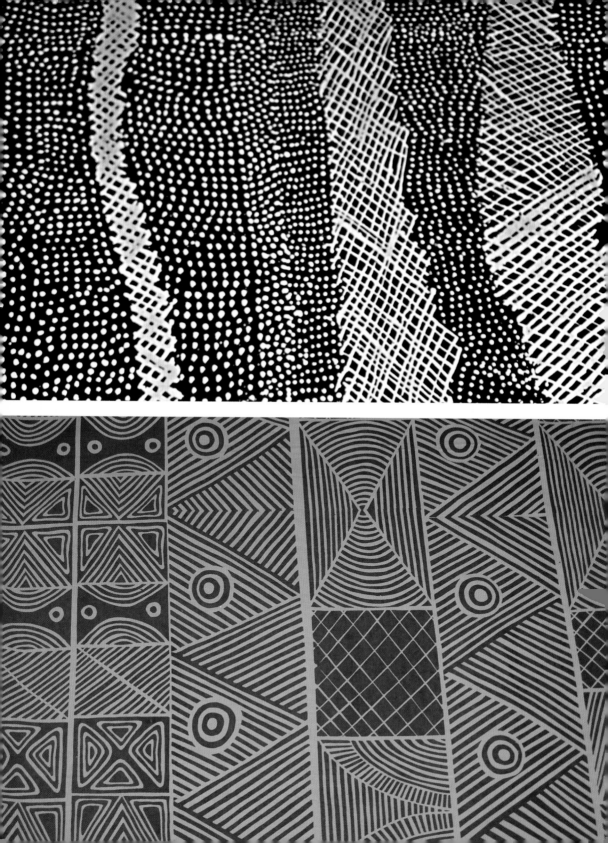

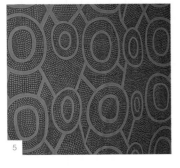

1 Osmond Kantilla, *Yilinga*, 2005
Printed and designed by Osmond Kantilla,
combination of Declan Apuatimi,
Carpet Snake (c.1981), and Angelo Munkara,
Fish (c.1981).
Screen-printed chantung silk (gold, yellow,
ochre, brown).
1100 x 2000mm
2 Jean Baptiste Apuatimi, *Jilamara*, c.1991
Screen-printed heavy cotton (white and black).
1150 x 3000mm
3 Osmond Kantilla, *Pandanus 1*, c.1990
Screen-printed cotton (lime and dark green light).
1180 x 3000mm
4 Jock Puautjimi, *Stoneaxe*, c.1986
Screen-printed linen (turquoise and green).
1307 x 3000mm
5 Declan Apuatimi, *Carpet Snake*, c.1981
Turquoise and chocolate cotton.
1015mm
6 Bede Tungatalum, *Snake*, c.1981
Screen-printed cotton drill (ochre and brown).
1180 x 3000mm
7 Tiwi Design fabric rolls and screens, 2005

Possessed of a quiet integrity, the simultaneously functional and sculptural porcelain objects of Prue Venables (b.1954) resonate with a self-assured simplicity. However, the cultivated quietness and apparent minimalism of her work masks an intricacy of making, in which particular pieces are carefully supported and fired on porcelain trays or setters.

Prue Venables

Other thrown forms are altered (and hand-rolled bases applied) at the leather-hard stage – a finicky process requiring meticulous timing and deft handling. Working in incremental stages, Venables savours the explicit 'sprung tension' of the wheel-thrown sections that exist in confounding alignment with their manipulated bases, rendering 'the origins of the forms uncertain'. In a 2005 catalogue essay, the renowned Australian potter Gwyn Hanssen Pigott alluded to the artful combination of stillness and the 'sense of risk, of fragility' that is central to Venables' work. 'Sometimes it is a single object – a pierced ladle with a precariously long stem, perhaps, or a scoop with an elegant, daring, ribbon-like handle, that surprises and then calms.' Such dynamism of form is derived from pushing the tolerance of her medium to its limits, and Venables habitually experiences a high failure rate. Critical to Venables' work and philosophy of making was a period of study undertaken at Harrow School of Art (1981–83) in the intensely rigorous and stimulating Studio Pottery course, with influential lecturers including Walter Keeler, whose technique of altering thrown forms has proven formative. A further area of investigation into eighteenth and nineteenth-century industrial techniques was initiated by observing industrial ware – such as insulators and laboratory equipment – in the potteries at Stoke-on-Trent. At Harrow, she became aware for the first time not only that many of these items were hand-thrown, but that they were also finely worked in a way that required extremely advanced levels of skill. For Venables, who had hitherto been taught to throw in a manner that masqueraded as the handmade, such precision of finish was a revelation. It was only on her return to Australia in 1989 from Britain (where she

had been resident for almost 13 years) that she began to work with Limoges porcelain – discovering that the luminous beauty of the material precluded the need for decoration. Logically, inevitably, form assumed a more primary role, as Venables explored the aesthetics of simple utilitarian objects from laboratory funnels to exquisitely minimal Shaker brooms. In particular, she was fascinated by the manner in which handles made possible the augmentation of a form, effectively shifting it into and activating the surrounding space. Like the rich aubergine interior of a silken-black basket form, forays into colour are highly considered. The unexpected pale yellow interior of a white funnel is intended to generate the effect of a lustrous shadow – an effect only achievable, Venables notes, 'when the form is to some extent contained'. In 2004 she was invited for five weeks to Gifu City in Japan[1] by the Oribe Design Centre, in order to develop a 13-piece range of white (recycled) porcelain tableware – cups, saucers, plates, bowls and a stirrer – for production. She does not distinguish between exhibition work and design for production, believing that one feeds into the other without segregation, since, as she says, 'the thinking is the same'. Collaboration also interests Venables, and she has developed a tea set prototype – including a tray, cups, tea strainer and tea-bag holder – with Simon

Lloyd, whose unconventional approach to materials is notable for its innovation. In the last few years she has also begun studying metalsmithing techniques, in anticipation of the possible incorporation of metallic elements into her ceramic groupings. ▪ For almost two decades, the multi-award-winning Venables has shown regularly in Europe, the United States and Japan: in 2005, for example, she held a solo exhibition at London's Galerie Besson, and in 2006 she participated in Australian Contemporary's *Bare & Beyond* for Collect at the Victoria & Albert Museum. ▪ It is instructive that a contemporary object that inspires her with a sense of wonder is a (perplexingly) flexible porcelain spring designed for use in industrial furnaces, in which the excessively high temperatures would melt its metallic counterpart. Venables' ceramic pieces – strong, assured, beautiful – frequently appear to be not only fragile, but too precious to use, and she consciously cultivates such anomalies in her work. Ultimately, in honouring a still extant, but rapidly disappearing culture of making,[2] Venables challenges viewers' perceptions (and preconceptions) about utility, and about the way in which we consider and use functional objects. ▪ *Wendy Walker*

1. Like her colleague Simon Lloyd, Prue Venables was a prize-winner in the 2004 *Jan Ken Pon World Design Competition* – an attempt to revitalise the crafts and local industry of Gifu Prefecture in Japan, by inviting design students and professional designers from around the world to submit design concepts.
2. In a November 2005 lecture at the Art Gallery of South Australia, Tanya Harrod observed that: 'The ceramics industry in Britain has undergone devastating change ... as formerly great firms like Royal Doulton and Wedgwood ... have relocated production to Indonesia and China ... We are all aware that in the future very little industrial pottery will be made in Europe. A whole culture will vanish.'

1 *White Bottle and Cups,* 2003
Hand-thrown and altered porcelain.
Average: 200 x 280 x 120mm
2 *White Basket* (detail), *Yellow and White Funnel,* 2005
Hand-thrown and altered porcelain.
Tallest: 280mm
3 *Black Dish, White Sieve with Handle,* 2005
Hand-thrown and altered porcelain.
Tallest: 200mm
4 *Oliva Bowl, Large Cup and Saucer, Small Cup Saucer, Small Plate,* 2004
Recycled Porcelain.
Prototype manufactured in Japan.
Tallest: 200mm
5 *White Scoop, Sieve, Spoon, Dish, Jug and Bowl,* 2005
Hand-thrown and altered porcelain.
Tallest: 270mm
6 *Black Bowl, Bottle and Jug,* 2005
Hand-thrown and altered porcelain.
Tallest: 270mm

Photography Terence Bogue

Georgia Chapman (b.1970) is passionate about textiles and their potential to express individual aesthetics. Since establishing the fashion label Vixen in 1992, she has brought textile design to the forefront of our consciousness, making distinctive printed fabrics for clothing and homewares.

Georgia Chapman

Vixen

After completing a degree in textile design at Melbourne's RMIT University in 1990, Chapman worked in the fashion industry, but was disillusioned by the lack of originality presented by the mass market. Chapman started to collaborate with Meredith Rowe, and they produced their first range of accessories for an exhibition at the former Meat Market Craft Centre in Melbourne. 'We started designing scarves and sarongs because they're an uninterrupted piece of fabric, and therefore a great way to feature our prints,' Chapman says 'We were completely driven by the surface decoration rather than the product, and both scarves and sarongs required very little in terms of manufacturing.' ▮ At first, Vixen did a lot of design and hand-printing for other fashion labels, such as Scanlan and Theodore, Collette Dinnigan and bigger companies like Country Road. 'Mainly we would design for them and then they would print offshore, but we were also doing a lot of hand-printing … We eventually pulled back from producing for other labels. It got to the point where we felt we had become fabric printers.' In the early stages of the company, the commissioned work enabled Chapman and Rowe to build up the business, and to gradually employ more staff and create a full range of accessories. Then they were able to print purely for their own production. This also allowed them an opportunity develop Vixen's 'signature' look, 'our first active step to define what our business was about'. ▮ In 2000, Chapman took sole ownership of the company and continues to be involved in the design and production, from start to finish, which allows her a lot of creative control. She maintains a supportive staff, and has set up relationships with local pattern cutters, fabric agents, retail clients and manufacturers. In an unusual arrangement for a textile designer, she employs a fashion designer,

Maureen Sohn. Chapman also works closely with Melanie Sohn on the homeware designs. At present, Vixen employs eight staff members. 'We have an amazing pattern-maker and seamstress, and staff who specialise in printing fabrics and managing the daily running of the business.' They mix their own dyes, develop new printing techniques and make samples in-house. 'We've got dye books for all the colours and small swatches for the sample range, but fabric can change so there are lots of different variables.'

To create the ranges, Chapman translates her ideas onto paper, spending a lot of time working with photocopies, painting, or using woodblocks or collages. Initially she designs with small screens, and trials with lengths of fabric. Exploring imagery and scale, she mainly works in black and white. Simultaneously, Maureen Sohn will be working on patterns and garment shapes, so even from that early stage there are conversations about possible garments and outfit combinations. Through working with hundreds of different swatches of fabric and multiple prints, a story starts to emerge and they decide on which prints to put onto full screens. They print the samples at the same time as completing all the patterns for the garments. Fabrics and base cloths are bought to finish the fashion range. The garments are either cut in-house or sent to local makers. 'There may be four different fabrics that make one garment, so we need to work with makers with high levels of skill. There may also be hand-beading or detailing required.' By the end of each season, Vixen will have produced over 1,000 metres of fabric.

Every season evolves from the last. There is a beautifully feminine and hand-crafted quality to the textiles. Chapman is particularly interested in the idea of body adornment: 'I love the whole idea of people telling a story by what they are wearing.' The work is as much about one fabric as the combination of a few. Part of the Vixen look is its eclectic mix of patterns and colours. 'People personalise what we do. I love it when someone walks in, and they might have a couple of garments from different ranges worn together and they'll just do it in their own way … a way that I would never think of and it looks great.' Vixen fashion and homewares are now stocked in over 25 stores in Australia and overseas. Although the company has sold to stores in the United States, United Kingdom, Singapore and New Zealand, it retains its strong local focus. The Melbourne market provides Vixen with its largest proportion of sales. One of Chapman's dreams for the future is to open a combined studio and retail outlet. Moving in 2006 from their large central location in Melbourne to Fitzroy has already impacted on the level of in-house production. However, Chapman remains committed to designing in Australia. 'Design is so fresh here and a lot of a people are forging new areas and doing their own thing. There is a freedom and I never felt like I couldn't do it … because it is a smaller market it's easier in a sense to make a difference.'

Annabel Moir

1

2

1 *Crazy daisy top and crazy daisy skirt,* 2004
Secret Garden Winter Collection
Hand-printed nylon mesh, hand-printed
cotton elastine.
2 *Baroque beaded jacket, Honey comb shirt,*
Sojourn dress, 2005
Sojourn Collection
Hand-beaded, hand-printed silk georgette.
3 *Japonism,* 2003
Hand-printed silk georgette, devore velvet,
silk jacquards.
Largest 100mm
4 *Sojourn vest and delta skirt,* 2005
Sojourn Collection
Hand-printed silk georgette, pintucked linen
skirt, hand-printed silk linen border.
5 *Crazy daisy scarf,* 2004
Secret Garden Winter Collection
Hand-printed silk georgette, devore velvet.
6 *Mae ling top, Ophelia halter top,*
Lovella wrap skirt, 2004
Secret Garden Winter Collection
Hand-printed nylon mesh, cotton lace,
devore velvet, hand-printed silk satin.

Photography Kalimna Mohamed

Industrial designer Charles Wilson (b.1968) is his own definitive client: 'I avoid designing anything I wouldn't want for myself. If I design for a group that doesn't include me, I end up doing rubbish.' Though such a propensity might be, as he says, 'anti-marketing', it ensures that his work is motivated by a genuine sense of worthiness.

Charles Wilson

Wilson subscribes to the theory that it is the designer's duty to recognise opportunities for innovation, to reinterpret problems and to tangibly contribute by discovering the design solutions. 'It's about the way objects make people feel,' he says. 'So that brings into ergonomics the notion of comfort, as well as vanity, and a relationship between a person and an inanimate object.' ■ Wilson manifests this philosophy in his work by employing innovative features that are sensitive to the user's needs, both functional and aesthetic. His saucepan, designed in 2004, for instance, contains a notch in its rim that acts as a stand for the lid, erasing the need to find a surface on which to place the lid as well as providing a hygienic alternative to a hinge. A bar stool seamlessly creates a footrest by way of a void in the stand. The back and armrests of his *Boulder* sofa (2005) have been smoothed and integrated to cradle the seated body, providing comfort and a sense of nurturing. ■ These examples also illustrate Wilson's breadth of design applications, which encompasses furniture, objects and spaces. Despite this, he claims it is not his deliberate intention to work across a variety of formats. 'Perhaps more the case is that I have a limit to the number of interesting ideas I can have on one particular format,' he says. 'I've designed more sofas than any other object, and I don't know that I have many more in me. There's only so much I can do and still make it relevant.' ■ Though he employs computer-based modelling to draw and test his designs, Wilson breathes life into the intangible confusion of lines and pixels by way of exquisitely crafted scale models. They are perfectly formed treasures, and might be the centrepiece in a particularly groovy doll's house. 'People love models, so if you want to sell them a

1

design it is like giving them a gift,' he says. The models also play a pivotal role in his design process, allowing him to spatially explore the design. 'I don't really trust the worth of ideas until they are represented in three dimensions,' he comments. ■ Wilson's furniture has made it to the marketplace under the umbrella of Woodmark International, an Australian company that began by importing European furniture and progressed to manufacturing the designs under licence. In recent years, however, the company has been increasingly shifting its focus to develop projects with Australian designers on a freelance basis, manufacturing and

distributing the results, and granting the designer a royalty. Though this format is the standard among most European design companies, it is very rare in Australia. **The relationship began when Woodmark's founder and head, Arne Christiansen, approached Wilson to design a compact sofa. Recognising a sterling opportunity, Wilson ultimately presented to him not only a compact sofa but also several considerably less compact sofas, ranges of chairs, tables and more. His gamble paid off. Christiansen liked the lot of it and made the significant investment in Wilson's work to release the entire range, which Wilson credits as 'singularly the biggest break that I've had'.** It may be that the value of a company such as Woodmark is magnified in Australia because of its role as intermediary between the designer, and manufacturers, retailers and the marketplace – domains that are notoriously difficult for designers to penetrate. For Wilson, Woodmark's support has led to opportunities outside of Australia. 'With a certain body of work behind you people start taking you seriously, even if you're living on the other side of the world,' he says. He is in the process of establishing a number of relationships with companies overseas, and an Australian distributor is investigating the United States as a good destination for his work. Wilson reveals that the plan is for the work to be produced in the US. He says, 'it's rare and exciting for US manufacturers to be taking on Australian design.' *Emily Howes*

1 *Oil Burner,* 2006
Computer rendering, prototype aluminium, stainless steel.
83 x 70mm
2 *Canisters,* 2004
Resin.
Prototypes.
Tallest: 150mm
3 *Boulder* sofa, 2004
Cold-molded foam over plywood, upholstery.
Manufactured by Woodmark International, Australia
600 x 2450 x 900mm
4 *Boulder* ottoman, 2004
Cold-moulded foam over plywood, upholstery.
340 x 800 x 800mm
5 *Candelabra,* 2005
Electroplated silver, rare earth magnets.
Prototype.
170 x 430 x 430mm

4

5

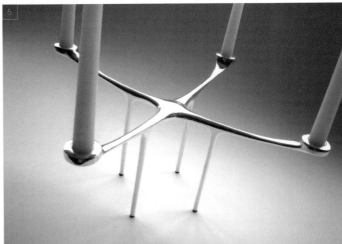

Sisters Nicole (b.1967) and Simone (b.1965) Zimmermann began their creative and business partnership in 1991. Fifteen years later, they have created a well-known name for themselves amongst Australia's leading fashion brands. Since opening their first store in Sydney in 1992 in South Dowling Street, Darlinghurst, Zimmermann has steadily expanded its business.

Nicole and Simone Zimmermann

Zimmermann

It now has seven stores around Australia, sells though David Jones stores nationally and has an impressive list of international stockists, including Bergdorf Goodman, Intermix and The Big Drop in the United States, Harrods and Fenwicks in the United Kingdom, and major departments stores CK Tangs Singapore and Lane Crawford Hong Kong, as well as selected boutiques in Asia. Initially forging its reputation through swimwear, Zimmermann has developed a distinctive style that crosses day and night. With a strong Sydney sensibility, Zimmermann clothes satisfy a full life, from the beach, to cafes and bars. The designs started as a response to Nicole Zimmermann's life, what she wanted to wear and how she wanted to feel. This feminine, sexy look now defines the brand, with Nicole's heart and soul still present in every garment. With a degree in fashion from East Sydney Technical College, Nicole continues to manage the creative process and is head of the Zimmermann design department; Simone, with her background in marketing, oversees production and sales. Together they collaborate on the broader direction of the Zimmermann brand. With Nicole Zimmermann's eye for unique fabrics and clever cutting, Zimmermann clothes are a vibrant mix of style and originality. Colour is key, as are bold designs and striking silhouettes. The brand develops its own prints, inspired by everything from tea-towels to artworks and vintage clothes. Zimmermann has also made a collection drawing on the extensive Florence Broadhurst print archives, licensed through Signature Prints. In silk or Lycra, the patterns and shapes are used confidently with daring attitude. 'If Sydney was personified, she'd be bronzed, brazen and almost certainly wearing a Zimmermann bikini, so synonymous has the sunny

label become with Australian style.'[1]  Since 1996, Zimmermann has been showing seasonal collections in Australia, creating two swimwear and ready-to-wear collections each year. Comments following their ready-to-wear parade at Mercedes Australian Fashion Week in 2006 predicted Zimmermann as Australia's next major international success.[2] With international outlets already established in London, New York, Singapore and Hong Kong, there is plenty of scope to expand their markets there and beyond. 'Our next step is to open a Zimmermann boutique in New York, a place we have a personal affiliation with and responsive markets,' says Simone. Based in the semi-industrial Sydney suburb of Zetland, Zimmermann produces its garments in Australia and offshore. The sisters have found that the challenge of running a profitable business has required them to expand their offshore manufacturing. Simone remarks, 'Idealistically we'd like to produce things here, but we still need to be economical and efficient … our main consideration is quality'. Zimmermann creates patterns and samples in-house, while working with a range of technical experts on the printing screens and cutting, as well as with external contractors for labour components. Zimmermann is now at a point of employing 17 dedicated staff at head office, and 55 staff in total. There is a constant hive of activity behind the scenes at Zimmermann head office. Producing hundreds of designs each season, the business is ready to take on growing international demand. 'We see the fashion industry starting to evolve. Australian brands are being recognised overseas', says Simone, and Zimmermann is well-placed to sell its identity as a dynamic Australian brand. Yet there is a welcome casualness to the sisters, a light-heartedness that defies their brilliant success. As Australia's leading swimwear designers, they are regularly invited to sell through *Victoria's Secret* catalogues. Fashion houses Marks & Spencer (United Kingdom) and Be Be (United States) have commissioned Zimmermann to develop in-house swimwear lines. While retaining its focus on women's wear, Zimmermann has also started producing clothing for young girls and children. With a loyal following, Zimmermann is maturing with its market. The label receives extensive and enthusiastic editorial coverage, and has graced the pages of *Vogue, Harper's Bazaar, Elle, W, Glamour, Nylon, Marie Claire* and the international swimwear bible, *Sports Illustrated*. The latest Zimmermann designs feature printed chiffons, electric colours, ruffles, bows, tartans, love-heart prints, cutaway one-piece swimsuits and jersey gowns with Grecian detailing. With Zimmermann's fashion in the spotlight, new opportunities are arising for this thriving fashion label.

Annabel Moir

2

1 *Slinky Cross Over Frill* one-piece, Magenta, 2005–06
Cruise Swim Collection
Tactel/elastane.
2 *Havana Knotted* long dress, Taupe, 2005–06
Spring Summer LOVE Collection
Poly/elastane.
3 *Collection Swim*, Panel cut-out one-piece, Taupe and Teal, 2005–06
Spring Summer LOVE Collection
Tactel/elastane.
4 *Collection Swim Knotted* one-piece, Taupe, 2005–06
Spring Summer LOVE Collection
Tactel/elastane.
5 *Varadero Platted* long dress, Ocean, 2005–06
Spring Summer LOVE Collection
Poly/elastane.
6 *Collection Swim Cross* frill one-piece, Magenta, 2005–06
Spring Summer LOVE Collection
Tactel/elastane.
7 *Collection Swim Gathered* cross one-piece, Ocean, 2005–06
Spring Summer LOVE Collection
Tactel/elastane.

1. 'Sisters on the springboard, with designs on a ripple effect,' Anthea Loucas, *Sydney Morning Herald,* 5 May 2003, Sydney.
2. 'Swimwear brand makes a big splash in haute couture scene,' Patty Huntington, *Sydney Morning Herald,* 28 April 2006, Sydney.

What would happen if you could cross a Bauhaus-esque rigour with the whimsical ponderings of Mother Goose? If the owl and the pussycat went, instead, to Weimar? A chandelier that evokes Rapunzel's tumbling hair, or a fruit bowl that apes an Elizabethan ruff, a lamp that harks to a cluster of trees? Such is the work of zuii, a Melbourne-based design partnership comprising of Alana Di Giacomo (b.1979) and Marcel Sigel (b.1976), whose creativity and professional gumption have set them on an exponential trajectory.

Alana Di Giacomo and Marcel Sigel

zuii

Sigel and Di Giacomo met as students in Perth and relocated to Melbourne to launch their design careers together. They established an international mandate from the start and, with typically adventurous spirit, aimed to debut zuii at the 2004 Milan International Furniture Fair's *Salone Satellite*. When they were accepted, the news was welcome, but cast the harsh light of day on their ambitious vision. Sigel reflects, 'We thought "what are we going to do now?" We had about three months before we had to be in Milan. So we went there without anyone ever having seen our work.' ■ 'We thrust ourselves in the deep end and didn't know what to expect,' Di Giacomo adds. 'But we found lots of different people from different countries in the same position as us, which was a big comfort. Everyone's trying to do their own thing and so are we.' ■ Their name, 'zuii', is sourced from the title of a Japanese manuscript, *Karakuri Zuii*, which details the Edo period's ingenious mechanical puppets and clocks, and aptly reflects their eclectic and quirky approach to design. Sigel and Di Giacomo often begin their process with a self-motivated brief, developing it independently before establishing a candid dialogue between them to refine the design. They apply their idiosyncratic style to ordinary objects such as furniture, lighting and homewares, mutating them and bestowing them with quirky, unexpected twists that challenge the end-user, surprising and delighting. 'For example the woodland light is structurally different and innovative,' Sigel illustrates, 'but we didn't want to take it too far away from a traditional lampshade. That way people know what it is – they are not too scared of it or distanced from it – but it's got an edge and a certain character.' ■ For zuii, the self-motivated work provides an opportunity to be more ideas-

driven than market-driven, liberating them from the limitations of saleability, economy and mass appeal. 'We want to mark objects with their own personal identity and beauty, giving them a character so they stand out from other objects in the market,' says Di Giacomo. 'That's why companies would hopefully come to us, wanting us to carry that through to represent them.' In this way, zuii's self-initiated works also act as showpieces for their creativity and skill, and provide them with further professional opportunities.

Recently, just such an encounter materialised when a representative from Royal Selangor, impressed by zuii's showing in Milan, approached them to design a range of homewares in pewter. Released in late 2006, the range incorporates bowls, vases, photograph frames, a tray and salt and pepper shakers. It provided them with valuable on-the-ground experience in designing for mass-production within a client's framework. **Sigel comments, 'With this we have to think more about the end-user and whether it is going to sell in the target market**. **'But we're still putting in our interpretation as to what a pewter object today could be and what people might appreciate,' adds Di Giacomo.**

This experience illustrates the value, too, of exhibiting at the Milan International Furniture Fair, as Milan exposes them to companies and manufacturers that would be impossible to reach from home. Sigel and Di Giacomo agree that they need to look overseas if they are to achieve their professional goals, as Australia is perceived to be under-supplied with support for ambitious young designers. 'We've been told by European manufacturers to get out of Australia!' Sigel exclaims, but goes on to clarify that their international focus is not solely one of manufacturing convenience. 'One of the reasons we are looking overseas is, because if we go international, it flows back locally as well. Whereas if we started locally, it wouldn't flow so easily to the international level.' Still at the beginning of their careers, the pair have distinguished themselves with their professional fearlessness, their inventive output and in the diversity of design applications they explore. Though bold, they also acknowledge their newness and vulnerability. As Di Giacomo comments, 'We're still discovering a lot. We're still really new to this industry.' Their youth sustains their freshness and optimism, which can be precious qualities in a sometimes cynical industry.

Emily Howes

1 *Henry's Collar – fruit bowl*, 2005
Moulded polyester fibre or stainless steel.
Prototype.
100 x 420 x 420mm
2 *Carbon Sapphire*, 2005
Aluminium or fibre composites.
Prototype.
700 x 670 x 500mm
3 *Untitled vase*, salt and pepper shakers, bowl and tray, 2006
Manufactured by Royal Selangor, Malaysia.
Pewter.
Tallest: 220mm
4 *Woodland (table light)*, 2004
Aluminium.
Prototype.
520 x 490 x 490mm

Designer Biographies

1

Ari Athans

BORN: 3 December 1965, Sydney, Australia
CONTACT: Ari Jewellery; 1/760 Brunswick Street
New Farm, QLD, 4005; ari@arijewellery.com.au;
www.arijewellery.com.au **EDUCATION/TRAINING**:
Diploma Jewellery and Object Design, 1992,
Randwick Tafe; Bachelor Applied Science (Geology),
1988, University of Technology, Sydney
SELECTED EXHIBITIONS: 2005 *Arc, Art Design and
Craft Biennial,* Brisbane City Gallery, Brisbane; 2004
Self, Angel Row Gallery, Nottingham and toured
the United Kingdom; 2002 *Stonewear,* Jan Murphy
Gallery, Brisbane; 2001 *Schhmuck 2001*, International
Handwerksmesse, Munich; 2000 *Bodyguards,* Craft
Queensland, Brisbane **SELECTED BIBLIOGRAPHY**:
2005 *Craft Unbound*, Kevin Murray, Craftsman House,
Melbourne; 2005 'Ari Jewellery', Cameron Bruhn,
Artichoke, Issue 13, Melbourne; 2000 'Bodyguards',
Tim Morell, *Object* Magazine, Issue 4/00, Sydney;
1998 'Diagnostic imaging in silver and glass', Rhana
Devenport, *Object* Magazine, Issue 1/98, Sydney
SELECTED COLLECTIONS: Toowoomba Regional
Gallery, Queensland **SELECTED STOCKISTS**:
Ari Jewellery, Brisbane; e.g.etal, Melbourne

Jonathan Baskett

BORN: 6 October 1969, Canberra, Australia
CONTACT: Jonathan Baskett Creative; PO Box 242
Murrumbateman, ACT, 2582; info@jonathanbaskett.com;
www.jonathanbaskett.com **EDUCATION/TRAINING**:
Master of Visual Arts, 2003, Canberra School of Art,
Australian National University; Bachelor of Visual Arts
(Honours), 1996, Canberra School of Art, Australian
National University **SELECTED EXHIBITIONS**:
2005 *New Directions in Glass,* Australian Embassy,
Washington; 2004 *Bombay Sapphire Design Discovery
Award,* Space Furniture, Sydney; 2004 *Tyranny of
Distance,* Tokyo Designers Block, Gallery Piazza
Harajuku, Tokyo, Seoul; 2004 *Geometry, Rhythm, Light,*
Object Gallery, Sydney; Craft ACT, Canberra; Gaffer
Studio Glass, Hong Kong; 2003 *Ranamok*, Beaver
Galleries, Canberra, toured nationally, Anna Bibby
Gallery, Auckland **SELECTED BIBLIOGRAPHY**:
2005 *Australian Glass Today,* Margot Osborne,
Wakefield Press, Kent Town, South Australia; 2000
Review, Corning Museum of Glass, *New Glass Review,*
Issue 21, New York; 1997 *Review,* Corning Museum
of Glass, *New Glass Review,* Issue 19, New York
SELECTED COLLECTIONS: Glasmuseum, Ebeltoft,
Denmark; Ishikawa Design Collection, Kanazawa;
Kunst & Gewerbe Museum, Dresden; Australian
National University Glass Workshop Collection, Canberra

bernabeifreeman
Rina Bernabei and Kelly Freeman

BORN: Rina Bernabei, 14 November 1968, Sydney, Australia; Kelly Freeman, 23 October 1976, Cooma, Australia ▮ **CONTACT**: bernabeifreeman Pty Ltd; 12 Nicholls Ave Haberfield, NSW, 2045; info@bernabei freeman.com.au; www.bernabeifreeman.com.au ▮ **EDUCATION/TRAINING**: Rina Bernabei, Bachelor of Design, 1991, University of Technology, Sydney; Kelly Freeman, Bachelor of Industrial Design (Honours), 1998, University of New South Wales ▮ **SELECTED BIBLIOGRAPHY**: 2006 *The Presence of Things: Sense, veneer and guise,* Monash University Faculty Gallery, Melbourne and toured regional galleries; 2005 *Bombay Sapphire Design Discovery Award,* Space Furniture, Sydney, Melbourne, Brisbane; 2005 *Powerhouse Museum Australian Design Award*, Powerhouse Museum, Sydney; 2004 *Design 2004*, Melbourne Museum, Melbourne; 2004 *Sydney Style,* Object Gallery, Sydney Opera House, Sydney ▮ **SELECTED BIBLIOGRAPHY**: 2005 'Western Front', *Monument*, Issue 68, Melbourne; 2005 'Posterboard', *Poster Magazine*, Issue 07, Melbourne; 2004 'IDEA 2004 Winner Product Design', *(inside) Architectural Design Review,* Issue 34, Sydney; 2004 'Tell-tale textures', Jennifer Verrall, *The Age Domain,* 14 July, Melbourne; 2004 'Design Island', Georgie Bean, *Thirty4*, July/ August, Holland; 2004 'Creative tension', Julia Richardson, *Sydney Morning Herald Metropolitan,* Sydney ▮ **SELECTED STOCKISTS**: Object Store, Sydney; FORM, Perth; Living Edge, nationally

Caroline Casey

BORN: 19 January 1964, Melbourne, Australia ▮ **CONTACT**: Caroline Casey Design; Level 1, 63 William Street East Sydney, NSW, 2010; cb@caseybrown.com.au; www.caseybrown.com.au ▮ **EDUCATION/TRAINING**: Associated Science Degree (Interior Design), 1991, Parsons School of Design, New York; Bachelor of Arts (Fashion and Textile Design), 1986, Sydney College of the Arts, University of Sydney ▮ **SELECTED EXHIBITIONS**: 2003 Aram Design Store, London; 2001 Galleria Design Store, Nuernberg; 1998–99 *Process,* Powerhouse Museum, Sydney; 1996 *Arts and Industry,* Anibou, Sydney; 1995 *Caroline Casey,* Anibou, Sydney ▮ **SELECTED BIBLIOGRAPHY**: 2003 'Origin of pieces', Lucia van der Post, *The Times,* London; 2003 'Casey cracks Europe', Davina Jackson, *Sydney Morning Herald,* Sydney; 2003 'Take it home', Madelaine Lim, *The Independent*, London; 2002 'Design and conquer', Guy Allenby, *Sydney Morning Herald,* 19 January, Sydney; 2001 'Kunststuke', Anke Kote, *Elle Decoration,* Germany ▮ **SELECTED COLLECTIONS**: Victoria & Albert Museum, London; San Francisco Museum of Modern Art; Powerhouse Museum, Sydney; National Gallery of Australia, Canberra; Art Gallery of South Australia, Adelaide ▮ **SELECTED STOCKISTS**: Anibou, Sydney, Melbourne; Aram, London; Studio Willmann Nuernberg, Germany

Nicola Cerini

BORN: 27 July 1969, Warrnambool, Victoria, Australia **CONTACT:** Nicola Cerini Australia; 39 Little Hoddle Street Richmond, VIC, 3121; info@nicolacerini.com; www.nicolacerini.com **EDUCATION/TRAINING:** Bachelor of Art (Textile Design), 1991, RMIT University; Summer Apprentice Program, 1995, The Fabric Workshop, Philadelphia; New Enterprise Incentive Scheme, 1995, Melbourne **SELECTED EXHIBITIONS:** 2006 *The Presence of Things: Sense, veneer and guise,* Monash University Faculty Gallery, Melbourne and toured regional galleries; 2003 *Cecily & Colin Rigg Contemporary Design Award,* Ian Potter Centre, National Gallery of Victoria, Melbourne; 2002 *Australian Fashion & Textile Design Exhibition,* Fashion Centre Korea, Daegu, Korea; 2000 *Masters of Technique: Creators on cloth,* Monash Gallery of Art, Melbourne and regional galleries; 1998 *Putting It in Print*, Craft ACT, Nara, Japan, JamFactory, Adelaide and toured regional galleries **SELECTED BIBLIOGRAPHY:** 2006 'Furnished with the fabric of ideas', *Herald-Sun* Business Profile, 27 January, Sydney; 2006 'Special Report: Fibres & fabrics', *Ragtrader,* 13 January, Sydney; 2005 'Cutting it in the textile design trade', *The Age*, 19 November, Melbourne; 2005 'Make Me: Emotional baggage', *Object* Magazine, Issue 47, Sydney; 2005 'Out there: news, views, trends and goings on', *Inside Out,* March/April, Sydney **SELECTED COLLECTIONS:** National Gallery of Victoria, Melbourne; Museum and Art Gallery of the Northern Territory, Darwin **SELECTED STOCKISTS:** Australian National Gallery, Canberra; Art Gallery of New South Wales, Sydney; Museum of Contemporary Art, Sydney; Made in Japan, Melbourne; Kleen, Melbourne

Lucas Chirnside

BORN: 9 January 1976, Clyde, New Zealand moved to Australia 1990 **CONTACT:** 847 Rathdowne Street Carlton North, VIC, 3054; design@smlwrld.com; www.smlwrld.com **EDUCATION/TRAINING:** Bachelor of Architecture (Honours), 2002, RMIT University **SELECTED EXHIBITIONS:** 2006 *Bombay Sapphire guest designer,* Superstudio Piu, Salone Internazionale del Mobile, Milan; 2005 Salone Internazionale del Mobile – *Salone Satellite* with Melbourne Movement, Milan; 2004 *A Molecular History of Everything* (*well not everything), Australian Centre for Contemporary Art, Melbourne; 2004 *Tyranny of Distance,* Tokyo Designers Block, Gallery Piazza Harajuku, Tokyo, Seoul; 2003 *Hybrid Objects: Recent directions in Australian design,* Melbourne Museum, Melbourne **SELECTED BIBLIOGRAPHY:** 2006 'Time travel', Y-L. Dann, *Monument,* April/May, Sydney; 2006 'Time for design', K. Holt, *POL Oxygen,* March, Sydney; 2006 'Clocking on', L. Keens, *Belle,* February/March, Sydney; 2005 *A Molecular History of Everything* (*well not everything), J. Engberg, Australian Centre for Contemporary Art, Melbourne; 2002 'Orient express', S. Braun, *Blueprint* Magazine, Issue 202, London

Bianca Looney

BORN: 21 July 1977, Brisbane, Australia
CONTACT: 847 Rathdowne Street Carlton North, VIC, 3054; xenolith@fastmail.fm
EDUCATION/ TRAINING: Bachelor of Arts (Visual Arts), 1997, Queensland University of Technology **SELECTED EXHIBITIONS:** 2005 *Next Stop Milano – Australian Designers of Promise,* Triennale di Milano, Milan; 2005 *Salone Internazionale del Mobile – Salone Satellite* with Melbourne Movement, Milan; 2004 *A Molecular History of Everything* (*well not everything),* Australian Centre for Contemporary Art, Melbourne; 2004 *Tyranny of Distance,* Tokyo Designers Block, Gallery Piazza Harajuku, Tokyo, Seoul; 2004 *Design 2004,* Melbourne Museum, Melbourne

SELECTED BIBLIOGRAPHY: 2005 'Wisdom of Bianca Looney', J. Brown, *The Age,* September, Melbourne; 2005 *Everyday Objects and Other Narratives,* C. Vignando, Craft Australia, August, Canberra; 2005 'Salone Internazionale del Mobile, Milan', D. Neustein, *Monument,* Issue 68, Melbourne; 2005 'On even ground', S. Crafti, *SDQ,* Winter Issue 18, Sydney; 2005 *A Molecular History of Everything* (*well not everything),* J. Engberg, Australian Centre for Contemporary Art, Melbourne

cloth

Julie Paterson

BORN: 15 October 1963, Taunton, England, arrived Australia 1989 **CONTACT:** cloth Pty Ltd; 35 Buckingham Street Surry Hills, NSW, 2010; cloth@clothfabric.com; www.clothfabric.com
EDUCATION/TRAINING: Postgraduate Diploma of Art Education, 1985, Goldsmiths College, University of London; Bachelor of Arts (Honours – Multi-Disciplinary Design), 1984, Trent University, United Kingdom **SELECTED EXHIBITIONS:** 2005 *In The Shed,* Collect, Sydney; 2005 *In The Shed Prototypes,* Spence + Lyda, as part of *Sydney Esquisse,* Sydney; 2003 *Encounters,* Tokyo Designers Block, Spiral Gallery, Tokyo; 2003 *Of the Land from the Air,* Living Edge, Melbourne, Sydney **SELECTED BIBLIOGRAPHY:** 2005 'Julie Paterson fabric designer', *Creative Homes,* December, Sydney; 2005 'Woman of cloth', *Vogue Living,* May/June, Sydney; 2004 'Weaving the magic', *Belle,* December, Sydney; 2004 'cloth', *Casa Arbitare,* July, Milan; 2001 'Woman of the cloth', *Wallpaper,* October, London **SELECTED STOCKISTS:** cloth, Sydney; Object Store, Sydney; Deka, Brisbane; Taylor + Taylor, Melbourne; Décor design, Perth

Susan Cohn

BORN: 1 August 1952, Sydney, Australia  **CONTACT:**
Workshop 3000; 183 Flinders Lane Melbourne, VIC,
3000; www.cohnartist.com ■ **EDUCATION/TRAINING:**
Candidate for Doctorate of Fine Art Theory, 1999–
2006, College of Fine Arts, University of New South
Wales; Graduate Diploma of Fine Art, 1986, RMIT
University; Diploma of Art (Gold and Silversmithing),
1980, RMIT University ■ **SELECTED EXHIBITIONS:**
2004 *I protest I object*, Anna Schwartz Gallery at
Depot Gallery, Sydney; 2003 *Black Intentions,* Ian
Potter Centre, National Gallery of Victoria, Melbourne;
2003 *Clemenger Contemporary Art Award,* Ian Potter
Centre, National Gallery of Victoria, Melbourne;
2000–03 *Techno Craft: The work of Susan Cohn
1980–2000,* National Gallery of Australia, Canberra,
toured nationally; 1999 *Techno Craft 33.3%,* Glasgow
School of Art, Glasgow, Idée Gallery, Tokyo
SELECTED BIBLIOGRAPHY: 2005 'Indesign luminary',
Jan Howlin, *Indesign,* Vol. 22 August, Sydney; 2003
Black Intentions catalogue, National Gallery of Victoria,
Melbourne; 2003 'The meaning of things', Deyan
Sudjic, *Domus 861,* July/August, Italy; 2002 *Request,
Response, Reaction: the designers of Australia
and New Zealand,* Stephen Crafti, Images Publishing
Group, Melbourne; 2000 *Techno Craft: The work of
Susan Cohn 1980–2000,* National Gallery of Australia,
Canberra ■ **SELECTED COLLECTIONS:** National
Gallery of Australia, Canberra; National Gallery
of Victoria, Melbourne; Victoria & Albert Museum,
London; National Museum of Scotland, Edinburgh;
Art Gallery of South Australia, Adelaide ■ **SELECTED
STOCKISTS:** Anna Schwartz Gallery, Melbourne;
RG Madden, Melbourne and Sydney; National Design
Centre, Melbourne

Crumpler

Stuart Crumpler, Will Miller, Dave Roper

BORN: Stuart Crumpler, 12 January 1973, Rochester,
Victoria, Australia; Will Miller, 24 July 1970, Adelaide,
Australia; Dave Roper, 13 January 1970, Adelaide,
Australia ■ **CONTACT:** Crumpler Bags; 6 Chelmssford
Street Kensington, VIC, 3031; enquiries@crumpler.com.au;
www.crumpler.com.au ■ **EDUCATION/TRAINING:**
Stuart Crumpler (Principal Designer), Bachelor
of Visual Arts (Sculpture), 1993, Ballarat University,
Victoria ■ **SELECTED BIBLIOGRAPHY:** 2005
'A bagful of money', *The Age,* 29 May, Melbourne ■
SELECTED STOCKISTS: Crumpler stores, nationally
and New York, Singapore; Apple Centre, nationally;
Brunswick Street Cycles, Melbourne; Camera Action
Camera House, Melbourne; Snowgum, nationally

10

Janet DeBoos

BORN: 1 March 1948, Melbourne, Australia
CONTACT: Brindabella Pottery; 261/2 Endeavour
House Manuka, ACT, 2603 **EDUCATION/TRAINING:**
Bachelor of Science, 1969, Sydney University; Ceramics
Certificate, 1971, East Sydney Technical College;
Diploma in Education, 1972, Sydney Teachers College
SELECTED EXHIBITIONS: 2005 *Porcelaine à l'ère
de la Postmodernitié,* Musée Royal de Mariement,
Belgium; 2004 Collect (Narek Galleries), Victoria
& Albert Museum, London; 2005 *Table Manners,*
Crafts Council Gallery, London; 2002 *Material Culture,*
National Gallery of Australia, Canberra; 2001
A Composite of Opposites (with Alan Watt) Narek
Galleries at The Drill Hall Gallery, Australian National
University, Canberra **SELECTED BIBLIOGRAPHY:**
2006 'Sublime pottery captures life's everyday rituals
and routines', Meredith Hinchliffe, *Canberra Times
(Times 2),* 12 April, Canberra; 2006 'Whiter than white,
a marriage of materials and desire', *Object* Magazine,
Issue 48, Sydney; 2002 *Porcelain,* Jack Doherty, A&C
Black, London; 1998 *Ceramic Form, Design and
Decoration* (revised), Peter Lane, A&C Black, London;
1988 *A Collector's Guide to Modern Australian
Ceramics,* Janet Mansfield, Craftsman House, London
SELECTED COLLECTIONS: National Gallery of
Australia, Canberra; Canberra Museum and Gallery,
Canberra; Powerhouse Museum, Sydney; Musée
Royal de Mariemont, Belgium; Taipei County Yingge
Ceramics Museum, Taipei **SELECTED STOCKISTS:**
Narek Galleries, Tanja, NSW

11

Dinosaur Designs
Louise Olsen, Stephen Ormandy, Liane Rossler

BORN: Louise Olsen, 24 January 1964, Sydney,
Australia; Stephen Ormandy, 9 March 1964,
Melbourne, Australia; Liane Rossler, 7 May 1965,
Sydney, Australia **CONTACT:** Dinosaur Designs
585 Elizabeth Street, Strawberry Hills, NSW, 2012;
dinosaur@dinosaurdesigns.com.au;
www.dinosaurdesigns.com.au **EDUCATION/
TRAINING:** Graduate Diploma Professional Art Studies,
1986, College of Fine Arts, University of New South
Wales; Bachelor of Visual Arts, 1985, College of Fine
Arts, University of New South Wales **SELECTED
EXHIBITIONS:** 2003–05 *Dinosaur Designs,* Object
Gallery, Sydney, toured nationally, Tokyo, Bangkok,
Taipei, Singapore; 2002–04 *Tokyo Designers Block,*
Japan; 2002 *Objects of Desire,* Object Gallery, Sydney;
1998 *Personal Effects/The Collective Unconscious,*
Museum of Contemporary Art, Sydney; 1989 *Australian
Fashion: The contemporary art,* Victoria & Albert
Museum, London **SELECTED BIBLIOGRAPHY:**
2005 *Studio: Design at Work,* Donald Williams,
McGraw-Hill, Sydney; 2003 *Dinosaur Designs,* Object
Gallery, Sydney; 2002 *Request, Response, Reaction:
the designers of Australia and New Zealand,* Stephen
Crafti, Images Publishing Group, Melbourne; 1998
Contemporary Jewellery in Australia and New Zealand,
Patricia Anderson, Craftsman House, Sydney; 1992
The Crafts Movement in Australia: A history, Grace
Cochrane, NSW University Press, Sydney
SELECTED COLLECTIONS: Powerhouse Museum,
Sydney; National Gallery of Victoria, Melbourne
SELECTED STOCKISTS: Dinosaur Designs, Sydney,
Melbourne, New York; Museum of Modern Art Design
Store, New York; National Gallery of Australia, Canberra;
FORM and Aspects of Kings Park, Perth; Idée, Tokyo

12

Easton Pearson
Pamela Easton and Lydia Pearson

BORN: Pamela Easton, 23 April 1958, Charters Towers, Queensland, Australia; Lydia Pearson, 27 August 1957, Liverpool, United Kingdom, moved to Australia 1963  **CONTACT:** Easton Pearson; 725 Ann Street Fortitude Valley, QLD, 4006; eastonpearson@eastonpearson.com **EDUCATION/ TRAINING:** Lydia Pearson, Bachelor of Arts, 1978, University of Queensland **SELECTED EXHIBITIONS:** 2005 *Transforming Traditions,* VCUQ Gallery of Art, Virginia Commonwealth University, School of the Arts, Qatar; 2004 *Sailor Style,* Fashion Film, Australian National Maritime Museum, Sydney; 2003 *Un Wrapped, Australian Fashion and Textile Design*, Bendigo Art Gallery, Victoria, Asialink Travelling Exhibition; 2002 *Sourcing the Muse,* Powerhouse Museum, Sydney; 2005 *TAG,* Craft Queensland, Brisbane **SELECTED COLLECTIONS:** Powerhouse Museum, Sydney; National Gallery of Victoria, Melbourne **SELECTED STOCKISTS:** Easton Pearson, Brisbane, Sydney; David Jones, nationally; Browns, London; Bergdorf Goodman, New York; Via Bus Stop, Tokyo

13

Edols Elliott
Benjamin Edols and Kathy Elliott

BORN: Benjamin Edols, 19 June 1967, Sydney, Australia; Kathy Elliott, 3 July 1964, Sydney, Australia **CONTACT:** Edols Elliott; 12/111 Old Pittwater Road Brookvale, NSW, 2100; edolselliott@ozemail.com.au; www.edolselliott.com **EDUCATION/TRAINING:** Benjamin Edols, Bachelor of Visual Arts, 1991, Sydney College of the Arts, Sydney University; Postgraduate Diploma, 1992, Canberra School of Art, Australian National University; Kathy Elliott, Bachelor of Visual Arts, 1991, Canberra School of Art, Australian National University **SELECTED EXHIBITIONS:** 2006 Collect, Victoria & Albert Museum, London; 2005 SOFA, Navy Pier, Chicago; 2004 *Sydney Style,* Object Gallery, Sydney Opera House, Sydney; 2004 *Recent Work,* de Vera, New York; 2002 *Cultivate,* William Traver Gallery, Seattle **SELECTED BIBLIOGRAPHY:** 2005 *Australian Glass Today,* Margot Osborne, Wakefield Press, Kent Town, South Australia; 2001 *Artists in Glass,* Dan Klein, Mitchell Beazley, London; 2000 *Craft from Scratch,* 8th Triennale Form and Matters Australia + Germany; 1999 *Contemporary Australian Craft,* Powerhouse Museum, Sydney **SELECTED COLLECTIONS:** Victoria & Albert Museum, London; Powerhouse Museum, Sydney; Toyama Art Museum, Japan; Auckland Museum, New Zealand; Corning Museum of Glass, New York **SELECTED STOCKISTS:** de Vera, New York; Sabbia Gallery, Sydney; William Traver Gallery, Seattle; Schurenberg, Aachen; Masterworks, Auckland

14

F!NK & Co.
Principal Designer Robert Foster

BORN: 23 August 1962, Kyneton, Victoria, Australia
CONTACT: F!NK & Co.; 25 Endurance Avenue
Queanbeyan, NSW, 2602; finkdesign@iimetro.com.au;
www.finkdesign.com **EDUCATION/TRAINING:**
Bachelor of Fine Arts (Gold & Silversmithing), 1981,
Canberra School of Art, Australian National University;
Postgraduate Studies (Gold & Silversmithing), 1985,
Canberra School of Art, Australian National University
SELECTED EXHIBITIONS: 2005 *Vast Terrain,*
FORM, Perth, Object Gallery, Sydney Opera House,
Sydney, Melbourne Museum, Melbourne; 2005
Transformations: The language of craft, National
Gallery of Australia, Canberra; 2001–02 *A Motion
in Time,* JamFactory, Adelaide, Craft ACT, Canberra,
Anibou and Qantas domestic terminal, Sydney,
RG Madden, Melbourne, CraftWest Gallery, Perth;
2000 *Australia and Germany: 8th International Frankfurt
Craft Triennale,* Museum für Angewandte Kunst,
Frankfurt, Germany; 1999 4+1, Powerhouse Museum,
Sydney **SELECTED BIBLIOGRAPHY:** 2006
'Fostering design', Merryn Gates, *Object* Magazine,
Issue 49, Sydney; 2002 *Request, Response, Reaction:
the designers of Australia and New Zealand,* Stephen
Crafti, Images Publishing Group, Melbourne; 2001
International Design Year Book, Michele De Lucchi
(ed.), Laurence King, London; 1992 *Design Visions,*
Robert Bell, Art Gallery of Western Australia, Perth
SELECTED COLLECTIONS: Victoria & Albert
Museum, London; Lisbon Design Museum, Portugal;
National Gallery of Australia, Canberra; Powerhouse
Museum, Sydney; National Gallery of Victoria,
Melbourne **SELECTED STOCKISTS:** Museum
of Modern Art Design Store, New York; San Francisco
Museum of Modern Art, San Francisco; National
Gallery of Australia, Canberra; RG Madden, Melbourne,
Sydney; Object Store, Sydney

15

Adam Goodrum

BORN: 21 May 1972, Sydney, Australia
CONTACT: 25 John Street Waterloo, NSW,
2017; agoodrum@pacific.net.au **EDUCATION/
TRAINING:** Bachelor of Design (Industrial Design),
1993, University of Technology, Sydney
SELECTED EXHIBITIONS: 2006 20/20 *Vision,* NSW
Parliament House, Sydney; 2005 *Folding House,*
Canberra Biennial, Canberra; 2005 *Superstudio,*
Milan International Furniture Fair, Milan; 2005
… and the serpent tempted Eve, Object Gallery,
Sydney; 2004 Tokyo Designers Block, Tokyo
SELECTED BIBLIOGRAPHY: 2006 'Form & function',
Lino Magazine, Issue 13, Australia/New Zealand;
2005 'Stitch chair', *ID Annual Design Review,*
Issue 51, United States; 2005 '100% Australian,
The Glamorous', *Schoner Wohnen Decoration*, July/
August, Germany; 2005 'All about Eve', *Black and
White Magazine,* Issue 76, Sydney; 2004 'Way to go',
The (Sydney) Magazine, Sydney Morning Herald,
Issue 16, Sydney

16

Jon Goulder

BORN: 7 October 1970, Bowral, NSW, Australia
 **CONTACT:** Jon Goulder; jon@jongoulder.com; www.jongoulder.com ■ **EDUCATION/TRAINING:** Apprenticeship upholstery-furniture making, 1992; Diploma Fine Wood and Design, 1999, Canberra School of Art, Australian National University ■ **SELECTED EXHIBITIONS:** 2005 *Inspired! Design Across Time,* Powerhouse Museum, Sydney; 2004 *Hobart Art Prize,* Tasmanian Museum and Art Gallery, Hobart; 2004 *40 Degrees,* Stilwerk Centre, Berlin; 2004 *Sydney Style,* Object Gallery, Sydney Opera House, Sydney; 2003 *Bombay Sapphire Design Discovery Award,* Space Furniture, Sydney ■ **SELECTED BIBLIOGRAPHY:** 2005 '100% Australian', *Schoner Wohnen Decoration*, 4/2005, Hamburg; 2005 'Against the grain', *Surface,* Issue 54, New York; 2005 'Design special', *Australian Financial Review Magazine,* November, Sydney; 2003 *Sydney Style,* Brian Parkes, Object: Australian Centre for Craft and Design, Sydney ■ **SELECTED COLLECTIONS:** Powerhouse Museum, Sydney; Tasmanian Museum and Art Gallery, Hobart ■ **SELECTED STOCKISTS:** Anibou, Sydney, Melbourne; Co Design, Adelaide; Fuse, Brisbane; Design Farm, Perth; BW, Hong Kong

17

Lorinda Grant

BORN: 13 July 1974, Melbourne, Australia
■ **CONTACT:** Eternal U; 9 Belinda Ave Golden Square, VIC, 3555; lorindagrant01@hotkey.net.au ■ **EDUCATION/TRAINING:** Product Design and Development, 1999, Melbourne School of Fashion; New Enterprise Incentive Scheme, 1998, Melbourne ■ **SELECTED EXHIBITIONS:** 2004 *Pins and Needles,* National Gallery of Victoria, Melbourne; 2003 *Un Wrapped, Australian Fashion and Textile Design,* Bendigo Art Gallery, Victoria, Asialink Travelling Exhibition; 2003 *Holes Surrounded by Threads,* Immigration Museum, Melbourne; 2002 *Following Lorinda,* Bendigo Art Gallery, Victoria; 2000 *A Thread and Two Sticks,* Craft Victoria, Melbourne ■ **SELECTED BIBLIOGRAPHY:** 2002 *Herald Sun,* 11 November, Melbourne; 2002 *Australian Women's Weekly,* July, Sydney; 2002 *The Weekly Times,* 13 February, Melbourne; 2001 *Sunday Telegraph,* 11 March, Sydney; 2001 'Talent scout', *Harper's Bazaar,* May, Sydney ■ **SELECTED COLLECTIONS:** National Gallery of Victoria, Melbourne ■ **SELECTED STOCKISTS:** Christine Accessories, Melbourne; Empire Rose, Perth, Melbourne; Inese, Sydney; Strelitzia, Sydney; Wheel and Loom, Maldon, Victoria

1B

Julie Blyfield
Gray Street Workshop

BORN: 13 September 1957, Melbourne, Australia
CONTACT: Gray Street Workshop; 10 Sydney
Place Adelaide, SA, 5000; jblyfield@adam.com.au;
gsw@senet.com.au **EDUCATION/TRAINING:**
Associate Diploma Jewellery and Metalsmithing, 1988,
South Australian College of the Arts and Education;
Diploma in Teaching (Secondary Fine Art), 1978,
Torrens College of Advanced Education, Adelaide
SELECTED EXHIBITIONS: 2006 Collect, Australian
Contemporary Gallery, Galerie ra, Amsterdam, Victoria
& Albert Museum, London; 2005 *Transformations:
The language of craft,* National Gallery of Australia,
Canberra; 2005 *Signs taken for wonders – Gray Street
Workshop celebrates 20 years,* South Australian
School of Art Gallery, University of South Australia,
Adelaide, Galerie ra, Amsterdam; 2004 *Schmuck
2004,* Internationale Handwerksmesse, Munich,
Germany; 2003 *Flourish,* Gallery Funaki, Melbourne
SELECTED BIBLIOGRAPHY: 2006 *Bare and Beyond,*
Australian Contemporary at Collect 2006, Wendy
Walker, Visual Arts Board of Australia Council,
Australia; 2006 'London calling', Margot Osborne,
The Advertiser Review, 28 January, Adelaide; 2005
500 *Brooches: Inspiring adornments for the body,*
Marthe le Van (ed.), Lark Books, New York; 2003
'Blyfield raises the stakes', Penny Webb, *The Age,*
19 November, Melbourne; 1998 *The International Design
Year Book 1998*, Richard Sapper (ed.), Laurence King,
London **SELECTED COLLECTIONS:** National
Museum of Scotland, Edinburgh; National Gallery
of Australia, Canberra; National Gallery of Victoria,
Melbourne; Art Gallery of South Australia, Adelaide;
Queensland Art Gallery, Brisbane **SELECTED
STOCKISTS:** Galerie ra, Amsterdam; Gallery Funaki,
Melbourne; JamFactory, Adelaide; Object Store,
Sydney; Beaver Galleries, Canberra

Leslie Matthews
Gray Street Workshop

BORN: 23 April 1964, Puerto Rico, arrived Australia
1968 **CONTACT:** Gray Street Workshop; 10 Sydney
Place Adelaide, SA, 5000; lesliem@picknowl.com.au;
gsw@senet.com.au; **EDUCATION/TRAINING:**
Bachelor of Design (Jewellery & Metalsmithing),
1985, School of Design, South Australian College
of Advanced Education; Masters of Visual Art, Masters
by Research, 2006, School of Art, University of South
Australia **SELECTED EXHIBITIONS:** 2005 *Signs
taken for wonders – Gray Street Workshop celebrates
20 years,* South Australian School of Art Gallery,
University of South Australia, Adelaide, Galerie ra,
Amsterdam; 2005 Collect, Victoria & Albert Museum,
Lesley Craze Gallery, London; 2004 *Looking Over My
Shoulder, 20th Anniversary Exhibition,* Lesley Craze
Gallery, London; 2003 *Metal Element of Six Countries –
The Circumference of Metal,* International Design
Centre, Nagoya, Japan; 2002 *Goldfields OZGold
Award 2002,* Quadrivium Gallery, Sydney, toured
nationally **SELECTED BIBLIOGRAPHY:** 2005 *Signs
taken for wonders – Gray Street Workshop celebrates
20 years,* Margot Osborne, Gray Street Workshop,
Adelaide; 2005 'Parallel Universe: The Gray Street
Workshop @ 20', Margot Osborne, *Artlink* Magazine,
Vol. 25, no 1, Adelaide; 2005 'Shades of gray', Louise
Nunn, *The Advertiser Arts,* 27 June, Adelaide; 2004
'The gentle wash of memory', Wendy Walker, *Object*
Magazine, Issue 44, Sydney; 2004 'Limbs of steel',
Paul McGillick, *Indesign*, Issue 16, Sydney
SELECTED COLLECTIONS: National Gallery of
Australia, Canberra; Art Bank, Canberra; Art Gallery
of South Australia, Adelaide; Museum of Arts and
Sciences, Darwin; Art Gallery of the Northern Territory,
Darwin **SELECTED STOCKISTS:** Lesley Craze
Gallery, London; Velvet da Vinci, San Francisco; Object
Store, Sydney; JamFactory, Adelaide

Catherine Truman

Gray Street Workshop

BORN: 8 October 1957, Adelaide, Australia
CONTACT: Gray Street Workshop; 10 Sydney Place Adelaide, SA, 5000; ctsl@senet.com.au; gsw@senet.com.au ■ **EDUCATION/TRAINING:** Masters of Fine Art candidate, 2006, Monash University, Melbourne; Feldenkrais® Training, 1999, Australian Feldenkrais® Foundation, Perth; Studied Netsuke carving techniques, 1990, Tokyo, Japan; Associate Diploma Jewellery and Metalsmithing, 1985, University of South Australia; Diploma of Teaching, Bachelor of Education (Secondary Fine Art), 1978, University of South Australia ■ **SELECTED EXHIBITIONS:** 2005 *Signs taken for wonders – Gray Street Workshop celebrates 20 years,* South Australian School of Art Gallery, University of South Australia, Adelaide, Galerie ra, Amsterdam; 2004 *2004: Australian culture now,* National Gallery of Victoria, Melbourne; 2003–04 *Light Black,* JamFactory, Adelaide, Museum of Contemporary Art, Tokyo, Museum of Contemporary Art, Kyoto; 1999 SOFA, New York; 1998 *Seppelt Contemporary Art Award,* Museum of Contemporary Art, Sydney ■ **SELECTED BIBLIOGRAPHY:** 2005 *Signs taken for wonders – Gray Street Workshop celebrates 20 years,* Margot Osborne, Gray Street Workshop, Adelaide; 2004 *2004: Australian culture now,* National Gallery of Victoria, Melbourne; 2003 *Light Black,* JamFactory, Adelaide; 2002 *Australian Art in the National Gallery of Australia,* Anne Gray (ed.), National Gallery of Australia, Canberra; 2001 'Supple: The work of Catherine Truman', Christine Nicholls, *Art Monthly,* Issue 139, Canberra ■ **SELECTED COLLECTIONS:** Danner-Stiftung, Pinakothek der Moderne, Munich; National Gallery of Australia, Canberra; National Gallery of Victoria, Melbourne; Powerhouse Museum, Sydney; Art Gallery of South Australia, Adelaide ■ **SELECTED STOCKISTS:** Gallery Funaki, Melbourne; Charon Kranson, New York; JamFactory, Adelaide

19

Akira Isogawa

BORN: 25 December 1964, Kyoto, Japan, moved to Australia 1986 ■ **CONTACT:** Akira; Suite 5, Level 1, 2–12 Foveaux Street Surry Hills, NSW, 2010; akira@akira.com.au; www.akira.com.au ■ **EDUCATION/TRAINING:** Fashion Design, 1986, East Sydney College, Sydney Institute of Technology ■ **SELECTED EXHIBITIONS:** 2005 *Akira Isogawa Printemps-été,* National Gallery of Victoria, Melbourne, Asialink Travelling Exhibition; 2003 *Un Wrapped, Australian Fashion and Textile Design,* Bendigo Art Gallery, Victoria, Asialink Travelling Exhibition; 2002 *Sourcing the Muse,* Powerhouse Museum, Sydney; 2001 *Akira Isogawa,* Object Gallery, Sydney; 1998 *Seppelt Contemporary Art Award,* Museum of Contemporary Art, Sydney ■ **SELECTED BIBLIOGRAPHY:** 2006 'The boy who would be king', Jamie Huckbody, *Harper's Bazaar,* March, Sydney; 2005 *Akira Isogawa Printemps-été,* National Gallery of Victoria and The Asialink Centre, Melbourne; 2003 *Un Wrapped, Australian Fashion and Textile Design*, Bendigo Art Gallery, Victoria; 2001 *Akira Isogawa,* Object: Australian Centre for Craft and Design, Sydney ■ **SELECTED COLLECTIONS:** National Gallery of Victoria, Melbourne; Powerhouse Museum, Sydney ■ **SELECTED STOCKISTS:** Akira, Sydney, Melbourne; David Jones, nationally; Browns, London; Barney's Japan, Tokyo; Villa Moda, Dubai; Saks, London

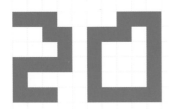

Sheridan Kennedy

BORN: 2 April 1964, Winton, Queensland, Australia
CONTACT: PO Box 650 Darlinghurst, NSW, 1300; shri@sheridankennedy.com; www.sheridankennedy.com
EDUCATION/TRAINING: Diploma of Art (Jewellery), 1984, Queensland College of Art; Bachelor of Art (Jewellery), 1987, Queensland College of Art; Commenced PhD 2005, Sydney College of the Arts, Sydney University **SELECTED EXHIBITIONS:** 2005 *The Specious Voyages,* JamFactory, Adelaide, Museum of Brisbane, Brisbane; 2004–05 *The HAT Project: Here and There Australia/UK,* toured venues in United Kingdom, Object Gallery, Sydney, JamFactory, Adelaide, Melbourne, Queensland; 2004 *Sydney Style,* Object Gallery, Sydney Opera House, Sydney; 2002 *Future Factor,* Craft Queensland, Brisbane, Object Gallery, Sydney, toured nationally; 1997 *Contemporary Vessels & Jewels – Australian Fine Metalwork,* Shanghai Museum, China, Queensland Art Gallery, Brisbane, toured regional galleries in Queensland **SELECTED BIBLIOGRAPHY:** 2005 'A match made in heaven', S. Ostling, *Interact*, Craft Australia, Canberra; 2004 'Dazzling pretenders', Crystal James, *Poster* Magazine, Issue 4, Melbourne; 2002 'All that glitters', Isabella Reich, *Object* Magazine, Issue 40, Sydney; 2002 'Site Upfront', *Monument*, Issue 46, Melbourne; 2000 *Virtual Gallery of Contemporary Jewellery,* Quickenden, Kenneth, Birmingham Institute of Art & Design, Birmingham **SELECTED COLLECTIONS:** National Gallery of Australia, Canberra; Art Gallery of Western Australia, Perth; Queensland Art Gallery, Brisbane; Art Gallery of South Australia, Adelaide **SELECTED STOCKISTS:** Object Store, Sydney; Akira, Sydney, Melbourne; Katerine Kalaf Gallery, Perth; Zu Design, Adelaide; Sculpture to Wear, Los Angeles

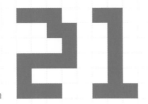

korban/flaubert
Janos Korban and Stefanie Flaubert

BORN: Janos Korban, 13 April 1961, Port Augusta, SA, Australia; Stefanie Flaubert, 13 December 1965, London, moved to Australia 1966 **CONTACT:** korban/flaubert; 8/8–10 Burrows Road Alexandria, NSW, 2044; info@korbanflaubert.com.au; www.korbanflaubert.com.au **EDUCATION/TRAINING:** Janos Korban, Bachelor of Arts, 1988, University of Adelaide; Stefanie Flaubert, Bachelor of Architecture (Honours), 1988, University of Adelaide **SELECTED EXHIBITIONS:** 2005 *Adventure*, Object Gallery, Sydney; 2003, 2005 Milan International Furniture Fair, *Salone Satellite,* Milan; 2004 *Tyranny of Distance,* Tokyo Designers Block, Australian Embassy, Tokyo; 2003 *Sway With Me,* London; Designers Block, Selfridges, London; 2002 *Mood River,* Wexner Center for the Arts, Columbus, Ohio **SELECTED BIBLIOGRAPHY:** 2006 *Transmaterial,* Blaine Brownell (ed.), Princeton Architectural Press, New York; 2005 *Young Asian Designers,* Joachim Fischer, Fusion Publishing, Cologne; 2005 *Studio: Design at Work,* Donald Williams, McGraw Hill, Melbourne; 2005 'Tangled in light', *Frame* Magazine, Issue 47, Netherlands; 2005 'Korban/Flaubert and the adventure laboratory', *Object* Magazine, Issue 46, Sydney **SELECTED COLLECTIONS:** Pinakothek der Moderne, Munich; Powerhouse Museum, Sydney

Stefan Lie

BORN: 23 August 1968, Sydney, Australia
CONTACT: Stefan Lie Design Studio; PO Box 7466 Bondi Beach, NSW, 2026; stefan@stefan-lie.com; www.stefan-lie.com ■ **EDUCATION/TRAINING:** Bachelor of Industrial Design (Honours), 1997, University of Technology, Sydney ■ **SELECTED EXHIBITIONS:** 2005 *workshopped 05,* Strand Arcade, Sydney; 2005 *Work in Progress,* ACUDE, Sydney; 2004 *Sydney Style,* Object Gallery, Sydney Opera House, Sydney; 2003 *No Dust Ring,* Plimsoll Gallery, Hobart; 2003 *workshopped 03,* Strand Arcade, Sydney ■ **SELECTED BIBLIOGRAPHY:** 2005 *Vogue Living,* September/October, Sydney; 2005 *Vogue Living,* March/April, Sydney; 2005 'Good blings', *Sunday Telegraph Magazine,* 20 February, Sydney; 2004 'On the Verge'*: Stefan Lie, Sunday Telegraph Magazine,* 10 October, Sydney; 2004 *Wallpaper* Navigator* 02, October ■ **SELECTED COLLECTIONS:** Powerhouse Museum, Sydney ■ **SELECTED STOCKISTS:** de de ce, Sydney, Melbourne, Brisbane; Poepke, Sydney; Chiodo, Melbourne; moochi, Auckland

Simone LeAmon

BORN: 16 April 1971, Melbourne, Australia ■
CONTACT: O.S Initiative; PO Box 12485 A'Beckett Street Melbourne, VIC, 8006; simone@osinitiative.com; www.osinitiative.com ■ **EDUCATION/TRAINING:** Master of Design, School of Architecture and Design, 2004, RMIT University; Bachelor of Fine Art, 1992, Victorian College of the Arts, University of Melbourne; Advanced Certificate of Art and Design, 1989, Box Hill Institute of TAFE, Melbourne ■ **SELECTED EXHIBITIONS:** 2005 *Anytime Soon. Australia,* 1000 Eventi, Milan; 2005 *Beyond Fashion,* Australian National Wool Museum, Geelong, Victoria; 2004 Australian Digital Design Biennale, Melbourne Museum, Melbourne; 2003 *Quiet Collision,* Via Farini Gallery, Milan; 2003 *MOTO Showroom,* Gertrude Contemporary Art Spaces, Melbourne ■ **SELECTED BIBLIOGRAPHY:** 2006 'Forms of desire and comfort', Belinda Stenning, *CURVE,* Issue 14, Melbourne; 2006 'It's only the beginning', Stephen Crafti, *Indesign,* Issue 25, Sydney; 2005 'Profile', Din Heagney, *Desktop,* Issue 203, Melbourne; 2004 'Moto design', Patrizia Coggiola, *Mood,* Issue 59, Milan; 2003 'Get your motor running', Ashley Crawford, *The Age,* 30 August, Melbourne

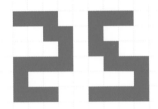

Alexander Lotersztain

BORN: 8 October 1977, Buenos Aires, Argentina, moved to Australia 1998 **CONTACT:** Alexander Lotersztain Studio; PO Box 3662 South Brisbane, QLD, 4101; info@derlot.com; www.derlot.com **EDUCATION/TRAINING:** Bachelor of Design (Industrial Design), 2000, Queensland College of Art, Griffith University **SELECTED EXHIBITIONS:** 2005 *Coral light + sound,* Space Furniture, Brisbane; 2005 *Plastic Fantastic,* Craft Queensland, Brisbane; 2004 *Sputnik Travel 'Sputniks',* Tokyo; 2003 Sputnik Hotel, Tokyo; 2003 *Hall 03,* Popcork, Milan **SELECTED BIBLIOGRAPHY:** 2006 'Success Alexander Lotersztain', *MAP*, Design Issue, February, Australia; 2006 'Australian design', *Vogue Living*, March/April, Sydney; 2005 'Satellite out of Africa', *Indesign,* Issue 20, Sydney; 2003 'Where is my space age', Sean Topham, *Prestel,* United Kingdom; 2001 'Japan design to the new generation', Akari Matsuura, Gap Publication Co., Japan **SELECTED COLLECTIONS:** Soft Sofa, Japan; Idée, Tokyo; Pompidou Museum, Paris **SELECTED STOCKISTS:** Idee, Tokyo; Sputnik, Tokyo; Artquitect, Barcelona; Street and Garden Furniture Company, Brisbane; InAfrica Community Foundation, IACF, Brisbane-Swaziland

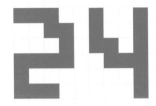

Khai Liew

BORN: 5 December 1952, Kuala Lumpur, moved to Australia 1971 **CONTACT:** Khai Liew Design; 166 Magill Road Norwood, SA, 5067; enquiries@ khailiew.com.au; www.khailiewdesign.com.au **EDUCATION/TRAINING:** Self taught **SELECTED EXHIBITIONS:** 2006 Collect, Victoria & Albert Museum, London; 2003 *20th Century Style: Furniture,* Art Gallery of South Australia, Adelaide; 2001 *(X)po[sit]ion,* Museum of South Australia, Adelaide; 2001 *Long Weekend,* JamFactory, Adelaide; 1999 *Innerspace,* JamFactory, Adelaide **SELECTED BIBLIOGRAPHY:** 2006 *Collect*, British Crafts Council, London; 2005 'Joss sticks and rosary beads', Wendy Walker, *Indesign*, Issue 22, Sydney; 2002 'Something for the weekend?', Albert Hill, *Wallpaper* Magazine, Issue 47, London; 2001 'Inspired simplicity', Wendy Walker, *Object* Magazine, Issue 3/01, Sydney **SELECTED COLLECTIONS:** Art Gallery of South Australia, Adelaide **SELECTED STOCKISTS:** Khai Liew Design, Adelaide

Maningrida Arts & Culture

CONTACT: Maningrida Arts & Culture; PMB 102 Winnellie, NT, 0821; info@maningrida.com; www.maningrida.com

Elsie Marmanga
Maningrida Arts & Culture

BORN: 1960 (Language Group Burarra) **SELECTED EXHIBITIONS:** 2003 *Threads of Time,* Burrinja Gallery, Upwey, Victoria; 2002 *Wild Nature in Contemporary Australian Art and Craft,* JamFactory, Adelaide; 2001 *Art on a String: Threaded objects from the Central Desert and Arnhem Land,* Object Gallery, Sydney, toured nationally **SELECTED BIBLIOGRAPHY:** 2001 *Art on a String: Threaded objects from the Central Desert and Arnhem Land,* L. Hamby and D. Young, Object: Australian Centre for Craft and Design, Sydney and Centre for Cross-Cultural Research, Canberra **SELECTED COLLECTIONS:** Museum Victoria, Melbourne

Mabel Mayangal
Maningrida Arts & Culture

BORN: 1945 (Language Group Burarra) **SELECTED EXHIBITIONS:** 2003 *Maningrida Threads,* Museum of Contemporary Art, Sydney; 1998 *Interwoven: Fibre art from Australia and the Pacific,* Flinders Art Museum, Campus Gallery, The Flinders University of South Australia, Adelaide; 1995–97 *Crossing Border: Contemporary Australian textile art,* Kemper Museum of Contemporary Art and Design, Kansas City; 1995 *Maningrida: The language of weaving,* A.E.T.A touring exhibition throughout Australia and New Zealand **SELECTED BIBLIOGRAPHY:** 1998 *Origins and New Perspectives: Contemporary Australian textiles,* G.K. Lawrence, D. Mellor, Queen Victoria Museum and Art Gallery and Craft Australia, Launceston; 2001 *MCA Unpacked,* Museum of Contemporary Art, Sydney; 1995 *Crossing Borders: Contemporary Australian textile art,* S. Rowley and C. Leitch, University of Wollongong, Wollongong **SELECTED COLLECTIONS:** Flinders Art Museum, Adelaide; Museum of Contemporary Art, Sydney; Museum Victoria, Melbourne

Lorna Jin-gubarrangunyja
Maningrida Arts & Culture

BORN: 1952 (Language Group Burarra – Martay) **SELECTED EXHIBITIONS:** 2004 *Divas of the Desert: Maningrida, Minymaku,* Gallery Gondwana, Alice Springs; 2003 *20th Telstra National Aboriginal and Torres Strait Islander Art Award,* Museum and Art Gallery of Northern Territory, Darwin; 2003 *Maningrida Threads,* Museum of Contemporary Art, Sydney; 1995 *Maningrida: The language of weaving,* A.E.T.A touring exhibition throughout Australia and New Zealand **SELECTED BIBLIOGRAPHY:** 1995 *Maningrida: The language of weaving,* M. Carew, M.K.C. West, Australian Exhibition Touring Agency, Maningrida Arts & Culture and Museum and Art Gallery of Northern Territory, South Melbourne **SELECTED COLLECTIONS:** Museum Victoria, Melbourne; Myer Foundation, Melbourne; Queensland Art Gallery, Brisbane

Nellie Nambayana
Maningrida Arts & Culture

BORN: 1934 (Language Group Burarra – Martay)
SELECTED EXHIBITIONS: 2005 *Fibreforms,* Grantpirrie
Gallery, Sydney; 2004 *Bark Paintings, Carvings and
Fibre Works from Maningrida,* Hogarth Galleries,
Sydney; 2002 *Fibre: An exhibition of woven art,* Raft
artspace, Darwin; 1995 *Maningrida: The language of
weaving,* A.E.T.A touring exhibition throughout Australia
and New Zealand **SELECTED BIBLIOGRAPHY:**
1995 *Maningrida: The language of weaving,* M. Carew,
M.K.C. West, Australian Exhibition Touring Agency,
Maningrida Arts & Culture and Museum and Art Gallery
of Northern Territory, South Melbourne; 1996 *Women
Hold Up Half the Sky,* Monash University Gallery,
Melbourne **SELECTED COLLECTIONS:** Helen Read
Collection, Darwin

Agnes Djunguwana
Maningrida Arts & Culture

BORN: 1945 (Language Group Na-Kara) **SELECTED
EXHIBITIONS:** 2004 *Contexture,* Framed Gallery, Darwin;
2004 *Fibre and Sculptures,* Indigenart, Freemantle; 2002
Maningrida Fibre, Redback Art Gallery, Queensland

Alice Djulman Dalman
Maningrida Arts & Culture

BORN: 1955 (Language Group Rembarrnga)

Marc Pascal

BORN: 11 May 1959, Melbourne, Australia
CONTACT: Marc Pascal; 73 Newman Street
Thornbury, VIC, 3071; info@marcpascal.com;
www.marcpascal.com **EDUCATION/TRAINING:**
Bachelor of Industrial Design, 1991, RMIT University;
Bachelor of Fine Art (Painting and Printmaking),
1981, Victorian College of the Arts **SELECTED
EXHIBITIONS:** 2005 *Anytime Soon. Australia,* 1000
Eventi, Via Farini Gallery, Milan; 2003 Tokyo Designers
Block, Spiral Gallery, Tokyo; 2002 *Glow,* Object
Gallery, Sydney; 2000 *Designing Minds,* Object Gallery,
Sydney; 1998 *Objects for Dynamic Living,* Craft
Victoria, Melbourne **SELECTED BIBLIOGRAPHY:**
2002 *Request, Response, Reaction: the designers
of Australia and New Zealand,* Stephen Crafti, Images
Publishing, Melbourne; 2000 *Ripe: New design in
Australia,* Steven Cornwell, Craftsman House, Sydney;
2000 *Humanism & Materialism,* Anu Kumar, *Art 4D,*
December/January, Bangkok; 2000 *Designing Minds,*
Object: Australian Centre for Craft and Design, Sydney
SELECTED COLLECTIONS: Lisbon Design
Museum, Lisbon; Queensland Institute of Technology,
Rockhampton; RMIT University, Melbourne
SELECTED STOCKISTS: Object Store, Sydney;
RG Madden, Melbourne; Deka, Brisbane; Apartmento,
Wellington, Auckland; Air, Singapore

Preston Zly

Johanna Preston and Petr Zly

BORN: Johanna Preston, 8 October 1967, Melbourne, Victoria; Petr Zly, 3 August 1961, Czech Republic, moved to Australia 1968 **CONTACT:** Preston Zly Design; Rear 219 Smith Street Fitzroy, VIC, 3065; info@prestonzlydesign.com; www.prestonzlydesign.com **EDUCATION/TRAINING:** Johanna Preston, Certificate of Orthopaedic and Bespoke Footwear, 1993, Pascoe Vale TAFE (now RMIT); Intensive training with Bulgarian Master Shoemaker, 1992–94, Adelaide; Petr Zly, Bachelor of Arts (Fine Art, Sculpture), 1987, Phillip Institute of Technology (now RMIT) **SELECTED EXHIBITIONS:** 2005 *Timber,* de de ce, Melbourne; 2004 *Gang of Five,* Paris; 2003 *w6rds,* State Library of Victoria, Melbourne; 2003 *Top to Toe,* Ian Potter Centre, National Gallery of Victoria, Melbourne; 2002 *Twister,* Ian Potter Centre, National Gallery of Victoria, Melbourne **SELECTED BIBLIOGRAPHY:** 2005 'Hands on', Edwina Preston, *State of the Arts,* July/August, Sydney; 2005 *Harper's Bazaar,* April, Sydney; 2004 *123, The Art of Counting,* National Gallery of Victoria, Melbourne; 2004 Dewi Cooke, *The Age,* 6 September, Melbourne; 2003 *Top to Toe,* National Gallery of Victoria, Melbourne **SELECTED COLLECTIONS:** National Gallery of Victoria, Melbourne **SELECTED STOCKISTS:** Bitchinslacks, London; Kelly's Closet, Atlanta; Montage, Brighton, Melbourne; Paper Doll, Melbourne; Ricarda, Albany

Nick Rennie

BORN: 23 November 1974, Bougainville, Papua New Guinea, moved to Australia 1976 **CONTACT:** happy finish design; 21 Hillcrest Avenue Kew, VIC, 3101; nick@happyfinishdesign.com; www.happyfinishdesign.com **EDUCATION/TRAINING:** Bachelor of Industrial Design, 1999, RMIT University **SELECTED EXHIBITIONS:** 2004 *100% Design London,* 2004 design boom, London; 2004 *Tyranny of Distance,* Tokyo Designers Block, Tokyo; 2002–04 *happy finish design, Salone Satelite,* Milan International Furniture Fair, Milan; 2002 *Hybrid Objects,* Australian Embassy, Tokyo Designers Block, Tokyo, Melbourne Museum, Melbourne; 2000 Milan International Furniture Fair *Salone Satellite*, RMIT, Melbourne **SELECTED BIBLIOGRAPHY:** 2004 *Wallpaper* Magazine, London; 2004 *Abitare* Magazine, Issue 441, Milan; 2004 *SDQ,* Issue 14, Sydney; 2003 *International Design Yearbook 2003,* Bradford, UK; 2002 *Intramuros,* 102 September, Paris **SELECTED STOCKISTS:** Zoo design and fine art, Melbourne

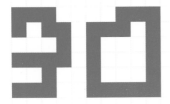

Jennifer Robertson

BORN: 5 April 1962, Somerset, England, moved to Australia 1986 ■ **CONTACT:** Jennifer Robertson; 2 Shannon Circuit Kaleen, ACT, 2617; jennifer.robertson@anu.edu.au; www.anu.edu.au/ITA/CSA/textiles ■ **EDUCATION/TRAINING:** Bachelor of Arts (Honours – Woven Textiles), 1984, West Surrey College of Art and Design, Farnham, Surrey, United Kingdom; Postgraduate Studies, 1985, Royal College of Art, London ■ **SELECTED EXHIBITIONS:** 2004 *Miniartextil,* Como, Montrouge, Nule; 2004 *Collect,* Victoria & Albert Museum, London; 2004 *Tripleweave,* Craft ACT, Livingstone Studio, London; 2002 *Australian Craft,* Mokkumto Gallery, Seoul; 1997 and 1994 – *4th and 5th International Textile Competition,* Kyoto ■ **SELECTED BIBLIOGRAPHY:** 2002 'Jennifer Robertson's textiles', *Craft Arts International,* Oct/Nov, Sydney; 2001 'Weaving in Binary: Digital technology in Jennifer Robertson's double cloth', *Fiberarts,* Dec/Jan, Asheville, NC, United States of America; 1997 *Masters of Their Craft,* Noris Ioannou, Craftsman House, Melbourne; 1991 *International Crafts,* Martina Margetts, Thames and Hudson, Melbourne; 1989 'Divine inspiration', *Interior Architecture and Design,* Issue 21, YPMA, Sydney ■ **SELECTED COLLECTIONS:** National Gallery of Australia, Canberra; Art Gallery of Western Australia, Perth; Art Gallery of South Australia, Adelaide; Renwick Alliance, Smithsonian Institute; the Surrey Institute of Art and Design University College ■ **SELECTED STOCKISTS:** Livingstone Studio, London; NUNO Corporation, Tokyo; Object Store, Sydney; Beaver Galleries, Canberra; Craft Victoria, Melbourne

S!X
Denise Sprynskyj and Peter Boyd

BORN: Denise Sprynskyj, 11 September 1960, Warragul, Victoria; Peter Boyd, 28 December 1971, Mornington, Victoria ■ **CONTACT:** S!X; 41 A'Beckett Street Melbourne, VIC, 3000; denise.sprynskyj@rmit.edu.au ■ **EDUCATION/TRAINING:** Denise Sprynskyj, Masters of Fashion, 2000, RMIT University; Bachelor of Fashion, 1992, RMIT University; Peter Boyd, Bachelor of Design, 1992, RMIT University ■ **SELECTED EXHIBITIONS:** 2005 *Textile Wearables,* Fusion Gallery, Tokyo; 2004–06 *A matter of time,* Tamworth Textile Biennale, Tamworth, then toured nationally; 2002 *Recent Acquisitions,* National Gallery of Australia, Canberra; 2002 *Sourcing the Muse,* Powerhouse Museum, Sydney; 2001 *Cycle of Decomposition,* Creation Baumann, Paris and Melbourne ■ **SELECTED BIBLIOGRAPHY:** 2004 *The Design Issue, State of the Arts,* Stephen Crafti, July – September, Sydney; 2003 'Eve of deconstuction', Robert Mckenzie, *SLAVE,* Issue 1, Melbourne; 1999 Tokyo *Vogue,* Margot Riley, Griffiths University, Queensland; 1998 *Catwalk The Designer Collections Mercedes Australian Fashion Week,* Debbie Coffey (ed.), Sydney; 1997 'Spring flowers and summer shows', Jim Logan, *Object* Magazine, Issue 4/97 Sydney ■ **SELECTED COLLECTIONS:** Powerhouse Museum, Sydney; National Gallery of Australia, Canberra; National Gallery of Victoria, Melbourne; Hobart City Gallery, Hobart ■ **SELECTED STOCKISTS:** Milly Sleeping, Melbourne; Blondies, Melbourne; Embellish, New Zealand; Strelitzia, Sydney; Felt, Singapore

Marc Schamburg
Schamburg + Alvisse

BORN: 15 October 1965, Southport, Queensland
CONTACT: Schamburg + Alvisse; Level 1,
116 Kippax Street Surry Hills, NSW, 2010;
m.schamburg@schamburgalvisse.com.au;
www.schamburgalvisse.com.au **EDUCATION/
TRAINING:** Bachelor of Arts Design (Interiors),
1987, University of Technology, Sydney
SELECTED EXHIBITIONS: 2005 *The New
Fluidity in Design,* San José Museum of Art, San
Francisco; 2001 *Eco-Logic,* Powerhouse Museum,
Sydney; 2000 *Olympic Arts Festival,* Object Gallery,
Sydney; 2000 *Salone Satellite,* Milan International
Furniture Fair, Milan; 1999 *4+1,* Powerhouse
Museum, Sydney **SELECTED BIBLIOGRAPHY:**
2005 'SPWY', *ID* Magazine; 2005 'Blobjects +
Beyond', S + M Holt-Skov; 2001 'Idées lumineuses',
French *Vogue,* October, France; 2001 *Designing
the 21st Century,* Taschen Books, Köln; 2000
'Profile: Schamburg + Alvisse', *Elle Décor,* June;
1999 'Golden years', *Wallpaper,* July/August,
London **SELECTED COLLECTIONS:** Powerhouse
Museum, Sydney **SELECTED STOCKISTS:**
Schamburg + Alvisse, Sydney

Michael Alvisse
Schamburg + Alvisse

BORN: 11 September 1963, Singapore, Malaysia,
moved to Australia 1970 **CONTACT:** Schamburg
+ Alvisse; Level 1, 116 Kippax Street Surry Hills,
NSW, 2010; m.alvisse@schamburgalvisse.com.au;
www.schamburgalvisse.com.au **EDUCATION/
TRAINING:** Bachelor of Arts (Architecture), 1985, Curtin
University **SELECTED EXHIBITIONS:** 2005 *The
New Fluidity in Design,* San José Museum of Art,
San Francisco; 2001 *Eco-Logic,* Powerhouse Museum,
Sydney; 2000 *Olympic Arts Festival,* Object Gallery,
Sydney; 2000 *Salone Satellite,* Milan International
Furniture Fair, Milan; 1999 *4+1,* Powerhouse Museum,
Sydney **SELECTED BIBLIOGRAPHY:** 2005 'SPWY',
ID Magazine; 2005 'Blobjects + Beyond', S + M
Holt-Skov; 2001 'Idées lumineuses', French *Vogue,*
October, France; 2001 *Designing the 21st Century,*
Taschen Books, Köln; 2000 'Profile: Schamburg
+ Alvisse', *Elle Décor,* June; 1999 'Golden Years',
Wallpaper, July/August, London **SELECTED
COLLECTIONS:** Powerhouse Museum, Sydney
SELECTED STOCKISTS: Schamburg + Alvisse, Sydney

Oliver Smith

BORN: 10 March 1974, Sydney, Australia **CONTACT:** Oliver Smith; GPO Box 2066 Canberra, ACT, 2601; info@oliversmith.com.au; www.oliversmith.com.au **EDUCATION/TRAINING:** Master of Philosophy, Gold & Silversmithing Workshop, 2003, National Institute of the Arts; Gold & Silversmithing Workshop (Honours), 2000, National Institute of the Arts; Bachelor of Visual Arts (Jewellery & Object Design), 1995, Sydney College of the Arts **SELECTED EXHIBITIONS:** 2005 *Banquet: A collaboration,* part of Art Gallery of South Australia's 'An Artful Feast', Adelaide; 2004 *Oliver Smith Product Launch: The best of craft and industry,* Craft ACT, Canberra; 2004 14th Silver Triennial, Deutsches Goldschmiedehaus Hanau, Hanau/Solingen/Chemnitz/ Gottingen, Kolding, Schoonhoven, Antwerpen; 2002 *Defining the Object IV,* Quadrivium Gallery, Sydney; 2001 *new design 2001,* Object Gallery, Sydney **SELECTED BIBLIOGRAPHY:** 2006 'Sharp cheese – F!NK Fatware', *Gourmet Traveller,* February, Sydney; 2006 'Cool metal hot shop', *Monument,* December/ January, Melbourne; 2006 'F!NK & Co. new releases – Oliver Smith Fatware Knives', *Object* Magazine, Issue 48, Sydney; 2005 'Food for thought – Ilia serving utensils', *Vogue Living,* November/December, Sydney; 2005 'In my mind's eye – Oliver Smith: Silversmith', *Artlook,* June, Canberra **SELECTED COLLECTIONS:** Government House, Canberra; Admiralty House, Sydney **SELECTED STOCKISTS:** National Gallery of Australia, Canberra; Metalab, Sydney; All Hand Made Gallery, Sydney; Object Store, Sydney

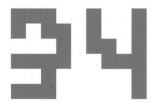

Brian Steendyk

BORN: 4 June 1970, Brisbane, Australia **CONTACT:** Steendyk; 27 Isaac Street Spring Hill, QLD, 4000; contact@steendyk.com; www.steendyk.com **EDUCATION/TRAINING:** Bachelor of Architecture, 1993, Queensland University of Technology; Masters of Architecture, 1996, Illinois Institute of Technology, Chicago **SELECTED EXHIBITIONS:** 2005 *Inspired! Design Across Time,* Powerhouse Museum, Sydney; 2004 *State of Design Festival,* Melbourne Museum, Melbourne; 2004 *40 Degrees*, Stilwerks, Berlin, Germany; 2003–04 *Salone Satellite*, Milan International Furniture Fair, Milan, Italy; 2003–04 *Australian Style,* Tokyo Designers Block, Australian Embassy, Tokyo, Japan **SELECTED BIBLIOGRAPHY:** 2006 'Profiles – Brian Steendyk', *ARC Art, Design & Craft Biennial,* Artworkers Alliance, Brisbane; 2005 'Steendyk', *Tabypet* Magazine, 5'2005 (65), Russia; 2004 'Brian Steendyk – A reason to design', *Indesign* Magazine, Vol.19, Sydney; 2003 'Design dream', *Casa Vogue,* number 15, Italy; 2003 *Australian Design Awards,* Standards Australia, Sydney **SELECTED COLLECTIONS:** Powerhouse Museum, Sydney **SELECTED STOCKISTS:** Space Furniture, Brisbane, Sydney, Melbourne; Stilwerks, Berlin; Printemps, Paris

Tiwi Design

Established 1969 ■ **CONTACT:** Tiwi Design; PMB 59 Nguiu via Winnellie, NT, 0822; tiwides@octa4.net.au; www.tiwiart.com

Jock Puautjimi
Tiwi Design

BORN: 27 November 1962 (Skin Group Wantarringa) ■ **SELECTED EXHIBITIONS:** 2004 *Yikwani – Fire*, Alcaston Gallery, Melbourne; 2002 *Yikwani*, National Gallery of Victoria, Melbourne, toured to regional Victoria and Sydney; 2000 *Tiwi Dreaming*, Taos, New Mexico; 2000 *Tiwi 2000*, Gallery Gondwana, Alice Springs; 1990 *Solo exhibition, Shades of Ochre*, Darwin ■ **SELECTED COLLECTIONS:** Museum and Art Gallery of the Northern Territory, Darwin; Queensland Art Gallery, Brisbane; Art Gallery of South Australia, Adelaide

Maria Josette Orsto
Tiwi Design

BORN: 30 October 1962 (Skin Group Japajapunga) ■ **SELECTED EXHIBITIONS:** 2003 *20th Telstra National Aboriginal and Torres Strait Islander Art Award*, Museum and Art Gallery of the Northern Territory; 2002 *Kiripuranji*, National Art Bank, toured Australian embassies on four continents; 2000 *Tiwi Dreaming*, Taos, New Mexico; 1997 *Tiwi Art*, Museum of Contemporary Art, Sydney; 1993 *Mamunukuwi Jilarmara, Tiwi Women's Art*, Drill Hall Gallery, National Gallery of Australia, Canberra ■ **SELECTED COLLECTIONS:** National Gallery of Australia, Canberra; Queensland Art Gallery, Brisbane

Jean Baptiste Apuatimi
Tiwi Design

BORN: c.1940 (Skin Group Tapatapunga) ■ **SELECTED EXHIBITIONS:** 2006 *Makatingari*, solo exhibition, Aboriginal and Pacific Art Gallery, Sydney; 2002 *19th Telstra National Aboriginal and Torres Strait Islander Art Award*, Museum and Art Gallery of the Northern Territory; 2001 *Islands in the Sun*, National Gallery of Australia, Canberra; 2000 *Tiwi Dreaming*, Taos, New Mexico; 1994 *Power of the Land, Masterpieces of Aboriginal Art*, National Gallery of Victoria, Melbourne ■ **SELECTED COLLECTIONS:** National Gallery of Australia, Canberra; Art Gallery sof South Australia, Adelaide; Museum Victoria, Melbourne; National Gallery of Victoria, Melbourne; Museum and Art Gallery of the Northern Territory, Darwin ■ **SELECTED BIBLIOGRAPHY:** 1994 *Art of the Tiwi from the Collection of the National Gallery of Victoria*, National Gallery of Victoria, Melbourne; 1993 'Narrative and Decoration in Tiwi Painting: Tiwi representations of Purukuparli Story', J. Bennet, *Art Bulletin of Victoria*, 33, Melbourne; 1993 *The Body Tiwi Aboriginal Art from Bathurst and Melville Islands*, the University Gallery, University of Tasmania, Launceston

Osmond Kantilla
Tiwi Design

BORN: 27 June 1966 (Skin Group Stone)
SELECTED EXHIBITIONS: 2002 *19th Telstra National Aboriginal and Torres Strait Islander Art ward*, Museum and Art Gallery of the Northern Territory, Darwin; 2002 *Material Thing Fabric and Textiles Exhibition,* Boomalli Aboriginal Artists' Cooperative, Sydney; 2000 *Tiwi Textiles – Translating Tradition,* London Printworks Trust, London; 1999 *Collection of screen-printing,* Framed Gallery, Darwin **SELECTED COLLECTIONS:** Powerhouse Museum, Sydney; University of Wollongong, NSW; Art Gallery of South Australia, Adelaide; Queensland University of Technology, Brisbane; Northern Territory University, Darwin

Bede Tungatalum
Tiwi Design

BORN: 1952 (Skin Group Yarinapinila) **SELECTED EXHIBITIONS:** 2003 *20th Telstra National Aboriginal and Torres Strait Islander Art Award,* Museum and Art Gallery of the Northern Territory, Darwin; 2001 *Islands in the Sun,* National Gallery of Australia, Canberra; 2000 *Telstra Indigenous Art Award,* Museum and Art Gallery of the Northern Territory, Darwin; 2000 *Fremantle Print Art Award* (1st Prize), Fremantle Arts Centre, WA; 2000 *Tiwi 2000,* Gallery Gondwana, Alice Springs

Prue Venables

BORN: 27 February 1954, Newcastle Upon Tyne, moved to Australia 1956 **CONTACT:** 27 Orchard Crescent Mont Albert North, VIC, 3129; prueven@melbpc.org.au **EDUCATION/TRAINING:** Masters Fine Art (Ceramics), 1995, RMIT University; Acset 1 – Teacher Training, 1988, ILEA, London; Harrow Diploma of Studio Pottery, 1983, Harrow College of Art, London; Bachelor of Science (Honours – Zoology), 1974, Melbourne University **SELECTED EXHIBITIONS:** 2006 Collect, Victoria & Albert Museum, London; 2005 *Prue Venables,* Rex Irwin Fine Art, Sydney; 2005 *Prue Venables,* Besson Gallery, London; 2005 *Table Manners Contemporary International Ceramics,* Crafts Council, London; 2002 *Prue Venables,* Nancy Margolis Gallery, New York **SELECTED BIBLIOGRAPHY:** 2004 *Contemporary Porcelain,* Peter Lane, Craftsman House, London; 2000 *Functional Pottery,* Robin Hopper, Krause Publishing, Iola. WI, USA; 1999 *Design Sourcebook: Ceramics,* Edmund de Waal, New Holland, London; 1997 *Masters of Their Craft,* Noris Ioannou, Craftsman House, London; 2004 *Shards: Garth Clark on Ceramic Art,* Garth Clark, Ceramic Arts Foundation, New York **SELECTED COLLECTIONS:** Shepparton Art Gallery, Victoria; Powerhouse Museum, Sydney; National Gallery of Australia, Canberra; National Gallery of Victoria, Melbourne; National Museum, Auckland **SELECTED STOCKISTS:** Rex Irwin Fine Art, Sydney; Besson Gallery, London; Christine Abrahams Gallery, Melbourne; Beaver Galleries, Canberra; Barret Marsden Gallery, London

Charles Wilson

BORN: 19 April 1968, Forbes, NSW, Australia
CONTACT: 5/5 Springfield Avenue Potts Point, NSW,
2011; c.s.w@bigpond.com; www.woodmark.com.au
EDUCATION/TRAINING: Industrial Design, 1991,
University of Technology, Sydney **SELECTED
EXHIBITIONS:** 2004 *40 Degrees*, Stilwerk, Berlin; 2004
Tyranny of Distance, Tokyo Designers Block, Tokyo;
2005 *LaunchPad,* source 490, Sydney; 2004–05
Bombay Sapphire Design Discovery Award, Space
Furniture, Sydney, Melbourne **SELECTED
BIBLIOGRAPHY:** 2002 'Profile, Charles Wilson',
Artichoke, Issue 2, Melbourne; 2005 'The soft sell',
Vogue Living, Sydney; 2005 'Pheonix rising', *SDQ,*
Issue 19, Sydney **SELECTED COLLECTIONS:**
Powerhouse Museum, Sydney; National Portrait Gallery,
Canberra; Sherman Galleries, Sydney **SELECTED
STOCKISTS:** Living Edge, Sydney, Melbourne; Fuse,
Brisbane; Co-Design, Adelaide; Design Farm, Perth;
Katalog, Auckland; BW, Hong Kong

Vixen

Georgia Chapman

BORN: 13 February 1970, Melbourne, Australia
CONTACT: Vixen; 121 Victoria Street Fitzroy, VIC,
3065; info@vixenaustralia.com; www.vixenaustralia.com
EDUCATION/TRAINING: Bachelor of Art (Textile
Design), 1990, RMIT University **SELECTED
EXHIBITIONS:** 1999 *Seppelt Contemporary Art
Award,* Museum of Contemporary Art, Sydney; 2000
Repetition: Vixen Australia reworked retrospective,
Craft Victoria, Melbourne; 2001 *Foundations Of Gold,*
RMIT University Storey Hall, Melbourne, Mumbai,
Osaka, Seoul, Manila, Singapore; 2002 *Sourcing
the Muse,* Powerhouse Museum Sydney; 2003
*The Cecily and Colin Rigg Comtemporary Design
Award,* Ian Potter Centre, National Gallery of Victoria,
Melbourne **SELECTED COLLECTIONS:** National
Gallery of Victoria, Melbourne; Powerhouse Museum,
Sydney **SELECTED STOCKISTS:** Andrea Gold
Studio, Melbourne; Blondies Boutique, Melbourne;
Husk Corporation, Melbourne; Montage, Brighton;
Perugia, Elsternwick

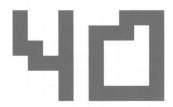

zuii

Alana Di Giacomo and Marcel Sigel

BORN: Marcel Sigel, 23 September 1976, Melbourne, Australia; Alana Di Giacomo, 2 March 1979, Freemantle, WA, Australia  **CONTACT:** zuii; GPO Box 5156 Melbourne, VIC, 3001; marcel@zuii.com; www.zuii.com **EDUCATION/TRAINING:** Marcel Sigel, Bachelor of Arts (Honours – Product Design), 2001, Curtin University of Technology; Alana Di Giacomo, Bachelor of Arts (Visual Communication), 2000, Curtin University of Technology **SELECTED EXHIBITIONS:** 2006 *Somewhere Between,* Object Gallery, Sydney; 2005 *Bombay Sapphire: Sapphire Inspired,* New York; 2004–05 *Salone Satellite,* Milan; 2004 *Sydney Morning Herald Young Designer of the Year,* Powerhouse Museum, Sydney; 2004 *The Edge: Australian International Furniture Fair,* Sydney **SELECTED BIBLIOGRAPHY:** 2005 'Best young designers 2004', *Wallpaper**, January/February, United Kingdom; 2005 'Fresh picked: Antipodean antics', *Surface,* Issue 53, United Stated; 2005 'Zuii – Ology', *CASAinternational*, Issue 31, China; 2005 'La Sinergia Creativa Di Zuii', *Ottagono*, Italy; 2004 'Design atlas: zuii – musical chairs', *Monument,* Issue 62, Melbourne **SELECTED COLLECTIONS:** Alessi Design Museum; Bombay Sapphire

Zimmermann

Nicole and Simone Zimmermann

BORN: Nicole Zimmermann, 18 September 1967, Sydney, Australia; Simone Zimmermann, 7 April 1965, Sydney, Australia **CONTACT:** Zimmermann; 48–56 Epsom Road Zetland, NSW, 2017; simone@zimmermannwear.com; www.zimmermannwear.com **EDUCATION/TRAINING:** Nicole Zimmermann, Fashion Design Diploma, 1993, East Sydney Technical College; Simone Zimmermann, Marketing, 1990, University of Technology, Sydney **SELECTED BIBLIOGRAPHY:** 2005 'Stars with red', *Marie Claire,* June, Sydney; 2005 'A decade of Australian design', *Marie Claire*, September, Sydney; 2005 'Zimmers have NYC in frame', Sarah Grant, *The Daily Telegraph,* 9 August, Sydney; 2005 'Style in the city', *Yen,* February/March, Sydney; 2005 'Designer Babies', *Weekend Australian,* 5 October, Sydney **SELECTED STOCKISTS:** David Jones, nationally; Figleaves, United States, United Kingdom; Harrods, United Kingdom; Victoria's Secret, United States; California Sunshine, United States

Contributor Biographies

Freestyle

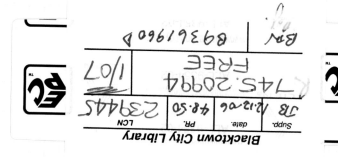

freestyle

NEW AUSTRALIAN DESIGN FOR LIVING

■ **Published by** Object: Australian
Centre for Craft and Design, Sydney
Melbourne Museum, Melbourne

■ **Edited by** Brian Parkes

Contents

First published in Australia in 2006
Published to coincide with the
exhibition, *Freestyle: new Australian
design for living* shown
5 October 2006 – 4 February 2007
at Melbourne Museum, then
10 March – 13 May 2007 at Object
Gallery, Sydney before touring
nationally and internationally.

Co-published by Object:
Australian Centre for Craft and
Design and Melbourne Museum

Object: Australian Centre
for Craft and Design
415 Bourke Street Surry Hills
Sydney NSW 2010 Australia
www.object.com.au

Melbourne Museum
Carlton Gardens Carlton
Melbourne VIC 3001 Australia
www.museum.vic.gov.au

© Object: Australian Centre
for Craft and Design and
Melbourne Museum 2006
© Individual texts by individual
authors 2006

Unless otherwise stated,
all quotes in profile texts
are from interviews between
the designer and author
conducted during the
preparation of this publication.

ISBN 0 9751759 4 7

Editor and Curator: Brian Parkes
(Associate Director, Object)
Project Manager: Juliet Wilson
(Coordinator Exhibitions – Design,
Melbourne Museum)
Project Coordination: Louise Ingram
(General Manager, Object)
Assistant Curator: Annabel Moir
(Assistant Curator, Object)
Copy Editor: Theresa Willsteed
Art Direction and Design:
Frost Design
Portrait Photography:
Anthony Geernaert
Image Management: Ingrid Unger,
Michael Pennell (Melbourne Museum)

Printing: Imago in Thailand

Distributed by Thames & Hudson
Australia Pty Ltd
Portside Business Park
Fishermans Bend VIC 3207
www.thamesandhudson.com

All rights reserved. No part
of this publication may be
reproduced, stored in a retrieval
system or transmitted in any
form or by any means without
the prior permission in writing
of the publishers. Please
forward all enquiries via e-mail
to object@object.com.au

Freestyle: new Australian design for living brings together the work and stories of forty outstanding Australian designers from the fields of furniture, lighting, textiles, homewares, fashion, jewellery and accessories. ■ This publication and the exhibition it accompanies aim to reflect the character, vibrancy and increasing maturity of contemporary design in Australia. ■ Handmade one-off and limited edition design objects are showcased and considered alongside industrially manufactured items and prototypes – reflecting the breadth and nature of design excellence and innovation in Australia. ■ Intriguing aspects of the personality, passion and processes of the individual designers are revealed, and their work is placed within broader personal and cultural contexts. ■ *Freestyle* provides a unique and timely overview of contemporary object design in Australia.

BRIAN PARKES

(curator and editor) has been Associate Director at Object: Australian Centre for Craft and Design since January 2000. He manages Object Gallery's exhibition program and his major curated exhibitions for Object Gallery include *Interiors*, 2001, *Akira Isogawa*, 2002, *Dinosaur Designs*, 2003, *Sydney Style*, 2004 and *Global Local*, 2005 (which toured to the Victoria & Albert Museum, London). He is one of ten curators recently invited by Phaidon Press, London, to contribute to *& fork*, a new book to be published in 2007 profiling 100 emerging product designers from around the world. Parkes is a graduate of the Tasmanian School of Art in Hobart and has a background in both the creative and commercial spheres within museums and galleries, having managed the merchandising and retail operations at the Museum of Contemporary Art, Sydney (1998–2000) and the National Gallery of Australia, Canberra (1995–98).

PAUL MCGILLICK

(essay author) is Editor of the quarterly architecture and design magazine, *Indesign*. Formerly Editor of *Monument*, he has published extensively on architecture, design, and the visual and performing arts. He was chief critic for Visual and Performing Arts for *The Australian Financial Review* (1985–2002) and Series Editor, Producer and Presenter with SBS TV's arts program, *Imagine* (1994–96) which pioneered design and architecture on television. He holds a PhD in drama and a Master of Architecture degree. His books include *Alex Popov: Buildings and Projects* and *Sydney Architecture*.

ROBYN HEALY

(essay author) is a Lecturer and Postgraduate Coordinator (Fashion) in the School of Architecture and Design, RMIT University, Melbourne, where she is completing her PhD on fashion and exhibition culture. She has worked with Australian public collections of fashion and textiles for over 20 years, and has held positions of Senior Curator at the National Gallery of Victoria and the National Gallery of Australia. She has curated over 30 major exhibitions relating to fashion and textiles. In 2002 she was awarded a Federal Government Centenary medal for her contribution to Australian society.

GRACE COCHRANE

(essay author) is a freelance curator and writer and currently the Editor of *Object* Magazine. From 1988–2005, she was Senior Curator of Australian Decorative Arts and Design at the Powerhouse Museum, Sydney. She has written and spoken extensively about the crafts over 30 years, and is the author of *The Crafts Movement in Australia: A history* (1992). In 2001 she received the Australia Council's Visual Arts/Craft Board's Emeritus medal. She was curator of the Powerhouse Museum's permanent exhibition, *Inspired! Design across Time*, 2005, and is working on the exhibition *Smart Work: Design and the handmade*, which will open at the Powerhouse Museum with a symposium in March 2007.

SARAH BOND

(profile author) is Visual Arts Manager at Asialink, the University of Melbourne. Responsible for the management and touring of exhibitions, she is also involved in developing and nurturing professional opportunities for Australian artists, curators and organisations within Asia. Bond has worked in the visual arts, crafts and museum sector for over a decade and was the Exhibition Manager at Craft Victoria for six years, where she developed and managed the exhibition program including works by some of Australia's leading craft practitioners.

MARGIE FRASER

(profile author) writes for some of Australia's leading journals in art, design, architecture and travel. She is currently Brisbane Editor of *Vogue Living* magazine, Contributing Editor to *Indesign* magazine, and a weekly columnist in the *Brisbane News*. She has worked within the arts industry as an advocate, exhibitions coordinator and consultant, and co-authored *Arts Management: A practical guide* with Jennifer Radbourne. She currently serves on the Board of Craft Queensland.

MEREDITH HINCHLIFFE

(profile author) has had a keen interest in visual arts and craft since working at the then Craft Association of the ACT (1979–1986). She has worked at artsACT in the ACT Government and for the National Campaign for the Arts (1996–97). She has also curated exhibitions and regularly writes for the *Canberra Times* and arts magazines, including *Craft Arts International* and *Textile Fibre Arts*. Hinchliffe received an ACT Women's Award in 2000 in recognition of her significant contribution to the ACT community in the arts.

EMILY HOWES

(profile author) is a freelance writer and editor based in Sydney. She completed a Bachelor of Design (Hons) at the University of New South Wales, focusing her studies on ceramics. Having developed a niche as a design writer, she worked at Craft Victoria and Object, coordinating and writing for their respective publications, *Craft Culture* and *Object* Magazine. She regularly contributes to a range of publications in Australia and internationally.

EWAN MCEOIN

(profile author) is Creative Director of Euroluce and works closely with the design industry in Melbourne. He is involved with communicating, writing and editing in the design arena. From 1998 to 2004 he was the Editor of *(inside) Australian Design Review*. A design teacher and critic, McEoin still mentors and teaches on design.

ANNABEL MOIR

(assistant curator and profile author) has been working at Object since 2001. Over the last five years she has gained experience in exhibitions and publishing (for *Object Magazine* and various exhibition catalogues). As Assistant Curator she has been involved in major exhibitions for Object Gallery including *Frost*bite: Graphic ideas by Vince Frost*, 2006 and *Birdsong: Janet Laurence with Ross Gibson*, 2006. Moir holds Bachelor of Arts/Bachelor of Commerce degrees from the University of Sydney.

WENDY WALKER

(profile author) is an Adelaide-based writer, art critic and occasional curator. Throughout 2006 she is the Samstag writer-in-residence at the University of South Australia, conducting research into the lives of Anne and Gordon Samstag for a forthcoming publication. She was the curator in 2006 of Australian Contemporary's *Bare & Beyond* for Collect at London's Victoria & Albert Museum. In 2004, her monograph *Beautiful Games*, on photo-based artist Deborah Paauwe, was published by Wakefield Press.

VINCE FROST

(art director and designer) runs his 25-plus creative studio, Frost Design, Sydney, having relocated from London in 2004. In 1995 he started Frost Design, London, creating award-winning work for clients from The *Independent* newspaper to Nike – working on anything from postage stamps to magazines, identities, TV advertising, on-line and the built environment. He continues to work for a range of international clients, including D&AD's magazine *Ampersand*, as well as Warner Music, Macquarie Bank and Sydney Dance Company. Frost's work was the subject of a retrospective exhibition presented by Object Gallery at the Sydney Opera House in 2006, and is also documented in a 500-page book *Frost*(sorry trees)*.

ANTHONY GEERNAERT

(portrait photographer) studied a Bachelor of Photography (Hons) at the London College of Printing, graduating in 1998. Geernaert specialises in portraiture, art, editorial and commercial photography, working for magazines including, *Monument, Vogue Living, Surface, Viewpoint, Oyster* and *More Space*. He regularly travels around Australia and internationally working on corporate briefs that require a twist in their perspective.

Message from
Senator The Hon. Rod Kemp
Federal Minister for the
Arts and Sport

The *Freestyle: new Australian design for living* exhibition is a showcase of Australian contemporary craft and design. Fashion, furniture, lighting, textiles and more, highlight the innovative and creative diversity of Australian designers. *Freestyle* brings together 40 designers featuring the latest in design ideas and craftsmanship and illustrates the breadth of Australian excellence in design and innovation. The Australian Government is proud to support the *Freestyle* exhibition through its Visions of Australia program. Visions of Australia aims to make high quality exhibitions more accessible to more Australians. Since it began in 1993 Visions of Australia has provided more than $21 million to assist with the development and touring of 540 exhibition projects, which have visited more than 3,500 venues across Australia. More than 68 million people have visited Visions funded exhibitions. Congratulations to the team at Object and Melbourne Museum for putting this exhibition together, especially Object's Associate Director, Brian Parkes, who has curated such an outstanding selection of Australia's most celebrated craftspeople and designers. I am sure visitors to *Freestyle: new Australian design for living* will be delighted by what they see and impressed by the quality and originality of Australian design and manufacture.

Message from
André Haermeyer MP
Minister for Manufacturing
and Export, Victoria

Freestyle: new Australian design for living is a selection of outstanding works by Australian designers focusing on objects for the home and items for the body. The exhibition – a visual and thought-provoking delight for those seeking inspiration in Australian design – will no doubt engender much discussion, and this book is one that will be referred to time and again. ▪ Increasing the accessibility, availability and enjoyment of design, and Victorian design in particular, is an objective that the Victorian Government has been pursuing and realising over the past four years. This is because we know that being a recognised design capital contributes to our community identity as well as to the business and economic achievements of our State. ▪ Further, the Victorian Government recognises that Victorian business and industry must be focused and pro-active in responding to a rapidly changing world economy. Design is a key enabler in achieving this, as the success of the established and emerging designers in this book clearly demonstrates. We are committed to cultivating the design capability of businesses to further develop and maintain Victoria's economic success. ▪ The Victorian Government has worked in partnership with Melbourne Museum since 2003 and a stimulating programme of exhibitions, presentations, workshops and design activities for people of all ages has successfully promoted the value, importance and innovation of Victorian design across our State. ▪ I am delighted that Melbourne Museum and Object Gallery will be presenting this exhibition in Melbourne and Sydney with a view to it touring nationally and internationally. ▪ *Freestyle* reflects the breadth and nature of design excellence in Australia, with handmade one-off and limited edition design objects alongside industrially manufactured items and prototypes. It also imparts a critical overview of contemporary object design in Australia including essays by leading writers in the field. ▪ I hope you will enjoy this extraordinary book. It captures the essence of the exhibition and the approach of Australian designers – free-spirited, distinctive and stylish.

Object and Melbourne Museum
would like to thank

Object: Australian Centre for Craft and Design

One of Australia's most innovative arts organisations, Object passionately supports and promotes design through exhibitions, publications and retail activities. From furniture to fashion, textiles to glass, from the newly discovered to the most established designers, Object showcases the work of hundreds of talented Australians every year. Object presents its acclaimed exhibitions at two prestigious Sydney venues – Object Gallery in Surry Hills, and the Sydney Opera House Exhibition Hall – and beyond. From Sydney to Singapore, Tokyo to London, Object Gallery exhibitions and *Object* Magazine take design across Australia and to over 70 countries around the world. Object also retails the work of hundreds of designers and makers through its retail activity. As a non-profit organisation, Object aims to heighten awareness of outstanding design and promote an appreciation of contemporary visual culture in Australia. Celebrating over 40 years of supporting the design community, Object continues its strong reputation as a dynamic, contemporary and progressive design centre. www.object.com.au

Melbourne Museum

Melbourne Museum is known for its innovative exhibitions and bold architecture, and attracts close to 700,000 visitors a year to the historic Carlton Gardens site. It is one of three dynamic museums operated by Museum Victoria, Australia's largest public museum organisation. Using the latest technology and interpretation methods, Melbourne Museum gives visitors an unforgettable insight into the nature of the culture of Victoria and Australia. It has won awards for excellence in tourism, exhibition development, architecture, marketing, public relations, engineering, filmmaking, multi-media and building construction. Melbourne Museum's *Designed to Inspire* program is the Museum's long-term commitment to offer public recognition of the work of talented emerging and practising designers. The role of the Museum is to increase design literacy in the general public, to broaden national and international awareness of the quality and diversity of contemporary Australian design, and to enhance Victoria as a centre of design excellence. www.museum.vic.gov.au

FREESTYLE PRINCIPAL SUPPORTERS

Principal Sponsor

Victoria
The Place To Be

An Australian Government Initiative

Freestyle is presented as part of the Victorian Government State of Design Initiative.

This project has also been supported by Visions of Australia. Visions of Australia is the Commonwealth Government's national touring exhibitions grant program. It assists with the development or touring of cultural exhibitions across Australia.

FREESTYLE SPONSORS

Media Sponsor

ORGANISATIONAL SUPPORTERS

arts nsw

Australian Government · Australia Council for the Arts

Australian Government · NSW Government · SYDNEY OPERA HOUSE
THE VISUAL ARTS AND CRAFT STRATEGY

This project has been supported through Object's National Exhibitions Strategy funded by the Australia Council.

Object: Australian Centre for Craft and Design is a non-profit organisation supported by the Visual Arts and Craft Strategy, an initiative of the Australian, State and Territory Governments. Object is assisted by the New South Wales Government – Arts NSW, and the Australian Government through the Australia Council, its arts funding and advisory body.

SPECIAL THANKS

Contributors: Grace Cochrane, Robyn Healy, Paul McGillick, Sarah Bond, Margie Fraser, Meredith Hinchliffe, Emily Howes, Ewan McEoin, Wendy Walker, Theresa Willsteed
Frost staff: Vince Frost, Catriona Burgess, Anthony Donovan, Beverley Hall, Bridget Atkinson, Ben Backhouse
Photographer: Anthony Geernaert
Bombay Sapphire: Stephanie Allen, Nicola Dexheimer
Momentum Strategies: Jenny Bonnin
Thames & Hudson: Peter Shaw
Vogue Living: David Clark, Rob Bevan
Cafe Sydney: Jan McKenzie
Video Education Australasia: Tim Power, Mark McAuliffe, Lisa Tancredi
Museum Victoria staff: Dr J. Patrick Greene, Barbara Horn, Robin Hirst, Brett Dunlop, Juliet Wilson, Meredith Trevillion, Andy Greenwood, Luke Simpkin, Dimitra Birthisel, Rose Hiscock, Ingrid Unger, Michael Pennell, John Broomfield, Trevor Mason, Ben Healley, Joe Coleman, Hayley Townsend, Ursula Richens, Fay Valcanis, Jessica Bendell, Emily Wrigglesworth, Mandy Jones, Peter Hunt, Tony Wood, Carolyn Meehan, Lyn Price, Sue Grieve, Melissa Loughnan, Jenni Meaney, Melinda Viksne, Helen Privett, Tim Rolfe, Deb Frost, Cameron Crowley
Object staff: Steven Pozel, Brian Parkes, Louise Ingram, Kathryn Hunyor, Annabel Moir, Kennie Ward, Malcolm Smith, Leanne Amodeo, Harry Richardson, Carolyn Johnstone, Jo Maunsell, Sandra Brown, Christina Neubauer, Jenni Ryall, Gillian Heathcote, Phil Cramley, Elizabeth Kelly, Joanna Lim, Daniel Weisz
Personal thanks: Lesley Jackson, Stephen Goddard, Cas Bennetto, Katie Somerville

Freestyle has also had the support of these dedicated donors: Sharlene Chin, Sarah Gardner and Ginny Green

CHAPTER II.

A Glance at the Ellis Family.

"I wish Charlie would come with that tea," exclaimed Mrs. Ellis, who sat finishing off some work, which had to go home that evening. "I wonder what can keep him so long away. He has been gone over an hour; it surely cannot take him that time to go to Watson's."

"It is a great distance, mother," said Esther Ellis, who was busily plying her needle; "and I don't think he has been quite so long as you suppose."

"Yes; he has been gone a good hour," repeated Mrs. Ellis. "It is now six o'clock, and it wanted three minutes to five when he left. I do hope he won't forget that I told him half black and half green—he is *so* forgetful!" And Mrs. Ellis rubbed her spectacles and looked peevishly out of the window as she concluded.—"Where can he be?" she resumed, looking in the direction in which he might be expected. "Oh, here he comes, and Caddy with him. They have just turned the corner—open the door and let them in."

Esther arose, and on opening the door was almost knocked down by Charlie's abrupt entrance into the apartment, he being rather forcibly shoved in by his sister Caroline, who appeared to be in a high state of indignation.

"Where do you think he was, mother? Where *do* you think I found him?"

"Well, I can't say—I really don't know; in some mischief, I'll be bound."

"He was on the lot playing marbles—and I've had such a

time to get him home. Just look at his knees; they are
worn through. And only think, mother, the tea was lying
on the ground, and might have been carried off, if I had
not happened to come that way. And then he has been
fighting and struggling with me all the way home. See,"
continued she, baring her arm, "just look how he has
scratched me," and as she spoke she held out the injured
member for her mother's inspection.

"Mother," said Charlie, in his justification, "she began
to beat me before all the boys, before I had said a word to
her, and I wasn't going to stand that. She is always storm-
ing at me. She don't give me any peace of my life."

"Oh yes, mother," here interposed Esther; "Cad is too
cross to him. I must say, that he would not be as bad as he
is, if she would only let him alone."

"Esther, please hush now; you have nothing to do with
their quarrels. I'll settle all their differences. You always
take his part whether he be right or wrong. I shall send him
to bed without his tea, and to-morrow I will take his marbles
from him; and if I see his knees showing through his pants
again, I'll put a red patch on them—that's what I'll do.
Now, sir, go to bed, and don't let me hear of you until
morning."

Mr. and Mrs. Ellis were at the head of a highly respectable
and industrious coloured family. They had three children.
Esther, the eldest, was a girl of considerable beauty, and
amiable temper. Caroline, the second child, was plain in
person, and of rather shrewish disposition; she was a most
indefatigable housewife, and was never so happy as when in
possession of a dust or scrubbing brush; she would have
regarded a place where she could have lived in a perpetual
state of house cleaning, as an earthly paradise. Between her
and Master Charlie continued warfare existed, interrupted
only by brief truces brought about by her necessity for his
services as water-carrier. When a service of this character
had been duly rewarded by a slice of bread and preserves, or

some other dainty, hostilities would most probably be recommenced by Charlie's making an inroad upon the newly cleaned floor, and leaving the prints of his muddy boots thereon.

The fact must here be candidly stated, that Charlie was not a tidy boy. He despised mats, and seldom or never wiped his feet on entering the house; he was happiest when he could don his most dilapidated unmentionables, as he could then sit down where he pleased without the fear of his mother before his eyes, and enter upon a game of marbles with his mind perfectly free from all harassing cares growing out of any possible accident to the aforesaid garments, so that he might give that attention to the game that its importance demanded.

He was a bright-faced pretty boy, clever at his lessons, and a favourite both with tutors and scholars. He had withal a thorough boy's fondness for play, and was also characterised by all the thoughtlessness consequent thereon. He possessed a lively, affectionate disposition, and was generally at peace with all the world, his sister Caddy excepted.

Caroline had recovered her breath, and her mind being soothed by the judgment that had been pronounced on Master Charlie, she began to bustle about to prepare tea.

The shining copper tea-kettle was brought from the stove where it had been seething and singing for the last half-hour; then the tea-pot of china received its customary quantity of tea, which was set upon the stove to brew, and carefully placed behind the stove pipe that no accidental touch of the elbow might bring it to destruction. Plates, knives, and tea-cups came rattling forth from the closet; the butter was brought from the place where it had been placed to keep it cool, and a corn-cake was soon smoking on the table, and sending up its seducing odour into the room over-head to which Charlie had been recently banished, causing to that unfortunate young gentleman great physical discomfort.

"Now, mother," said the bustling Caddy, "it's all ready.

Come now and sit down whilst the cake is hot—do put up the sewing, Esther, and come ! "

Neither Esther nor her mother needed much pressing, and they were accordingly soon seated round the table on which their repast was spread.

" Put away a slice of this cake for father," said Mrs. Ellis, " for he won't be home until late ; he is obliged to attend a vestry meeting to-night."

Mrs. Ellis sat for some time sipping the fragrant and refreshing tea. When the contents of two or three cups one after another had disappeared, and sundry slices of corn-bread had been deposited where much corn-bread had been deposited before, she began to think about Charlie, and to imagine that perhaps she had been rather hasty in sending him to bed without his supper.

" What had Charlie to-day in his dinner-basket to take to school with him ? " she inquired of Caddy.

" Why, mother, I put in enough for a wolf ; three or four slices of bread, with as many more of corn-beef, some cheese, one of those little pies, and all that bread-pudding which was left at dinner yesterday—he must have had enough."

" But, mother, you know he always gives away the best part of his dinner," interposed Esther. " He supplies two or three boys with food. There is that dirty Kinch that he is so fond of, who never takes any dinner with him, and depends entirely upon Charlie. He must be hungry ; do let him come down and get his tea, mother ? "

Notwithstanding the observations of Caroline that Esther was just persuading her mother to spoil the boy, that he would be worse than ever, and many other similar predictions, Esther and the tea combined won a signal triumph, and Charlie was called down from the room above, where he had been exchanging telegraphic communications with the before-mentioned Kinch, in hopes of receiving a commutation of sentence.

Charlie was soon seated at the table with an ample allowance of corn-bread and tea, and he looked so demure, and conducted himself in such an exemplary manner, that one would have scarcely thought him given to marbles and dirty company. Having eaten to his, satisfaction he quite ingratiated himself with Caddy by picking up all the crumbs he had spilled during tea, and throwing them upon the dust-heap. This last act was quite a stroke of policy, as even Caddy began to regard him as capable of reformation.

The tea-things washed up and cleared away, the females busied themselves with their sewing, and Charlie immersed himself in his lessons for the morrow with a hearty good-will and perseverance as if he had abjured marbles for ever.

The hearty supper and persevering attention to study soon began to produce their customary effect upon Charlie. He could not get on with his lessons. Many of the state capitals positively refused to be found, and he was beginning to entertain the sage notion that probably some of the legislatures had come to the conclusion to dispense with them altogether, or had had them placed in such obscure places that they could not be found. The variously coloured states began to form a vast kaleidoscope, in which the lakes and rivers had been entirely swallowed up. Ranges of mountains disappeared, and gulfs and bays and islands were entirely lost. In fact, he was sleepy, and had already had two or three narrow escapes from butting over the candles ; finally he fell from his chair, crushing Caddy's newly-trimmed bonnet, to the intense grief and indignation of that young lady, who inflicted summary vengeance upon him before he was sufficiently awake to be aware of what had happened.

The work being finished, Mrs. Ellis and Caddy prepared to take it home to Mrs. Thomas, leaving Esther at home to receive her father on his return and give him his tea.

Mrs. Ellis and Caddy wended their way towards the fashionable part of the city, looking in at the various shop-windows as they went. Numberless were the great bargains they saw there displayed, and divers were the discussions they held respecting them.

"Oh, isn't that a pretty calico, mother, that with the green ground?"

"'Tis pretty, but it won't wash, child; those colours always run."

"Just look at that silk though—now that's cheap, you must acknowledge—only eighty-seven and a half cents; if I only had a dress of that I should be fixed."

"Laws, Caddy!" replied Mrs. Ellis, "that stuff is as slazy as a washed cotton handkerchief, and coarse enough almost to sift sand through. It wouldn't last you any time. The silks they make now-a-days ain't worth anything; they don't wear well at all. Why," continued she, "when I was a girl they made silks that would stand on end—and one of them would last a life-time."

They had now reached Chestnut-street, which was filled with gaily-dressed people, enjoying the balmy breath of a soft May evening. Mrs. Ellis and Caddy walked briskly onward, and were soon beyond the line of shops, and entered upon the aristocratic quarter into which many of its residents had retired, that they might be out of sight of the houses in which their fathers or grandfathers had made their fortunes.

"Mother," said Caddy, "this is Mr. Grant's new house—isn't it a splendid place? They say it's like a palace inside. They are great people, them Grants. I saw in the newspaper yesterday that young Mr. Augustus Grant had been appointed an attaché to the American legation at Paris; the newspapers say he is a rising man."

"Well, he ought to be," rejoined Mrs. Ellis, "for his old grand-daddy made yeast enough to raise the whole family. Many a pennyworth has he sold me. Laws! how the poor old folk do get up! I think I can see the old man now, with his sleeves rolled up, dealing out his yeast. He wore one coat for about twenty years, and used to be always bragging about it."

As they were thus talking, a door of one of the splendid mansions they were passing opened, and a fashionably-dressed young man came slowly down the steps, and walked on before them with a very measured step and peculiar gait.

"That's young Dr. Whiston, mother," whispered Caddy; "he's courting young Miss Morton."

"You don't say so!" replied the astonished Mrs. Ellis. "Why, I declare his grandfather laid her grandfather out! Old Whiston was an undertaker, and used to make the handsomest coffins of his time. And he is going to marry Miss Morton! What next, I'd like to know! He walks exactly like the old man. I used to mock him when I was a little girl. He had just that hop-and-go kind of gait, and he was the funniest man that ever lived. I've seen him at a funeral go into the parlour, and condole with the family, and talk about the dear departed until the tears rolled down his cheeks; and then he'd be down in the kitchen, eating and drinking, and laughing, and telling jokes about the corpses, before the tears were dry on his face. How he used to make money! He buried almost all the respectable people about town, and made a large fortune. He owned a burying-ground in Coates-street, and when the property in that vicinity became valuable, he turned the dead folks out, and built houses on the ground!"

"I shouldn't say it was a very pleasant place to live in, if there are such things as ghosts," said Caddy, laughing; "I for one wouldn't like to live there—but here we are at Mr. Thomas's—how short the way has seemed!"

Caroline gave a fierce rap at the door, which was opened by old Aunt Rachel, the fat cook, who had lived with the Thomases for a fabulous length of time. She was an old woman when Mrs. Ellis came as a girl into the family, and had given her many a cuff in days long past; in fact, notwithstanding Mrs. Ellis had been married many years, and had children almost as old as she herself was when she left Mr. Thomas, Aunt Rachel could never be induced to regard her otherwise than as a girl.

"Oh, it's you, is it?" said she gruffly, as she opened the

door; " don't you think better break de door down at once—
rapping as if you was guine to tear off de knocker—is dat de
way, gal, you comes to quality's houses? You lived here
long nuff to larn better dan dat—and dis is twice I've been
to de door in de last half-hour—if any one else comes dere
they may stay outside. Shut de door after you, and come
into de kitchen, and don't keep me standin' here all night,"
added she, puffing and blowing as she waddled back into her
sanctum.

Waiting until the irate old cook had recovered her breath,
Mrs. Ellis modestly inquired if Mrs. Thomas was at home. "Go
up and see," was the surly response. " You've been up stars
often enuff to know de way—go long wid you, gal, and don't
be botherin' me, 'case I don't feel like bein' bothered—now,
mind I tell yer.—Here, you Cad, set down on dis stool, and
let that cat alone; I don't let any one play with my cat,"
continued she, " and you'll jest let him alone, if you please, or
I'll make you go sit in de entry till your mother's ready to go.
I don't see what she has you brats tugging after her for
whenever she comes here—she might jest as well leave yer at
home to darn your stockings—I 'spect dey want it."

Poor Caddy was boiling over with wrath; but deeming
prudence the better part of valour, she did not venture upon
any wordy contest with Aunt Rachel, but sat down upon the
stool by the fire-place, in which a bright fire was blazing.
Up the chimney an old smoke-jack was clicking, whirling,
and making the most dismal noise imaginable. This old
smoke-jack was Aunt Rachel's especial *protégé*, and she
obstinately and successfully defended it against all comers.
She turned up her nose at all modern inventions designed for
the same use as entirely beneath her notice. She had been
accustomed to hearing its rattle for the last forty years, and
would as soon have thought of committing suicide as con-
senting to its removal.

She and her cat were admirably matched; he was as snap-
pish and cross as she, and resented with distended claws and

elevated back all attempts on the part of strangers to cultivate amicable relations with him. In fact, Tom's pugnacious disposition was clearly evidenced by his appearance; one side of his face having a very battered aspect, and the fur being torn off his back in several places.

Caddy sat for some time surveying the old woman and her cat, in evident awe of both. She regarded also with great admiration the scrupulously clean and shining kitchen tins that garnished the walls and reflected the red light of the blazing fire. The wooden dresser was a miracle of whiteness, and ranged thereon was a set of old-fashioned blue china, on which was displayed the usual number of those unearthly figures which none but the Chinese can create. Tick, tick, went the old Dutch clock in the corner, and the smoke-jack kept up its whirring noise. Old Tom and Aunt Rachel were both napping; and so Caddy, having no other resource, went to sleep also.

Mrs. Ellis found her way without any difficulty to Mrs. Thomas's room. Her gentle tap upon the door quite flurried that good lady, who (we speak it softly) was dressing her wig, a task she entrusted to no other mortal hands. She peeped out, and seeing who it was, immediately opened the door without hesitation.

"Oh, it's you, is it? Come in, Ellen," said she; "I don't mind you."

"I've brought the night-dresses home," said Mrs. Ellis, laying her bundle upon the table,—"I hope they'll suit."

"Oh, no doubt they will. Did you bring the bill?" asked Mrs. Thomas.

The bill was produced, and Mrs. Ellis sat down, whilst Mrs. Thomas counted out the money. This having been duly effected, and the bill carefully placed on the file, Mrs. Thomas also sat down, and commenced her usual lamentation over the state of her nerves, and the extravagance of the younger members of the family. On the latter subject she spoke very feelingly. "Such goings on, Ellen, are enough to set me crazy

—so many nurses—and then we have to keep four horses—
and it's company, company from Monday morning until
Saturday night; the house is kept upside-down continually—
money, money for everything—all going out, and nothing
coming in!"—and the unfortunate Mrs. Thomas whined and
groaned as if she had not at that moment an income of clear
fifteen thousand dollars a year, and a sister who might die
any day and leave her half as much more.

Mrs. Thomas was the daughter of the respectable old gentleman whom Dr. Whiston's grandfather had prepared for
his final resting-place. Her daughter had married into a
once wealthy, but now decayed, Carolina family. In consideration of the wealth bequeathed by her grandfather (who
was a maker of leather breeches, and speculator in general),
Miss Thomas had received the offer of the poverty-stricken
hand of Mr. Morton, and had accepted it with evident pleasure, as he was undoubtedly a member of one of the first
families of the South, and could prove a distant connection
with one of the noble families of England.

They had several children, and their incessant wants had
rendered it necessary that another servant should be kept.
Now Mrs. Thomas had long had her eye on Charlie, with a
view of incorporating him with the Thomas establishment,
and thought this would be a favourable time to broach
the subject to his mother: she therefore commenced by
inquiring—

"How have you got through the winter, Ellen? Everything has been so dear that even we have felt the effect of
the high prices."

"Oh, tolerably well, I thank you. Husband's business, it
is true, has not been as brisk as usual, but we ought not to
complain; now that we have got the house paid for, and the
girls do so much sewing, we get on very nicely."

"I should think three children must be something of a
burthen—must be hard to provide for."

"Oh no, not at all," rejoined Mrs. Ellis, who seemed rather

surprised at Mrs. Thomas's uncommon solicitude respecting
them. "We have never found the children a burthen, thank
God—they're rather a comfort and a pleasure than otherwise."

"I'm glad to hear you say so, Ellen—very glad, indeed,
for I have been quite disturbed in mind respecting you during the winter. I really several times thought of sending to
take Charlie off your hands : by-the-way, what is he doing
now ? "

"He goes to school regularly—he hasn't missed a day all
winter. You should just see his writing," continued Mrs.
Ellis, warming up with a mother's pride in her only son—
"he won't let the girls make out any of the bills, but does it
all himself—he made out yours."

Mrs. Thomas took down the file and looked at the bill
again. "It's very neatly written, very neatly written, indeed ;
isn't it about time that he left school—don't you think he has
education enough ? " she inquired.

"His father don't. He intends sending him to another
school, after vacation, where they teach Latin and Greek, and
a number of other branches."

"Nonsense, nonsense, Ellen ! If I were you, I wouldn't
hear of it. There won't be a particle of good result to the
child from any such acquirements. It isn't as though he was
a white child. What use can Latin or Greek be to a coloured
boy ? None in the world—he'll have to be a common mechanic, or, perhaps, a servant, or barber, or something of that
kind, and then what use would all his fine education be to
him ? Take my advice, Ellen, and don't have him taught
things that will make him feel above the situation he, in all
probability, will have to fill. Now," continued she, "I have
a proposal to make to you : let him come and live with me
awhile—I'll pay you well, and take good care of him ; besides,
he will be learning something here, good manners, &c. Not
that he is not a well-mannered child ; but, you know, Ellen,
there is something every one learns by coming in daily contact

with refined and educated people that cannot but be beneficial—come now, make up your mind to leave him with me,
at least until the winter, when the schools again commence,
and then, if his father is still resolved to send him back to
school, why he can do so. Let me have him for the summer
at least."

Mrs. Ellis, who had always been accustomed to regard
Mrs. Thomas as a miracle of wisdom, was, of course, greatly
impressed with what she had said. She had lived many
years in her family, and had left it to marry Mr. Ellis, a
thrifty mechanic, who came from Savanah, her native city.
She had great reverence for any opinion Mrs. Thomas expressed; and, after some further conversation on the subject,
made up her mind to consent to the proposal, and left her
with the intention of converting her husband to her way of
thinking.

On descending to the kitchen she awoke Caddy from a de-
licious dream, in which she had been presented with the black
silk that they had seen in the shop window marked eighty-
seven and a half cents a yard. In the dream she had deter-
mined to make it up with tight sleeves and infant waist, that
being the most approved style at that period.

" Five breadths are not enough for the skirt, and if I take
six I must skimp the waist and cape," murmured she in her
sleep.

"Wake up, girl! What are you thinking about?" said
her mother, giving her another shake.

"Oh!" said Caddy, with a wild and disappointed look—" I
was dreaming, wasn't I? I declare I thought I had that silk
frock in the window."

" The girls' heads are always running on finery—wake up,
and come along, I'm going home."

Caddy followed her mother out, leaving Aunt Rachel and
Tom nodding at each other as they dozed before the fire.

That night Mr. Ellis and his wife had a long conversation
upon the proposal of Mrs. Thomas; and after divers objec-

tions raised by him, and set aside by her, it was decided that Charlie should be permitted to go there for the holidays at least ; after which, his father resolved he should be sent to school again.

Charlie, the next morning, looked very blank on being informed of his approaching fate. Caddy undertook with great alacrity to break the dismal tidings to him, and enlarged in a glowing manner upon what times he might expect from Aunt Rachel.

"I guess she'll keep you straight ;—you'll see sights up there ! She is cross as sin—she'll make you wipe your feet when you go in and out, if no one else can."

"Let him alone, Caddy," gently interposed Esther; "it is bad enough to be compelled to live in a house with that frightful old woman, without being annoyed about it beforehand. If I could help it, Charlie, you should not go."

"I know you'd keep me home if you could—but old Cad, here, she always rejoices if anything happens to me. I'll be hanged if I stay there," said he. "I won't live at service— I'd rather be a sweep, or sell apples on the dock. I'm not going to be stuck up behind their carriage, dressed up like a monkey in a tail coat—I'll cut off my own head first." And with this sanguinary threat he left the house, with his schoolbooks under his arm, intending to lay the case before his friend and adviser, the redoubtable and sympathising Kinch.

CHAPTER III.

Charlie's Trials.

CHARLIE started for school with a heavy heart. Had it not been for his impending doom of service in Mr. Thomas's family, he would have been the happiest boy that ever carried a school-bag.

It did not require a great deal to render this young gentleman happy. All that was necessary to make up a day of perfect joyfulness with him, was a dozen marbles, permission to wear his worst inexpressibles, and to be thoroughly up in his lessons. To-day he was possessed of all these requisites, but there was also in the perspective a long array of skirmishes with Aunt Rachel, who, he knew, looked on him with an evil eye, and who had frequently expressed herself regarding him, in his presence, in terms by no means complimentary or affectionate; and the manner in which she had intimated her desire, on one or two occasions, to have an opportunity of reforming his personal habits, were by no means calculated to produce a happy frame of mind, now that the opportunity was about to be afforded her.

Charlie sauntered on until he came to a lumber-yard, where he stopped and examined a corner of the fence very attentively. "Not gone by yet. I must wait for him," said he; and forthwith he commenced climbing the highest pile of boards, the top of which he reached at the imminent risk of his neck. Here he sat awaiting the advent of his friend Kinch, the absence of death's head and cross bones from the corner of the fence being a clear indication that he had not yet passed on his way to school.

Soon, however, he was espied in the distance, and as he

was quite a character in his way, we must describe him. His most prominent feature was a capacious hungry-looking mouth, within which glistened a row of perfect teeth. He had the merriest twinkling black eyes, and a nose so small and flat that it would have been a prize to any editor living, as it would have been a physical impossibility to have pulled it, no matter what outrage he had committed. His complexion was of a ruddy brown, and his hair, entirely innocent of a comb, was decorated with divers feathery tokens of his last night's rest. A cap with the front torn off, jauntily set on one side of his head, gave him a rakish and wide-awake air, his clothes were patched and torn in several places, and his shoes were already in an advanced stage of decay. As he approached the fence he took a piece of chalk from his pocket, and commenced to sketch the accustomed startling illustration which was to convey to Charlie the intelligence that he had already passed there on his way to school, when a quantity of sawdust came down in a shower on his head. As soon as the blinding storm had ceased, Kinch looked up and intimated to Charlie that it was quite late, and that there was a probability of their being after time at school.

This information caused Charlie to make rather a hasty descent, in doing which his dinner-basket was upset, and its contents displayed at the feet of the voracious Kinch.

"Now I'll be even with you for that sawdust," cried he, as he pocketed two boiled eggs, and bit an immense piece out of an apple-tart, which he would have demolished completely but for the prompt interposition of its owner.

"Oh! my golly! Charlie, your mother makes good pies!" he exclaimed with rapture, as soon as he could get his mouth sufficiently clear to speak. "Give us another bite,—only a nibble."

But Charlie knew by experience what Kinch's "nibbles" were, and he very wisely declined, saying sadly as he did so, "You won't get many more dinners from me, Kinch. I'm going to leave school."

"No! you ain't though, are you?" asked the astonished Kinch. "You are not going, are you, really?"

"Yes, really," replied Charlie, with a doleful look; "mother is going to put me out at service."

"And do you intend to go?" asked Kinch, looking at him incredulously.

"Why of course," was the reply. "How can I help going if father and mother say I must?"

"I tell you what I should do," said Kinch, "if it was me. I should act so bad that the people would be glad to get rid of me. They hired me out to live once, and I led the people they put me with such a dance, that they was glad enough to send me home again."

This observation brought them to the school-house, which was but a trifling distance from the residence of Mrs. Ellis.

They entered the school at the last moment of grace, and Mr. Dicker looked at them severely as they took their seats. "Just saved ourselves," whispered Kinch; "a minute later and we would have been done for;" and with this closing remark he applied himself to his grammar, a very judicious move on his part, for he had not looked at his lesson, and there were but ten minutes to elapse before the class would be called.

The lessons were droned through as lessons usually are at school. There was the average amount of flogging performed; cakes, nuts, and candy, confiscated; little boys on the back seats punched one another as little boys on the back seats always will do, and were flogged in consequence. Then the boy who never knew his lessons was graced with the fool's cap, and was pointed and stared at until the arrival of the play-hour relieved him from his disagreeable situation.

"What kind of folks are these Thomases?" asked Kinch, as he sat beside Charlie in the playground munching the last of the apple-tart; "what kind of folks are they? Tell me that, and I can give you some good advice, may-be."

"Old Mrs. Thomas is a little dried-up old woman, who